STUDIES IN AFRICAN LITERATURE
▼▼▼▼▼▼▼▼▼▼▼▼▼▼▼▼▼▼▼▼▼ ▼

Running towards Us

Recent Titles in Studies in African Literature

▼▼▼▼▼▼▼▼▼▼▼▼▼▼▼▼▼▼▼▼▼▼▼▼▼▼▼▼▼▼▼

Moving the Centre: The Struggle for Cultural Freedoms
Ngugi wa Thiong'o

Thresholds of Change in African Literature: The Emergence of a Tradition
Kenneth W. Harrow

Wole Soyinka: An Appraisal
Adewale Maja-Pearce, editor

African Popular Theatre: From Precolonial Times to the Present Day
David Kerr

The Marabout and the Muse: New Approaches to Islam in African Literature
Kenneth W. Harrow, editor

Bessie Head: Thunder Behind Her Ears
Gillian Stead Eilersen

New Writing from Southern Africa: Authors Who Have Become Prominent Since 1980
Emmanuel Ngara, editor

Ngugi wa Thiong'o: An Exploration of His Writings, Second Edition
David Cook and Michael Okenimkpe

Writers in Politics: A Re-Engagement with Issues of Literature and Society
Ngugi wa Thiong'o

The African Novel in English: An Introduction
M. Keith Booker

A Teacher's Guide to African Narratives
Sara Talis O'Brien

Women's Voices in a Man's World: Women and the Pastoral Tradition in Northern Somali Orature, c. 1899–1980
Lidwien Kapteijns with Maryan Omar Ali

▼▼

Running towards Us

New Writing from South Africa

Edited and with an introduction by Isabel Balseiro

HEINEMANN
Portsmouth, NH

Heinemann
A division of Reed Elsevier Inc.
361 Hanover Street
Portsmouth, NH 03801–3912
www.heinemann.com

ISBN 0–325–00231–2 (Heinemann cloth)
ISBN 0–325–00211–8 (Heinemann paper)

Library of Congress Cataloging-in-Publication Data

Running towards us : new writing from South Africa / edited and with an
introduction by Isabel Balseiro.
        p. cm.—(Studies in African literature, ISSN 1351–5713)
      ISBN 0–325–00231–2 (alk. paper)—ISBN 0–325–00211–8
(pbk. : alk. paper)
        1. South African literature (English)   2. South Africa—Literary
collections.   3. Afrikaans literature—20th century—Translations into
English.   I. Balseiro, Isabel.   II. Studies in African literature. New series.

   PR9364.9 .R86 2000
   820.9'968—dc21   99–049243

British Library Cataloguing in Publication Data is available.

Paperback cover photo: "passages," Cape Town, South Africa. Courtesy of the editor.

Printed in the United States of America on acid-free paper.

04 03 02 01 00 SB 1 2 3 4 5 6 7 8 9

To Stuart García,
in memoriam

Contents

Acknowledgments   xiii

Introduction   xv

PART ONE   1

"Running towards Us"
Jeremy Cronin   3

"Marilyn's Dress"
Graeme Friedman   6

"Memory"
Chris Van Wyk   14

"The Women Sing"
Luvuyo Mkangelwa   15

"I'm retelling a womanburning"
Roshila Nair   16

"Spiral Child"
Louise Green   20

"Homeland Banter"
Pumla Dineo Gqola   21

"The Awakening of Katie Fortuin"
Finuala Dowling   30

PART TWO   39

"The Puddle"
Immanuel Suttner   41

"Mind-Reader"
Maureen Isaacson   44

"moni"
Seitlhamo Motsapi   48

"At the Commission"
Ingrid de Kok   49

"Mending"
Ingrid de Kok   50

"TRC Stories: It Gets under the Skin"
Heidi Grunebaum-Ralph   51

"Truth Commission"
Joan Metelerkamp   52

"The Devil"
Achmat Dangor   55

"Emotions and the Delegates"
Jonathan Grossman   71

"What's in a Name?"
Bernadette Muthien   75

"Je To Mozny"
Edward Lurie   76

"The Day of the Boycott"
Felicity Wood   82

PART THREE   99

"The WHITES ONLY Bench"
Ivan Vladislavić   101

"land"
Antjie Krog   112

"Recognition"
David Medalie   113

Excerpt from *Freedom Lament and Song*
Mongane Wally Serote   119

"Fragments from the Life of Norman Rubarto"
Paul Mason   122

"This Carting Life"
Rustum Kozain   132

"The Naked Song"
Mandla Langa   137

"Telegraph to the Sky"
Sandile Dikeni   157

"Rituals for Martha"
Zachariah Rapola   160

"Habari Gani Africa Ranting"
Lesego Rampolokeng   169

"Tiresias in the City of Heroes"
Karen Press   172

"Eternity Is a Hell of a Thing to Waste"
Natasha Distiller   178

Glossary   185

About the Contributors and the Editor   191

Acknowledgments

Two visits to South Africa, first a half year sabbatical leave in 1996 and then a three-months stay the following year, afforded me the opportunity to assemble this book. On both occasions, I had the privilege of being a research associate at the Centre for African Studies at the University of Cape Town. I wish to thank Brenda Cooper and Mahmood Mamdani as well as everyone else at the Centre for making me feel welcome. Support from Harvey Mudd College, of The Claremont Colleges, where I teach Comparative Literature, and an Arnold L. Graves and Lois S. Graves Award in the Humanities made my travel to South Africa possible.

I trace my interest in this project to a series of readings I attended in June and July of 1996 entitled "At the Fault Line." Organized by the Department of Adult Education and Extra Mural Studies at the University of Cape Town, this event brought together a number of important voices in South African letters whose interventions opened my eyes to discussions about truth and about reconciliation. Ingrid de Kok, one of the event's organizers, whom I had the fortune to meet only some months later, was pivotal in helping me to contact many of the writers who read their work on that occasion. In long and rich conversations with poets and fiction writers, academics and activists, cultural voyeurs, intellectuals, and students of South African literature and society, this project took shape. Many people have helped me along the way. I especially wish to thank Rustum Kozain, Jeremy Cronin, Karen Press, David Medalie, Paul Mason, Pumla Dineo Gqola, Maleshoane Rapeane, and Heidi Grunebaum-Ralph. Pumla Mafeje at *Drum* Publications; David and Marie Philip, as well as their colleagues at David Philip Publishers; Robert Berold at *New Coin*; Michael King at *New*

Contrast; and Delia Rothnie-Jones at *herStoria* provided some of the publishing forums through which my appetite grew. I also wish to express my appreciation to Rachelle Greef and Annelie de Wet, who lent a hand in reaching Afrikaans-speaking writers; to André van Niekerk, who, unbeknownst to me, advertised a call for papers in the South African Scriptwriters Association; to Nomvula Meth, through whom I was able to meet a number of young writers; and to Peter Horn, Eva Hunter, Rob Gaylard, and Liz Mackenzie. Professor Mazisi Kunene and Tessa Dowling were untiring advisers on authors who write in indigenous African languages. I am thankful to Gabeba Baderoon for her friendship and support in myriad ways. Hawa Monier was generous in helping me to reach Johannesburg-based writers in Muslim and secular communities. Thanks also go to Johannesburg-based Lionel Abrahams, Maureen Isaacson, Claudia Braude, and Pam Nichols—friend for life. And in New York, thanks to Timothy J. Reiss, unfailing mentor, and to Mark Sanders. Finally, I wish to thank Jim Lance, my editor at Heinemann, who backed this project from the start.

To Ntongela Masilela, colleague and dear friend, and Tobias Hecht: Thank you!

Introduction

Like the figure representing the answer to the riddle of the Sphinx, South Africa could be seen as a nation walking on several sets of feet. From one perspective, it is young and still on all fours, reborn only recently through struggle and negotiation, sacrifice and good fortune; from another point of view, it is a country facing something like a mid-life crisis, for it is mired in an enduring social and economic apartheid and in unrelenting poverty and violence; and South Africa can also be seen as a land gazing backwards and bearing its history like an unwieldy knobkerrie.

The vestiges of apartheid are as difficult to avoid today as it once was to circumvent the Group Areas Act. Although the legal and political changes are revolutionary, the economic and social ones are not. The new South Africa is very new. Many have warned me that from such a slippery foothold in history, it is impossible to speak of *a* new South African literature. Indeed it is. Yet the evanescence of this moment in the country's history has done nothing to prevent the appearance of many forms of writing that both speak to the uncertain present and that, doubtless, will transcend it. The pieces included here illustrate how a new consciousness of being is emerging. This anthology is an invitation for readers to consider literary responses from some of the best South African writers of poetry and short fiction to the current dispensation, the past from which that dispensation emerges, and the possible futures it presages.

Some of the responses in this volume are intensely personal. This is the case of Chris Van Wyk's "Memory," Roshila Nair's "I'm retelling a womanburning," and Pumla Dineo Gqola's "Homeland Banter." Others are more outward looking, as for instance Seitlhamo Motsapi's "moni,"

Karen Press's "Tiresias in the City of Heroes," and Joan Metelerkamp's "Truth Commission." But throughout this book the personal and the social are enmeshed. In some way, all of the pieces speak to recent changes in South African society. Beyond that broad criterion of representing a literary response to the current social and political context, the only basis of inclusion was the quality of the particular pieces and their relationship to the volume as a whole.

This collection does not embrace the wealth of South Africa's eleven official languages. Persistent efforts to gather submissions in languages other than English and Afrikaans yielded few results. In a country where only a small minority of the population speaks English as a native language and at a time when traditionally marginalized indigenous African languages have taken on a very public role at the Truth and Reconciliation Commission, one must question why South African literature continues to be produced largely in English and, to a lesser extent, in Afrikaans. Who decides what the canon of South African literature does and does not comprise? What are the relationships among language, art, and power in such a fractured social space as South Africa? A number of recent books address these issues, among them Sarah Nuttall and Carli Coetzee's *Renegotiating the Past: The Making of Memory in South Africa* (1998), Johannes A. Smit and colleagues' *Rethinking South African Literary History* (1996), Michael Chapman's *Southern African Literatures* (1996), and D. B. Ntuli and C. F. Swanepoel's *South African Literature in African Languages: A Concise Historical Perspective* (1993). From my perspective, the expression of memory (and its comprehension) will remain stunted as long as the linguistic diversity is not incorporated into the evolving canon. Without polyvocality, South Africans will continue to "stutter on memories" (Kozain, 1997). Having said that, I think readers will agree that the range of historical and personal memory included here is as broad as it is revealing about contemporary South Africa.

The anthology is divided into three sections that correspond loosely to the three sets of legs upon which a man might walk in his lifetime, as suggested in the riddle of the Sphinx. Part One is the most intimate and personal section. At the centre of a number of pieces are children, children who take the readers back to a past very much alive in the present. The poverty and fear amidst which the young girl lives in Roshila Nair's "I'm retelling a womanburning" persist at the heart of contemporary religious, sexual, and social reality in South Africa. In Graeme Friedman's story "Marilyn's Dress," domestic power relations between men and women and adults and children are woven gracefully into a larger tale of isolation, oppression, and thwarted ambitions. In "Homeland Banter," Pumla Dineo Gqola writes of a young girl who is trying to make sense of the autocratic world of Bantu education and to stand up for herself within that world.

The pieces in Part Two tend to revolve around the present, around the fugue of a transition shaped by the past but recognizing itself uneasily in the everyday world of the institutions emerging from the negotiated settlement, in urban crime, in raised and battered expectations of change. Achmat Dangor's "The Devil" somberly evokes the vulnerability inherent to all when evil is so rampant that life becomes banal, while Immanuel Suttner takes the reader from the everyday concerns of a housesitter to the seemingly supernatural world of crime. Three poets, Ingrid de Kok, Heidi Grunebaum-Ralph, and Joan Metelerkamp, address in distinct ways the trauma of memory evoked by the Truth and Reconciliation Commission; Seitlhamo Motsapi warns of an emergent apolitical materialism.

Part Three of this volume brings the past and the present together, leaving open the question of the future but gesturing, nonetheless, in different directions. In "The WHITES ONLY Bench," Ivan Vladislavić, fast becoming one of South Africa's most important authors of prose, writes of the debate in a museum over whether to look for a past symbolized by a bench reserved for "Europeans" or to reinvent it, ultimately questioning the distinction between these two tendencies. At the heart of Zachariah Rapola's "Rituals for Martha" is the spectre of moral decay in relation to human—and social—reproduction. Mandla Langa's "The Naked Song" is the story of a South African exile who has come home and remains caught somewhere between his past and his country's present, between a loyalty to change and his growing awareness of betrayal by comrades. Natasha Distiller's enigmatic "Eternity Is a Hell of a Thing to Waste," which closes the book, brings together Greek mythology and everyday terror in the karoo, the flat semidesert of South Africa.

Throughout the process of assembling this book I had, as already suggested, one persistent doubt: What if it were too soon to expect writers to speak of the past and of this moment in history? Are, as Denis Hirson (1997) has suggested in the introduction to his recent anthology of South African poetry, the country's fibres still too raw for writers to start picking up from the havoc all about them? Who has the right to define the map literary history is charting for itself in the new (dare I say, "post-apartheid") South Africa? And yet, urged by the sheer immediacy of the talk in the street and along the corridors of academic halls (as humorously depicted here in Felicity Wood's "The Day of the Boycott"); by the violence of unsuspected encounters between South Africans who had never before met on an equal footing (as conveyed in David Medalie's "Recognition"); and by the incantatory verses of poetry (such as in Rustum Kozain's "This Carting Life"), I realized that despite its precociousness, this anthology had acquired a life of its own that reflects a moment in the historical life of South Africa. South African writers, like most members of their larger society, continue to grapple with the weight of the country's recent history. Whichever direction the particular pieces included here take us, history weighs heavily in them. Fuelled by fear, joy, rage, and occasional personally nostalgic pangs, the past and its sequelae are themes running through this book.

Somewhere between a stillborn present and the still-to-be-born future, this anthology looks nervously over its shoulder at a past that, as vividly evoked by Jeremy Cronin, is "Running towards Us." In the poem from which this collection takes its title, an apparent corpse rises from what was to have been his funeral pyre only to start running. The figure—somewhere between life and death, who could be victim or perpetrator or both at once in South Africa's internecine violence—brings together past and present, fiction and reality. New writing from South Africa is also running towards us and sheds much light on the country's predicament.

In 1996, arguing that South Africans "still live in the past," Mbulelo V. Mzamane urged writers to explore what he termed the "peculiar psychology" (13–14) of the transitional process. He considered taking such a step a prerequisite to reconciliation. Taking stock, as it were, of what needs to be clarified and expurgated before the future (people's aspirations) can be realized, Mzamane referred to the "new" South Africa as a myth and to post-apartheid South Africa as a hope while warning of an impending neo-apartheid phase that constitutes a threat. The country now inhabits that angst-ridden space between neo-apartheid reality and a post-apartheid dispensation. This is the terrain straddled by the poetry and fiction included here. In bringing these pieces together, I hope to have captured some of the ambivalence inherent to all memory and to have given flesh to the twists and turns of a past whose débris nurture the foundations of a literature in the making.

Isabel Balseiro
Claremont, California

Works Cited

Chapman, Michael. *Southern African Literatures*. London: Longman, 1996.

Hirson, Denis, ed. *The Lava of This Land: South African Poetry 1960–1996*. Evanston, Ill: Northwestern University Press, 1997.

Kozain, Rustum. "Memories of Revolutions." Unpublished poem. 1997.

Mzamane, Mbulelo Vizikhungo. "From Resistance to Reconstruction: Culture and the New South Africa." 27.1 *Ariel* (1996): 11–18.

Ntuli, D. B. and C. F. Swanepoel. *South African Literature in African Languages: A Concise Historical Perspective*. Pretoria: Acacia, 1993.

Nuttall, Sarah, and Carlie Coetzee, eds. *Renegotiating the Past: The Making of Memory in South Africa*. Cape Town: Oxford University Press, 1998.

Smit, Johannes, Johan van Wyk, and Jean-Philippe Wade, eds. *Rethinking South African Literary History*. Durban: Y Press, 1996.

PART ONE

Running towards Us

JEREMY CRONIN ▼▼▼▼▼▼▼▼▼▼▼▼▼▼▼▼▼▼▼▼▼▼▼▼▼▼▼▼▼▼▼▼▼▼

It's two days after the worst. We've just returned from Johannesburg. We drop comrades in the vicinity, and decide, as Trevor puts it, to have a look.

Along roads pitted with the remains of barricades, swerving and bumping we go, eyes unpeeled.

Mahobe Drive has become a patrol strip. Armoured personnel carriers move up and down its half kilometre. They ignore us. Or, perhaps, they are watching closely. The hooded, slit-windowed faces of the vehicles make us uncertain. We don't linger.

Mahobe Drive is the cut-line, beyond it: ash and buckled zinc as far as the eye sees. 80 dead, I have read. 2,000 shacks destroyed. 20,000 homeless. Dull numbers to guess three days of devastation that have just happened here.

In those three days the apartheid police and army have destroyed an entire shanty-town, unleashing black vigilantes (*witdoeke*), victims themselves turned perpetrators, to perform much of the dirty work.

After-shocks, neuralgic points, are all around us now. An old man stumbles along with a corrugated sheet of zinc on his back. His eyes are blank with terror. He is half running, but from whom, and to where?

Over by the church, which will itself be burnt down in the coming days, there is a milling of refugees. People are jumpy. Suddenly from their skittish midst a sprinting of three, twenty, some sixty youth hurl themselves off in a wheeling pursuit. Or are they fleeing?

We shouldn't, shouldn't be here.

Around the corner are the New Crossroads homes, formal
structures, the last line of sanctioned black poverty before
ground zero, the burnt-out acres of the shanty-town.

As we turn the corner, we see people in their front yards
watching a strip of empty veld. There is a corpse lying there.

It moves. One knee bends and keels over.

Across the field, a young man draped in a blanket approaches
the body. Casually he places sticks on its chest. Another figure
strolls up to dowse the body with petrol.

All of this is done unhurriedly. In broad daylight. In the middle
of an open field, before some hundred people, and around the
corner from the police and army.

The lackadaisical visibility of this execution is, must be, the
main point.

The executioners preparing the victim move back and forth,
leaving him untended for many minutes at a time. This is ritual.
A macabre human sacrifice on the lip of a still smouldering
volcano, as if to stake challenge to its monopoly on death.

The car tyre, that will burn and burn, immolating the victim in
its rubbery inferno, is now being rolled out and placed on his
chest.

Let's go! Please! I am pleading with Trevor. The words I have
been reciting finally spilling out.

But is it horror? Or rage at our own impotence? Or the self-
disgust of the voyeur? Or is it fear that, while we watch, we too
will be engulfed from behind, overpowered, knocked down and
carried off by the police, or the youth, or the *witdoeke*?

But now the executioners themselves are disappearing, not
running, not diminishing their authority, just melting away. The
hundred-odd observers in the front yards of their homes are
also fading off.

And just as suddenly the corpse in the middle of the field is up, and sprinting away. In our direction. A wild, hobbling dash.

The victory of life over death? Of the innocent small person caught in the middle?

But what is the middle?

Are you sure, in the thick of all this slaughter, he could be innocent?

Whom did he just betray? Whom will he still betray now as he runs away from the executioners?

Away from the spectators. Away from the police and army with fresh killings on their hands. A corpse covered in petrol, each stumbling pace one step more away from a death it has already died.

He is running towards us. Into our exile. Into the return of exiles. Running towards the negotiated settlement. Towards the democratic elections. He is running, sore, into the new South Africa. Into our rainbow nation, in desperation, one shoe on, one shoe off. Into our midst. Running.

(1986–97)

Marilyn's Dress

GRAEME FRIEDMAN ▼▼▼▼▼▼▼▼▼▼▼▼▼▼▼▼▼▼▼▼▼▼▼▼▼▼▼▼▼▼▼▼▼▼

The girl peeks out from behind the rock as her mother walks toward the breakers. The small beach, sheltered from the settlement by the slope of the island's rocky terrain, faces across the strait. Somewhere to the hinterland are the neat rows of warders' homes that stand outside the walls of the prison. Today the mainland's harbour with its cargo ships, oil tankers, liners, and cranes, the coastal belt of luxury flats and hotels, the promenade that acts as a moat between the sea and the sometimes visible suburb, all lie hidden within the mist. Josie and her mother, Margaret, could be the only people on earth.

The hem of the girl's skirt is damp from kneeling on the wet sand. She frowns, noticing the water-darkened edges of the floral pattern, and knows what her mother will say:

"Josie!" she'll scold, "You've gone and got your dress dirty. It's only just come back from the wash!"

"But Mom!"

"Listen to me now, my girl." But there will be nothing more for Josie to listen to, her mother's thoughts will wander off, distracted.

Steadying herself against the cold rock surface, Josie rises from her knees. She brushes at the grains of sand that cling to her dress. Her blonde hair—some say it is almost white—is pulled back by an Alice band, and falls just short of her shoulders. Her cheeks are flushed.

The tide is low, and her mother's feet make deep indentations in the wet, yielding sand . . . heel, ball, toe . . . heel, ball, toe . . . neither hurried nor slow, an unbroken rhythm of prints on their path into the sea. . . .

It is a Saturday, the day for spring-cleaning. A few hours before, Margaret had started her work in the kitchen, on the stove which had served the families of correctional department servicemen since before the war, and rubbed away at the metal until Josie could see her face in it. Margaret had worked her way around the house, wiping, rubbing, dusting, sweeping, items touched, moved, picked up and attended to, always in the same order.

It was a small house with a corrugated iron roof. Last summer the peeling red paint was scraped off and the roof repainted by the prisoners. Josie had heard her parents discussing it.

"They're sweating like pigs up there," Margaret had remarked.

There was a living room and two bedrooms, one for Josie and her little sister, Beth, and one for their parents. The family ate in the kitchen, around a wooden table. It was Josie's job to lay the table. All the warders' houses were not as small, but Josie's father, Brandt, was not senior enough to be allocated one of the bigger homes. They had only been on the island for eighteen months.

Josie was eight years old. She attended the little school that overlooked the parade-ground. Her afternoons were spent playing outside with the children of the warders' families, helping about the house, or at other times, getting underfoot. That's what her mother called it: *underfoot.*

"You're underfoot, Josie, go and entertain yourself," Margaret would say.

"What are you making, Mom? Can't I help you?" Perhaps her mother would be sewing, the old black Singer's brass wheel with its thick, stubby spokes spinning round like those giant wheels at a fairground.

"You're underfoot, Josie."

"I want to help you." The needle of the Singer would whirr up and down, invisible to the naked eye, disappearing as if under a magician's spell. Until it would slow down, and Josie would catch sight of its secret mission: the needle piercing the material, and drawing the thread through, and back.

In recent months Margaret had taken to singing while she worked. It was always the same song, the same far-away voice, as if she'd just woken up but was still in a dream. "Happy birthday, Mr President, happy birthday to you. . . . " Once she noticed Josie staring at her, and she said, "I'm singing for the president, Josie, in America. I'm singing for President Kennedy."

In the bedroom things were different between Josie and Margaret. There was more time for talk. The girl would lie on her tummy on the bed, her face propped up by her hands, her ankles crossing and re-crossing themselves. She would suck on the ends of her hair.

Looking at herself in the dressing table mirror, Margaret would toss her own hair. "What do you think, Josie? Do you like it?"

"Yes! It looks wonderful, Mom."

"Marilyn wore it this way, when she was alive."

Josie would watch her mother dyeing her hair platinum blonde over the kitchen sink. "You won't need to do this, not like Marilyn and me."

Those were their best times together, Josie hanging about the long, beautiful legs of her mother.

"Happy birthday, Mr President, happy birthday to you. . . . " Margaret, singing for the great man across the sea. President Kennedy was also dead.

There were no friends for Josie's mother on the island. The warders' wives were mostly older than her or, Margaret would say, "From the other side of the tracks. They don't like us because I'm English." When Brandt was at work she played The Beatles and Little Richard on the record player, and the wives didn't like that either.

Josie's best friend was Annetjie, the Colonel's granddaughter who came to
stay on the island, along with her mother and four siblings. Her father had
been killed in a mining accident. He was the only white man amongst forty-
five men who were in a lift when the cable snapped. It took a week before
the bodies could be recovered. People said what a shame he had to die in
that way.

The girls played hide-and-seek in the lepers' graveyard, and hopscotch on
the parade-ground when the men weren't using it. Sometimes they played
with the boys and once, after they dared her—four boys ranging in age from
five to eleven, their hands on their hips, crewcutted heads jaunty in expect-
ant triumph—Josie shimmied up the flagpole until she could touch the flag.

Best of all she enjoyed her private conversations with Annetjie behind the
rows of haphazard, overgrown piles of rocks that stood for gravestones in the
lepers' cemetery. A few weeks before they had been there, on the other side
of the island, between the old graves and the sea, where the land slopes
gently, then falls sharply away into the rumble of water. Josie had a stick in
her hand, and pointed to the north-west, where they could see only the
horizon.

"Look, you can see forever."

"Tell me about the pirates," said Annetjie.

"See there," Josie said. "There's an old pirate whose name is Blackbeard.
He's coming from far away across the ocean to fetch us. He'll bring his ship
offshore and row his skiff to the beach and take us away with him to find
treasure." She dug in the burnt sand with the stick. "He's the president of
his country . . . we'll take prisoners along to row and President Blackbeard'll
give us turns to whip them."

A large oil tanker sailed slowly past; they had been coming more frequently because of the troubles in the Holy Land.

"Josie, do you think we'd be able to swim out to President Blackbeard's
ship?"

"Sure." Josie shaded her eyes, scanning the ocean. They were quiet for a
few minutes; from the quarry came sounds of the men digging. Josie scratched
the lines of a boat in the earth. "My Dad says kaffirs can't swim, that's why
they put them here. My Dad's a good swimmer, he was champion when he
was in the navy. Mom can't swim, she hates the water." Margaret had been
pushed into a swimming pool when she was a little girl. "My Dad tells me
stories about Alcatraz and Devil's Island. He says all the best prisons are on
islands, it's the natural place to keep dangerous men."

Josie crouches behind the rock watching the water swirl around her mother's
well-formed dancer's calves. Her dress has again become trapped between

her knee and the wet sand. She sucks at the ends of her hair, the faint taste of Sunlight soap on her tongue. She watches her mother intently. The sea makes way for Margaret, the white water froths around her shins, splashes up against her knees and thighs. . . .

Sundays on the island were different. Sundays brought with them the approval of her father. Brandt liked it when Josie put on her church dress and Margaret helped do her hair into one long plait. This, he said, was her golden ponytail. She was a unicorn, and she wore her horn at the back of her head.

Sunday after Sunday, Brandt would tell Margaret, "I'm just going for a beer, Margie. I'll catch up with you at church." The rest of the week he called her Margaret. "Come on, champ," he'd call to Josie. And they'd walk hand-in-hand to one of the other warder's homes where the men would sit around on the small back porch looking at the orange earth, sipping from their beer glasses, talking about rugby, about handguns and rifles, and about women. That dress of Josie's, made on her mother's Singer, had lace cuffs and a lace collar and a mauve satin ribbon at the neck.

"Brandt, she's looking so pretty, hey!" someone would say as they passed her from one lap to another.

"Have a sip, skat. Hey, you don't mind do you Brandt?"

"Nee, wat. . . . "

Josie would screw up her face. "Ugh! It tastes awful!" And the men would laugh.

After a few drinks they'd forget about her. "You go ahead, champ," Brandt would say, after he'd noticed her hovering, her hands behind her back, trying not to move around in the dusty backyard in case she got her clothes and shoes dirty. "I'll catch up with you."

She'd look over her shoulder as she left the yard. Brandt, already oblivious of her, would be talking with the others. In the moments before Josie ran off to church to join her mother, her little sister Beth and God, her head would be filled with the sights and sounds of warders clinking beer bottles, scratching unshaven cheeks, bleary-eyed and comradely, each one drawn back into the circle of men. . . .

Sometimes Brandt's brother Albert came to visit on the island. He'd been on the police force in Rhodesia but they'd kicked him out. Brandt would take Josie down to the quay to meet the boat. She'd listen out for the barks of the seals, and try to find their dark, blubbery forms under the water's surface. They moved so well in their own world.

Albert arrived on Friday night. Brandt had taken Josie to meet him. Later, well after she had gone to bed, she'd heard the men come home.

They'd been at the pub, and Albert was shouting something about his boss at the factory where Brandt had found him a job. Josie had pretended to be asleep when they came into the room she shared with Beth.

"Ag, moenie worry nie, boet, there's room enough for the two of us, she's only little."

"Okay, boet, sien jou môre," Brandt had slurred before lurching off to bed.

It came back to Josie as she knelt behind the rock watching Margaret enter the sea: the sound of Uncle Albert taking off his clothes, the crumpled drop to the worn carpet, the movement of the sheets, the give of the mattress. He stank of fish and beer.

"Hullo, Josie. It's me, Uncle Albert." His beard had prickled against her neck, through her fine blonde hair.

Josie had kept quiet, breathing in a way she prayed would sound like sleep.

"It's so cold outside, let's snuggle warm. Here, make your uncle warm."

Dad was a champion swimmer. . . . Mom hated the sea. . . . Dad called her "champ," he loved her church dress, the collar of lace. . . . Blackbeard's gonna come from across the ocean . . . ag, moenie worry nie boet, there's room enough for the two of us . . . happy birthday, Mr. President, happy birthday to you. . . .

Beth had cried out, woken by Josie's muffled protests, and the cries had woken Margaret. There had been a great deal of shouting and screaming, the little girls' father telling their mother to calm down.

"You're hysterical, woman. Margaret, shut up! Calm down!" Then he'd hit her. With his fist. Against her eye. She fell down and he took her by the hair and dragged her out of the room.

As Josie watches Margaret wade deeper into the sea, against the misty wand that has made the mainland disappear—perhaps forever—she can't stop herself from remembering, and from not remembering. Lying in her bed, yes, the covers over her head, her shivering knees tucked in beneath her chin, sucking on her Sunlight-washed hair, an acrid, awful sweetness pervading the dark space beneath the blankets.

And in the morning she found Margaret cleaning the stove. Brandt was in his warder's trousers with his braces over his bare chest and shoulders, having breakfast with Uncle Albert and giving orders to Margaret about how they wanted their eggs. They were laughing about something. Margaret's hair was tied up in a doek. Her hands scrubbed faster and harder; when the brothers left the house Uncle Albert playfully slapped her bottom.

Margaret finished polishing the stove and the floors and went outside to do the stoep. After a while the red floor was so gleamy Josie could see her face in there too. She closed her eyes and tried to pretend that she could no longer see but the sights came through her ears: the soft scooping of the polish, the dull scraping of the tin on the stoep floor, her mother's panting for breath. She pushed her palms against her ears, tightly enough to hear the drone of the ocean. The little girl hung around waiting—hoping—for her mother to scold her for being underfoot.

When she was finished Margaret stood on the stoep for a long time with the tin of polish in one hand and her rags in the other, staring at the big palm tree in front of the house, her forehead wet with sweat, the rise and fall of her breasts gradually calming. People walked past, some greeted her. She just stared at the palm tree.

Finally she went into her bedroom and put on "Marilyn's dress." Before they'd come to the island she'd taken Josie on the train to Stuttafords in town with money she saved from her housekeeping. They had tea at the posh restaurant. Margaret said the dressmaker's pattern and the material were precisely what she'd been looking for. She'd be able to make an outfit just like the one Marilyn wore in *The Seven Year Itch*, in the famous scene where her skirt billowed up around her thighs.

Although she'd finished the dress before coming to the island, she'd not worn it before. It had a bodice that consisted of a halter-neck that gathered around the back of her neck, and from there descended frontwards, wrapping itself around each breast before being joined to the waistband and the pleated skirt below. Brandt had not allowed her to wear it.

When she had it on, she sat quietly in front of her dressing table doing her hair and putting on makeup. She didn't answer when Josie asked where she was going, not so much as a, you're underfoot, Josie.

When she left the house the girl followed her.

"Go back inside, Josie."

So Josie kept her distance as Margaret made her way down to the little beach where the warders' families swam, only not Margaret because she hated the sea. Josie watched from behind the rock, the hem of her skirt getting damp because her knees were in the sand, as her mother took off her smart shoes and with Marilyn's dress caught by the wind and flapping up around her thighs, walked into the sea. . . .

The water is rough as it comes up against the island. The beaches here are not like the ones on the mainland, they offer little shelter during the hot months of summer, and are stormier than the mainland's during winter. Today is a cold, autumn day, and none of the familiar landmarks of the city can be seen, not even the cablecar that takes people to the top of the mountain.

At first Margaret seems to manage as the waves break against her body, soaking her dress so that it clings to her, the salt must be like glue on her skin. She does not jump in the manner of bathers before a breaking wave, she only raises her arms slightly as the wall of water rolls into her. Each time she is rocked backwards. Now and then she loses her footing. The waves fall against her belly and breasts and move past her, leaving behind water that only reaches her knees. She wades further into the trough of sea before the next breaker hits her. The set of waves is reaching its climax, each line hitting higher than the last. Josie gasps as her mother is swept under, but then Margaret bobs up again, flicking water from her face. Her sodden platinum blonde fringe is in her eyes. Another wave breaks over her and takes her under.

Josie comes out from behind the rock calling, "Mom! Mom! Mommy!" She runs along the shoreline like a crab, sideways across the beach, gaining no sight of her mother, then moving back over her tracks, but there is only the white froth of the waves and beyond that, across a short expanse of water, the wispy beginnings of the sea mist.

"Mommy! Mommy!"

Josie wades into the water and is knocked over by a wave, then is drawn seaward by the backwash which seems more fierce than that with which her mother had to contend. There is water in her nose and mouth and throat, and the salt stings her eyes. There is a terrible noise in her ears. She does not know which way is up. She has been covered by a cold blanket of sea.

One moment she has scraped her head on something solid, it must be the sand at the bottom of the sea, and then the next she feels air on her face, and can take it into her lungs, and she is coughing. The set of waves seems finally to have spent itself, the sea becomes a little calmer, and Josie, falling to her knees, rising and lurching forward and falling again, scrambles out.

Margaret is there, between some rocks to the westward side of the beach, bent over with her hands on her knees. She too, as Josie comes up to her, is coughing like mad. There are scratches on her legs and arms and face. She straightens herself up when she sees Josie, and puts a hand to her hair. Her dress is torn, drenched, her flesh patterned with goose-pimples.

Josie sniffs hard, the mixture of snot and saltwater like angry little wasps inside her head. Margaret takes her hand. "Look at you," she says, "you've got your dress all wet."

The girl laughs. "You have too, Mom."

The noon gun from the mainland goes off, the wind brings the sound across the strait, and in its wake Josie hears, for the first time today, the screeches of the seagulls. Mother and daughter make their way over the rocks and onto the path that leads to the settlement.

"Mommy! You forgot your smart shoes!" Josie lets go her mother's hand and runs back to where she saw Margaret leave the shoes. She has them now, and rejoins her mother.

They walk between two rows of warders' houses where, despite the cold weather, people sit on their stoeps, warders and their wives and their children. The island's minister stands outside his house talking to the district surgeon who has come across from the mainland to conduct his medical tour. They all stare at Margaret and Josie. One of the warders whistles, an undulating, loud wolf whistle.

Josie sits on the quay, on one of the suitcases Margaret has packed during the night, while Brandt slept. The sun has not yet risen. Beth is asleep in Margaret's arms. They had to pick their way through the small, clean warder's house, around the sleeping forms of Brandt and his brother Albert, who slept in the sitting room. Now on the quay, waiting amongst their possessions, they listen to the water lapping against the wooden staves and the old tyres that buffer the sides of the boats as they dock alongside. They will have to wait until 10:00 a.m., when the boat leaves.

Without us to wake him, Josie thinks, he will not know. Brandt will still be asleep by the time the boat has disappeared into the mist on its way to the mainland.

Memory

CHRIS VAN WYK ▼▼▼▼▼▼▼▼▼▼▼▼▼▼▼▼▼▼▼▼▼▼▼▼▼▼▼▼▼▼▼▼

Derek is dangling from the kitchen chair
while I'm shuffling about in a flutter of flour.
Mummy is making vetkoek on the Primus.
Derek is too small to peer over the table,
that's why mummy has perched him on the chair.
His dummy twitters so he's a bird.

I'm not that small—I was four in July.
I'm tall enough to see what's going on;
I'm a giraffe and the blotches of shadow
on the ceiling and the walls
from the flames on the Primus and candle
are the patches on my back.

Daddy's coming home soon
from the factory where they're turning him
into a cupboard that creaks.
But the vetkoek are sizzling and growing
like bloated gold coins:
We're rich!

This is my first vivid memory of childhood.
Why have I never written it all down before?
Maybe because the pan falls with a clatter
and the oil swims towards the twittering bird
Mummy flattens her forearm on the table,
stopping the seething flood.

As she does so she pleads with the bird to fly away,
but quietly so as not to ruffle his feathers.
But my brother clambers off the chair
as if he has all the time in the world.
Sensing danger, the twittering gives way to a wail
and the giraffe's patches flare on the restive walls.

Ma gives a savage scream that echoes across the decades
and cauterizes my childhood like a long scar.

The Women Sing

LUVUYO MKANGELWA ▼▼▼▼▼▼▼▼▼▼▼▼▼▼▼▼▼▼▼▼▼▼▼▼▼▼

The women sing
songs of worship
to make their journey
only a step away

The women sing
banging carriage walls
and whacking their bibles
with their strong hands
for drum-like sounds

The women sing
to conquer the thoughts
of the day's orders

The women sing
The women sing
to be free!

The women sing
to possess themselves
for a moment
at least!

I'm retelling a womanburning

ROSHILA NAIR ▼▼▼▼▼▼▼▼▼▼▼▼▼▼▼▼▼▼▼▼▼▼▼▼▼▼▼▼▼▼▼▼▼▼▼▼▼

I was thinking *I will be eight years old when my father returns from the six-to-twelve shift at the mill* and drinking sweet cold Milo when Aunty Padma flew down the stairs burning. She isn't really my aunt—neither my father's sister nor my mother's real sister. But where I come from all the mothers are aunts.

Our blue kitchen door was wide open with the hope of letting in a breeze to cool our boiling little flat. The blue kitchen door opens onto the dull staircase leading to the upper floors of Lavender Flats. From where I was sitting I could see the viscous gleam of the staircase walls, oil painted bottle-green to hide the dirt marks left by the grubby hands of the many children who live here. The Town Board reckons bottle-green oil paint a shrewd victory against both the dirt and complaints of rate-paying tenants. And hidden dirt has never incited a revolution.

And if a light bulb is still left unbroken after the weekly Friday night of drunken husbands and man-sons returning home from a game of thunnee in the early hours of the morning, returning with the feel of young lions in their fists, the green walls glow slickly. Dance eerily with the hazy shadow men staggering home to a piss-logged sleep. The rite of Saturday night.

It was too, for us children, much awaited these weekly end traditions. Daringly defying the admonishments of a hairbrush-wielding mother, my brother and I would peer secretly through the faded net curtains. Snorting through our nostrils at soft-spoken Uncle Pather crawling on all fours up the wrong staircase, singing the latest Tamil film hits. Making salaam-alaikum gestures to each other as Muslim Uncle crept stealthily to his door, trying to keep to the shadows. Drawing in our breaths excitedly as we heard our heroes Eunis, Strini and Benson swearing loudly as they pissed in Aunty Suriya's doorway, she that black-toothed bitch who is always spitting at them and calling them corner-boys, dagga-roekers and swines.

And throughout the long night we would hear furniture crashing, glass breaking and the frightened cries of children in the middle of a torrent of abuse hurled across the kitchen table. Sometimes, my brother and I would take bets with bubblegum, guessing at who was catching it that night. Other nights, when the crying lasted too long, we would cover our heads with the heavy blankets and try desperately to fall asleep. One, two, three, four . . . four sheep over the fence and another child crying. Five, six, seven . . . one more table crashing. Eight, nine . . . someone's shoved out the door above our heads. Ten. . . .

The following morning we would gather conspiratorially with the other children at the side of the flat and act out the dramas secretly. Crawling in the sand and groping about the wall. The boys pissing like hose pipes trying to splash the girls who dash out of range with delighted screams. Link hands in a circle and chant the swear words in loud whispers like witches on a moonlit night. And we knew that our friends who were missing were the ones that had caught it badly last night. And we knew that they had to be kept indoors so bruised bodies could tell no tales.

On the previous Friday night all the light bulbs in our block had been broken. The Town Board had not replaced them and for three days and nights since the staircase had remained in darkness. Lighted up now and then when a kitchen door opened and someone stepped out briefly to throw dirt into the grey standard-issue bin just outside each flat.

That night as I sat waiting for my father to return there was a strange glow descending the staircase. Growing and growing brighter and brighter. And the oil green walls were throwing off brilliant big shadows. Shapes I had never seen before on the oily walls. I thought of Deepavali, when we gather on the upper flat balconies and throw fire crackers into the night below, lighting up the dark with brilliant bursts of colour and joy. The candle flames we used to light our cracker wicks with made the same kind of dancing shapes on the green walls. Only the candle shapes are much smaller than these gigantic shapes on the wall in front of me now. But Deepavali was still weeks and weeks away. And I could sense some spectacular thing thumping down the stairs.

I smelled her melting hair long before she came into view. The smell reminded me of when my mother sat with the other aunts at the side of the flat and cleaned sheep trotters and sheep heads on a Primus stove. It was the aunts' way of supplementing the household budget. And the sheep heads and legs we children could not sell when we went door-to-door with our blood smeared grass baskets, accompanied by a cloud of buzzing blue flies, became a tasty meal during the week. That peculiar smell. A mixing of women sweating in the heat, paraffin burning and dried, blood-crusted wool melting.

I heard her thudding feet in a hurry to get somewhere. Get down the stairs quickly. Get out. And I heard her long black hair crackling and these other strange yet familiar hissing, sizzling sounds. The sound of a red hot iron rod running determinedly over a sheep trotter. Searing away the tiny, niggling hairs that cause indigestion. Charring the skin beneath an even, silky black.

I did not see her for long, only a vision of her as she danced away past our open blue door. She was briefly, brightly there one moment. Gone the next.

There was not much of her to see. She is a flying angel, I think. The Angel Gabriel I'd seen pictures of in the Hymn Book for Good Children when I sat with the Christian children by the side of the flat every Sunday morning. Out-stretched arms beating, as if wanting to embrace someone. Her feathery, flaming wings glowing an orange-blue halo around her. A hallowed mother breathing out the smell of paraffin. And I was remembering a Sunday school lesson—that it was the glowing holy light of the Heavenly Father that surrounds Gabriel, not the crackling melting flames of sheep trotters.

I was off the cupboard top I had been sitting on in a flash. Running after her. Wanting to see the woman inside the flames. So eager to know the blue flames that swallowed the woman inside. My weary mother, drying dishes otherside our cramped kitchen, had not seen her dance past our door. But I heard her following swiftly her child escaping into the dark night. Following the path of a strange light ahead like a moth made golden by the flames.

Now I am following Aunty Padma burning. I hear my heavily pregnant mother calling for me to come back to her. Child . . . my child. . . . Child. . . . As if I have no name! And I am thinking that in a few minutes I will be eight years old. A big girl, my father would say.

We have reached the Sunday school ground at the side of the flat. She collapses suddenly. The dance has left her feet. Writhing on the ground. This way and that. It is a heap of flames moving on the ground below me. I see the fire eating greedily into her arms, her breasts, her thighs. And still she remains silent.

It is unbearable. I cannot call out until she does. Unless she does. Oh my mother's sister. I implore her. Silently too. With the blood that links my mother to her and her to me. Call out just once. Call out and set me free of the fire you have set on my tongue. But still she remained silent.

Now I reach out like a priest to throw onto her sweet cold Milo from the cup I find I am still clutching. The trickle that splashes onto her burning face is lapped up greedily. But she begins to scream. Her scream terrifies me—releases me from the silent bondage with this burning woman I do not know anymore. The cup has fallen into the flames and now there is also the smell of plastic melting. A foul, polluted smell.

Now my mother is here reaching out for me. I will not let her touch me. Cannot. Now the flat aunts and uncles are here. And the children are here too. Trying to get past the crowd of elders to see. There is much screaming and threatening and slapping as the children are pushed back. And I see the women's eyes are a desperate orange-blue. And I see the men's eyes are oddly shadowed. And I see that only the retreating children's eyes remain curious and excited. And I want to get away from the women as they all grab at me. Screaming as if it were I who is burning so treacherously below.

And my mother is still reaching for me with her face flushed by the fire on the ground. Her swollen body clutches at me. Presses my face into its hard roundness. Drags me away. Smothered in my mother's bigness, I can hear. The sound of running footsteps. Water splashing. Steam hissing. My aunts crying. The men silent, except for one who is giving orders for more water and blankets. The urgent wail of the ambulance. I heard it all as if through a thick blanket. The blanketing of my mother's body.

And the next day all the women gathered and made off for the next flat where they grabbed the bitch who was the cause of their sister's burning and they tore off her clothes and beat her until she lay bleeding and unable to move. But nobody said anything to Aunty Padma's husband. He had lost too much, perhaps.

We never held Sunday school at the side of the flat again. The corner-boys wouldn't sit there anymore at night to smoke their pipes. The Lavender uncles were never drunk enough to walk over that spot on Friday nights. And when Deepavali came the rains fell for a long time. And bathed the scorched earth where she had burned. And when the sun shone the next day it drew up into the sky the smell she had left behind. And then the aunts gathered there again to clean the weekly sheep heads and trotters.

And I still remember my mother had clutched me so tightly to her belly that I had felt it moving inside. Her unborn baby alarmed at the excitement. My unborn sister excited at the alarm. Wanting to come out and smell for herself the night of a woman's silence. And I was thinking, my mother, if ever my father comes home with the smell of another woman on his breath. If ever my father comes home drunk and beats us all. If ever my father ignores you silently if he did come home at all. Will you speak? How will you speak?

And I am thinking there must be another way for us to be heard.

Spiral Child

LOUISE GREEN ▼▼▼▼▼▼▼▼▼▼▼▼▼▼▼▼▼▼▼▼▼▼▼▼▼▼▼▼▼▼▼▼▼▼

I have caught
this spiral child
grey as smoke
curled in a curved
corner of my life.
How she has hidden
from me, year after
year—waiting worm
—coiled, with me
through all those
special hours of dread
threading my dream
with hers till she criss crossed my nights
and days, stealing
from my heart
everything that was
most precious.
Somewhere in the
stack of years that
leans unsteadily
against my life
I lost her. Now
she is unpacking
my days, laying out
forgotten objects
as if the slow
drag of time had
not altered them
beyond recognition.

Homeland Banter

Pumla Dineo Gqola ▼▼▼▼▼▼▼▼▼▼▼▼▼▼▼▼▼▼▼▼▼▼▼▼▼▼▼▼▼

"Bulumko, Phumela Doris."

"Present, Miss," I shout just in time. The cold from outside follows me in as I shut the door behind me. I join the row of children in front of the already seated class. Miss Faku looks up from her table and then continues to call out the names on the register. We stand there facing the class, our backs to the blackboard, waiting for her to resume the daily activities. I am now trying to think up an excuse for being late, which is not always required. It makes no sense; we will get punished anyway. I look at the hand that will receive my share of the caning, my hand, numb from the cold winter morning. Standing fifth in the line I watch in anticipation as the four in front of me get their lashes, it is no longer an excuse that my mind is focused on. I am half waiting for my turn to be over, half hoping that by some miracle it will not come. No miracle ever happens in this class. The time is quarter past eight which means that I am late enough to have missed the ten-minute assembly which takes place every morning.

I put my schoolbag down and in the mistiness of my eyes I knock my knee against the desk. My right hand is between my thighs in a desperate attempt to rub away the pain. My hand burns and feels hot on the inside of my thigh. It is an unspoken rule that you do not cry after a caning, some way of communicating to the others that you are a big girl or boy so you can take the pain. I suck my lips in and bite on the soft insides, close my eyes and feel droplets cling to my eyelashes.

"Take out your Mathematics homework," the teacher commands. I have to release my hand to open my bag. My fingers are numb. Miss Faku is standing in front of the blackboard waiting to fill in the blanks with the right answers. There are ten sums on the board. Our hands go up, for her to choose the pupil who will provide the answer to the first sum.

"Hands up, all those who got ten out of ten! Good, good! Nine out of ten, good, eight out of ten. . . ." She stops saying good for those with less than six. She puts up a new set of sums on the board under the heading "Classwork." You cannot start doing the classwork before writing out the corrections to the homework exercise. We make pencil ticks in our own books or crosses depending on whether the answer was right or wrong. For class work we queue to her table for her to mark our books in red ink. She explains why the answers are wrong, then you have to go back to write corrections and stand in the queue. Sometimes you have to go up and down five or six times before you get it right. There can be corrections for corrections for corrections. If you have less than five out of ten frequently, you are stupid. The big boys at the back often take someone else's book and copy from it when the teacher is not looking.

Miss Faku gets up from her desk, orders all of us to sit down because she is going to repeat yesterday's lesson. I am bored because I scored ten out of ten for my homework and more than five out of ten for classwork. It is easy to get more than five out of ten but many people in my class are stupid. Miss Faku only repeats a class if many people have wrong answers. Then she asks if there are any questions. I never ask questions in class because I'm clever. There are times when I ask Sinazo, my friend, during break because she is also clever. The two of us compete for the first two positions in class. That is why we get to sit in front.

Miss Faku has finished the lesson now so there is a queue at her table again. She is not looking at the class now. I turn to face the row of desks to my right. I call out to Sinazo to ask what she has brought for lunch; I tell her about mine. We are whispering because we do not want the teacher to catch us, otherwise we will be in big trouble.

"Phumela and Sinazo! Have you finished your classwork?"

In unison we jump up startled. We have to stand to talk to the teacher. We respond, "Yes, Miss."

We look at each other because we do not know. Miss Faku gets up and walks towards Sinazo's desk.

"Sit down," she says as she marks my friend's book. Sinazo gets nine, I get them all right.

Miss Faku tells Sinazo to stand and gives her one lash for making noise and not getting all the answers right. I am happy because I got the total but sad since Sinazo got caned. The teacher turns around and stands towering above me. I look up at her in anticipation of the unknown.

"What are you looking at? Stand up!" I stand. She lifts her arm with the cane above her head. I have to stretch out mine to receive it. I protest. I got the total. She is angry now because I talked back and that is rude. I am informed that my punishment is for talking to Sinazo, thereby preventing her from also getting the total. But I only talked to her afterwards. I am being rude again. That may earn me more lashes. It doesn't. Miss Faku saunters back to her table. I look at Sinazo and she looks back at me. We both fake a smile because to cry would be to acknowledge the pain, which would make us like small children.

The bell is ringing so it must be half nine. All the classroom doors fling open as children rush out like air expelled from a balloon. It is time for P. T. now but it is too cold to run in shorts. Miss Faku decides to have her weekly "inspection." The other classes have it too at different times. The girls always have their turns first. We stand in front of the class in our panties, vests and socks. Miss Faku wants to see if they are clean. When she finds a girl with dirty underwear she gives her a warning and the following day she will have a lone inspection. When the girls have finished, it's the boys' turn. The same routine. We have this inspection every week but we never know which day because Miss Faku changes it to confuse us. Today is Monday, last week it was on Wednesday. She says that way we will always wear clean clothes to school because she might have an inspection. She is a nice teacher who never canes people for wearing dirty clothes. My friends from standard 3B and 3C say that their teachers cane those with dirty clothes. Immediately after the boys finish, the bell rings again. It is break time. We do not wait for the teacher to dismiss us.

In the shade of the stairs behind the 3B class, we sit and share our lunch box contents. We always share our lunch—Sinazo, Pumza, Vuyo and me. Pumza is in 3B, Vuyo in 3C. After we finish eating, we play games with other children. We are not talking much today because Sinazo and I do not feel like laughing about what happened in class. It is too soon for us to find it funny. The boys stand in the sun leaning against the wall when they are not playing soccer with a tennis ball. We play something else also with a tennis ball. It is called rubeka. There are two teams. The aim is to hit the competition with the ball, which makes your team the one that gets chased. They now have to avoid the ball at all cost. There are no winners in this game and the teams change each time we play.

We can hear music in the background. It is the senior choir practising for the concert. I do not ever want to be in the senior choir because they practice all the time, even during break. Sometimes they even stay on after school. They are singing the same notes over and over again.

The dust forms a thin film on our polished black school shoes as we run around in the dusty playground. There is a big stone in my way as I run, but I only remember to notice it as I hit the ground. I look at my soiled, scraped knee. It is throbbing with pain as I make my way to the tap to wash off the dirt. Some of the children are laughing because I fell, but I don't feel hurt. I also laugh when somebody else falls. I don't find it amusing, but it is what you are supposed to do after you say you are sorry. I think maybe it makes it more difficult for the injured one to cry.

My tunic is dirty and water droplets cling to it. I rub the wet part, which only makes it worse. Now there is a muddy patch like you get when chocolate melts on your clothes in the heat. I have to try to get it off, otherwise the teacher will tell me I am dirty after break.

The bell rings and I run back to my class, my knee stinging as the skin pulls on the grazed part. I cannot afford to get to the class after the door has been closed. I make it and the door closes behind me.

It is now the Social Studies period, so Mr. Dambu is standing next to the chart with the map of South Africa on it. "How many provinces are there in South Africa, class?"

"There are four provinces in South Africa, Sir," we sing back to him.

Today we do the departments of the Ciskei and the ministers heading them. He has written on the board all the information we should write in at the back of our books. We are expected to memorise it all for Friday's test. I look at the list and read each line twice over to myself. I only recognise one name on the list. He is the Minister of Education. He came to our school concert last week and made a speech. Shortly before he arrived, we were told to line the sides of the road to form a guard of honour. The convoy drove in amidst a cloud of dust that blew in our faces. Then we had to go and sit in the hall. He made a very long speech. I don't remember what he was saying because I fell asleep. Many children just fall asleep when speeches are made because we are not allowed to talk. We are told that it is disrespectful to talk when a big person talks. The parents sit up and listen. Sometimes the speeches are made in English so we cannot understand. This English is not the same as when we learn it at school. It is difficult but we can pick up the odd word. During a speech, the audience will clap, waking up the children in the process. If your mother or father is clapping, then you also join in.

I am woken from my trance when Teacher Dambu asks if we have finished copying the list down. I have stopped halfway so I quickly try to finish. He is now handing out copies of a map which we must colour in. It is not the first time we are doing this. I remember doing this last year. There are two circles which must be left blank. I used to wonder why last year. The teacher is telling us now that they are not in the country. I think the person who drew the map was confused to put Swaziland and Lesotho inside another country. We must fill in the names of the provinces in block letters. The lesson is over, but before Teacher Dambu leaves, "Good afternoon, class."

We stand and say, "Good afternoon, Sir."

"Sit down," and he walks out.

There is no teacher in the classroom now. Mr. Dambu has neglected to appoint somebody to make sure we keep quiet and to take down the names of the noisemakers. Soon the whole class is abuzz with children moving away from their desks to visit friends. I go across to Sinazo's desk. She shifts up closer to her deskmate to make room for me to sit next to her on the bench. I am looking at her hair because her one plait at the back has come undone.

"Do you want me to fix it up for you?"

"Can you do it? Do you know how to?"

I do not answer her. Instead I divide her hair into two parts. I cross the left section over the right and vice versa until there is no more hair in my hand. Her deskmate, Nosipho, tells me to let her do it, "You should do it with three sections, not two. Otherwise it's not a real plait. Let me show you."

As soon as I let go of Sinazo's hair, my effort falls apart. Nosipho laughs, taking the hair into her own hands and doing it the proper way.

Sinazo gives me a sideward glance, "I thought you knew how to do it the right way." But I ignore her.

I am watching Nosipho's expertise. I wish I could do it like that. I also wish my hair would be divided into three parts, like Sinazo's. My hair is too short. It can only be divided into six plaits, or two rows of plaits.

Someone shouts, "Sout!" I run back to my place and Mam Dambu walks in. I heed the warning just in time.

As soon as Mam Dambu walks in, my deskmate, Thandeka, tells me that she needs to go to the toilet. I tell her to wait until the teacher is sitting down. The teacher greets us in the usual way. We stand up to recite "My Shadow," the English poem we were told to learn for today. After we finish, we sit down and take out our reading books. We do not have to be told this; every Monday we do reading, Wednesday we have spelling or dictation, Friday we do grammar or compositions.

Thandeka is bouncing on our bench. Her hand shoots up. Mam Dambu points at her. "Mam, ndicel' ukuy' etoilet?"

"I can't hear you," is the response Thandeka's response meets with.

"Please, Mam . . . " Thandeka stutters. She has forgotten how to say it in English.

I take my exercise book and scribble the required words on the plastic cover. I gently press my foot over hers to get her attention. She reads the message out aloud from my book.

"Thandeka, sit down. You have just come back from break. Phumela, am I the teacher or are you?"

"You are the teacher, Mam."

"Why don't we see how good your reading is today? Read!" I do not know what page we are on. Somebody notices and whispers, "Page 25."

I start reading it out. I read each word very slowly, neglecting the intonation that we have so often been told is crucial. I feel the temperature rise suddenly from my left bum but I need not look. Thandeka could hold it in no longer.

"Phumela, who told you to stop? You are cheeky! It looks like there are two teachers in this class. Why don't you and I exchange places," she is bellowing as she comes towards me.

I get up, "No, Mam. . . . "

Too late! She has already discovered the pool and shouts, "Thandeka, you silly girl! Go outside and clean yourself up. You are stinking up the whole class."

Thandeka crawls back into the class after the teacher has left. As she gets down on the bench next to me I try to find out where she has been all this time. Before she can give me a proper explanation, we are notified by the class prefect that unless we give her our lunch tomorrow our names will go down on the noisemakers' list. We do not really have a choice: starve tomorrow or get caned today. Thandeka continues explaining, but the class prefect warns us again. If we do not stop talking now, she will put our names down. So, we will not eat tomorrow and we still don't get to talk. The school bell rings, officially announcing that school is out.

Tuesday morning, I arrive at school just as the gate closes. The principal announces that the school inspector will be coming tomorrow. He preaches to us about the importance of presenting the proper school image. We sing a few hymns and The Lord's Prayer. Afterwards, we sing "We are marching over to Jerusalem" as we march to our classes. The standard fives go first followed by the standard four class, and so on all the way to the sub-A class. At other times it happens the other way round with the sub-A's leaving first.

When we get to our class, we start chanting the multiplication tables because Maths class is first. Forty-six children ranting at the top of their voices the multiples of one to twelve. We get to six times six and the number of voices goes into sharp decline. Those that sit at the back, the really stupid ones, shout, "Six times seven. . . . "

We respond from the front, "Forty two." It goes on like this until twelve times twelve, the last set of multiples. The multiplication tables are printed at the backs of our exercise books, but it is school policy that everyone should cover their books in both brown paper and plastic covers. I am not sure if this is so we do not peek or in order to keep the books looking tidy. Maybe it's for both reasons.

We have a free period. The standard 2A teacher is absent. Sinazo and I go to the class. I have been sent to make sure that the students do not end up walking around outside their classroom instead of staying inside and reading. Normally they would have been sent to join the other standard 2 class, had they not been writing a test. Sinazo has not been asked to accompany me, she comes anyway. I walk into the class. Sinazo is still outside when a 2A girl pushes the door in her face. They have a slinging match. The girl pushes my friend back and Sinazo retaliates. Their tunics are flying as excitement fills the air. The class is impossible to control now because everybody loves a fight. In the end Sinazo wins, which is good. Imagine people talking about her losing a fight to someone who is her junior. I do not tell the class to keep quiet which is why I am here in the first place, because I too like talking in class when it is forbidden. I know that if I were to be caught now I would be in big trouble, but I choose not to think about it too much. Not until it's too late!

The door swings open and the vice principal walks in. I realise that very few people are in the right places. I am told to go back to my class, scolded for bringing Sinazo along. Sinazo, in turn, is scolded for being "forward" and doing things without being asked to. We leave the room but stand listening outside the door. The vice principal is demanding that people hand themselves over for making noise. The class growls the kind of sound where you know that the students do not agree with the teacher. We have been doing it for years. You close your mouth when you do it; otherwise you get picked on and caned in front of the whole class as an example. The vice principal has now decided to cane the whole class. Another growl.

Sinazo and I walk back to our class in silence. It is almost break time and I suddenly remember that I am to have no food. Poni, the biggest boy in my class, is standing outside the classroom. He will get into trouble if a teacher walks by, but I don't think he really cares. He often talks back to the teachers when they scold him. He says he is a man. I don't know if he is telling the truth. He looks old enough to have been to the bush, but I don't really know. He says that he will make sure that I do not go hungry provided I give him half of my lunch. He will beat the class prefect up for me when she comes to collect. I agree and feel safe. The bell rings.

"Phumela, a promise is a promise." I turn around and there she is. My guardian angel comes to my rescue.

"Leave the child alone! Imagine a big girl like you eating her food. She also wants to grow up and be your age."

"Poni, this has nothing to do with you. Where do you come into it?"

"I come in where I say I do."

She stands there speechless. There's only so much that you can say to Poni because he is not scared of anybody. She wags her finger close to my face; I start thinking it will get into my eye.

"You and me . . . after school. Don't be a coward," she breathes into my face. I am so scared that for the first time I wish school would never come out.

After the needlework/gardenwork period, the teacher tells me to stay on after school to try out for the netball team. I start wishing I were somebody else so that I would not have to go. If I were a boy then I could leave as soon as gardenwork is over. Besides, gardenwork is not even compulsory. It has to be done outside. When it is summer, the teachers say it is too hot. When it is winter, they do not do it anyway. There doesn't have to be a finished plot to show at the end of the year. If you are a girl, you have to do needlework from standard two onwards. The needle pokes your finger when you try to sew. You have to bring it from home and make sure that it doesn't get lost. At the end of the year we must all have finished the dress we are making this year. I must admit that I am stupid in sewing, so that I always need help. I will probably finish last which makes me the most stupid in my class. We do not get caned in sewing unless we play truant.

I wish I were shorter like my friends so that I would not have to stay on after school.

"Phum, aren't you scared to go to netball practice? She is much bigger than you, you can't fight her and win."

As if my fears are not heavy enough, Sinazo has to rub salt in my wounds. I resolve to give netball a skip and to face the consequences the following day.

Today is Wednesday. I make Auntie call in to school to say that I am sick. It has been a long process because she would never have called in if she didn't believe me. Last night I had a terrible stomach ache, so bad that I could not even eat boerewors which is my most favourite thing. I went to bed almost in tears. When Auntie came in to wake me this morning, I got out of bed as usual. Then I remembered. The stomach ache came back with such force that I could barely stand up straight, let alone walk. She gave me medicine. I hate medicine and this one is especially bitter. Afterwards she told me to get into the bath because I would soon be feeling well enough to go to school. I complied even to the extent of putting on my black tunic with my white shirt underneath. Breakfast tasted better than anything I had eaten in a long time. I ate everything up and then informed her that I was going to throw it all back up because my stomach couldn't hold it. I ran to the bathroom and . . . nothing. My stomach was in knots at the thought of the double beating awaiting me at school. I cannot tell anyone the truth because to skip school is a bad thing. It is something that stupid or bad students do.

My stomach is fine by ten. I know that it is too late to force me to go to school now. I have outsmarted them, all of them. I really believe that I am clever, even out of class.

The big clock says it is twelve. I am not feeling so clever now. There is nothing to do around the house. My parents are at work. My sister is at school. I could play with my little brother but he is asleep. Besides, he cannot even talk. He cries, speaks baby talk, and eats. That is all he does. He cannot sing or talk properly yet. I get out of bed and walk around the house in search of something to do. I cannot wait till after school so I can go out and play. I don't think I will skip school again because it is so boring. It is almost as bad as being punished for missing netball. We get a beating almost everyday at school for one thing or another but I am still afraid of the cane. I try to avoid it. I do not do anything naughty if I think the teacher might catch me. I only cannot keep quiet. Sometimes I really try hard not to speak in class, but it never works. My name inevitably finds its way onto the noisemakers' list. I suddenly remind myself of the fight that I was supposed to be in yesterday afternoon. Now I have a real stomach ache. Tomorrow she will beat me up.

I am looking at the calendar now. Two more days left this week. Tomorrow is coloured pink even though it is not a Sunday. All the other days apart from Sundays are white.

"Phumela, you should have just gone to school. Your tummy ache seems to have disappeared now, and all you are doing is getting in my way. Stand on the other side, I want to put polish on the spot you are standing on.

"Auntie. . . ."

"Don't Auntie me . . . move."

"Why is tomorrow pink on the calendar?"

"Let me see," she walks towards the calendar, "it's a public holiday—Republic Day. No school or work tomorrow."

No school. That is what she said. On Friday, both the teacher and the prefect will have forgotten. I am sitting near the window and from a distance I can see my uncle coming home. Staying home is not so bad, I can play with Uncle. I miss my friends and on Friday there will be homework from today. Maybe they learnt something new and I will not understand. What if it is difficult?

I can hear my uncle talking in the kitchen. I run out of the room with my sleeping brother in it and go to meet Uncle.

The Awakening of Katie Fortuin

FINUALA DOWLING ▼▼▼▼▼▼▼▼▼▼▼▼▼▼▼▼▼▼▼▼▼▼▼▼▼▼▼▼▼▼▼

Today my auntie, Katie Fortuin, woke up. She fell asleep in 1969. Quite long to be asleep nearly 25 years.

We sort of knew Katie was going to wake up so we were all standing around her bed. Me, my wife Sandra, my Ma, Uncle Richard (Ma's second husband), my brother Stan, my sisters Rosie and Maria, their husbands Shane and Achmat, my half-brothers Vincent, Clive and Johnny, my half-sister Agnes, and all their offspring. The first thing Katie asked for was a cup of tea. I'm glad she didn't express an urgent need to look at herself in a mirror. Shock might have killed her.

Not that she'd aged badly. Her skin was quite smooth for a 54-year old, probably because she hadn't been yelling or smoking and had gotten plenty of beauty sleep. But Ma had let Katie's hair grow into this great big wiry bush, kind of Afro-style, and it was streaked with grey. Lying with her bushy head against Ma's best Edgars pillowslip, Auntie looked much paler than us. Because of not being in the sun, she looked almost white.

Anyway, Katie didn't want a mirror, she wanted tea. I was sure she recognized in me the little boy who used to do errands for her, running down Hanover Street with no money but my Auntie's fervent promises.

"And if there's still no sugar, run down to the babbie-shop and get some. You can tell that *ou Slams* to put it on credit and don't mind if his face looks like *asyn*. And by the by, it's very cheeky for a coloured boy to grow a moustache, you know." I remembered then that my aunt had always been a prejudiced woman.

"Katie," said Ma, "we've had just on a quarter of a century to replace the sugar so you can rest assured your tea will be sugared just the way you like it." Katie looked suspiciously at Ma.

"And who might you be?" she asked.

"Don't you remember me Katie? I'm your sister, Desiree. You've been asleep so long, you don't recognise me."

"I must've been asleep long enough for you to guzzle a hundred pounds worth of *vetkoek,*" replied Katie, looking pointedly at Ma's matronly girth.

"Is that the thanks I get for looking after you and keeping you clean and sanitary for twenty-five years? You know you peed on my sheets and in nappies till they put that bag on you? I swear you put out about a gallon a day."

"Well, I'll go to the toilet from now on by myself, thank you, and then I won't have to have my liquid output measured by the likes of you."

"Don't thank me, thank Gawd you know me."

I couldn't believe it. As a kid I always remember Ma and Auntie Katie *skelling* each other out. Now it was like they just picked up where they'd left off somewhere in November of 1969, when my auntie, who'd been feeling inexplicably tireder and tireder, finally fell into a sleep. That's how it happened. Not a car accident or a stroke. Not a blow on the head, we don't think, unless she and Ma were quietly boxing each other on the side.

I was nine years old at the time and we were all living together in a little cottage in District Six, and I can tell you there wasn't much room for doing anything quietly on the side, which does make me wonder, incidentally, how come there got to be so many of us. Not surprising Uncle Richard's favourite saying is, "Where there's a will, there's a way."

I don't think Ma and Katie would've chosen to live together. Katie thought Ma was a slut who killed her first husband with her excessive desires. (In fact, my father was washed overboard in a weekend fishing expedition.) Ma was overpopulating the world and directly contributing to the slum conditions we were living in; her legs were always open wide either receiving the wherewithal to make babies or spewing out the finished product. Ma thought Katie was an uptight spinster who needed a good you know what, and asked why didn't she get herself a nice man in a wheelchair from the hospital so they could qualify for a state pension and not live with Ma who had never wanted to live with Katie anyway.

Auntie Katie, before she fell asleep, worked at Groote Schuur Hospital in the kitchens. It used to depress her no end. Can you imagine a Cape coloured woman not being allowed to cook with spices or herbs or flavourings of any kind?

"But it will make them well," she used to argue to the Matrons, "if they just have a little *borrie* or a speck of cayenne pepper to stimulate the glands. These spices are medicinal. What about ginger? Didn't your mother give you ginger for your *maagpyn*?"

But the Matrons were adamant. No spices. No herbs.

Katie's only ally in that big teaching hospital was young Professor Powell. Katie usually held white people at arm's length. She wanted to respect them, she said, and she couldn't do that once she'd got to know them intimately and realised that there was nothing in them that wasn't also in the most hardened *skollie* or Fancy Boys gang member. But Edward Powell was obviously different, because it was always "Professor Powell this" and "Professor Powell that" until one day my mother put her hands on her hips and said,

"Why don't you just let the whitey *naai* you if he's so *bleddy* wonderful?"

Katie tightened her cardigan around her, pinched her lips and wouldn't speak to my mother for a week, which was a great relief as far as the rest of us were concerned.

The truth is that Auntie Katie had a kind of crush on Professor Powell. More than a crush, really. Katie may have worshipped our Lord every Sunday in Upper Buitenkant Street, but from Monday to Friday Edward Powell of the Neurology Department was her demi-god. He wasn't much older than her himself, but he always called Katie "Miss Fortuin." And if we'd heard it once, we'd heard it a million times how one day when it was bucketing down in a typical Cape winter rainburst, Professor Edward Powell of the Neurology Department held his umbrella over the lowly Katie, bottle-washer and cook, for at least five minutes before she dashed to her bus.

Auntie Katie told us with pride how Professor Powell determined who would live and who would die, whose head could be stitched together and whose had to be left like Humpty Dumpty. The ginger-haired Professor presided over the sanity of all who lived on the Peninsula and beyond. Men and women who entered his doors tied up in strait-jackets might leave walking freely once he'd waved his magic scalpel. According to Auntie Katie Fortuin.

As a token of her immense admiration, Katie brought Edward (who was from Natal, and consequently liked curry as much as Katie did) home-made roti and other delicacies, still warm, wrapped in greaseproof paper. I remember Katie getting up at dawn to fold the Professor's samoosas. Stan and Vincent and me would lie in our shared bed, judging from the aromas and the clink of saucepans how far advanced Auntie Katie's culinary preparations were. At the crucial moment we'd fight past each other and the bedclothes and crowd into the tiny kitchen, pleading for just one of these succulent parcels.

It was odd when Katie started to drop off for a zzz in the middle of meals or conversations. She was usually such a bustling, tireless woman. Ma said they were working her too hard at the hospital and that white people thought coloured people never needed to rest. But it was more. Katie's personality was changing, because she didn't want to do the things she used to love doing, like walking to Church and greeting everyone along the way, or bargaining with the fruit and vegetable hawkers, or chasing *skollies* who came to pee against our wall. She got into trouble at work, which was also not like her; she was the most law-abiding person. Then one November morning (when she'd already had twelve hours' sleep) Katie stopped folding the Professor's samoosas, climbed into her freshly-made bed, and went back to sleep for nearly twenty-five years.

At first Ma thought Katie was suffering from nervous exhaustion, so she moaned a bit about how certain people are allowed to have a breakdown but others have to stay on duty, and then sent me to the hospital to deliver the samoosas. A receptionist my aunt would have described as *kwaai* called

Professor Powell to collect the still-steaming package from this snotty urchin.

"Auntie couldn't come. Auntie's sleeping. It's 80c for the samoosas."

I had memorized these lines and repeated them all the way from Cross Street to the door of the hospital. Professor Powell, for all his deep understanding of the human brain, looked puzzled. He didn't get a chance to question me though, because I was already running back to District Six, hoping I wouldn't get a hiding for coming late to school.

When Auntie Katie had been asleep for three days, Professor Powell visited. The arrival of his smart Cortina in Cross Street created tumult. Children of the neighbourhood crowded round him, laughing and teasing because this was their place, where they held sway, and the tall, thin gingery man was the outsider. He maintained his dignity and was respectfully welcomed by Ma and Uncle Richard who had imbibed some of Auntie Katie's reverence for "the Professor."

Ma showed him into Katie's bedroom, which wasn't actually Katie's because it was the room where everybody except Uncle Richard and Ma and the new baby slept. It had a low ceiling and one small, low window with net curtains. There were three beds covered in crocheted spreads, all pushed together, and over the beds hung a plaque of praying hands. Our clothes were in trunks, stacked on top of each other and used as a table. When Ma spotted Edward Powell opening the little picket gate, she quickly slapped a doily on this stack.

Professor Powell stooped over Katie and shone a light in her eyes.

"Has she been lying in the same position all this time?"

"Oh no, Professor, she tosses and turns sometimes. I think she's having a very nice sleep. I do all the work around here, you know. Now I've got these sheets to worry about too," she added.

"I would like to have her brought in for testing. I'll have an ambulance sent."

So Auntie Katie was tested. Lights were shone in her eyes. Her pulse was taken and her heartbeat was checked. Her brain was scanned. There was nothing wrong with Katie. She was just a coloured lady sleeping. Eventually, Katie was brought home in nappies, with a special little button on her tummy through which liquidized food could be squirted. A gastrostomy, Professor Powell called it. A catastrophe, Ma said.

"She is doing this on purpose to make my life a misery," said Ma, tearfully grinding up meat and vegetables. The new baby was crying, Uncle Richard was drinking at a tavern in Horstley street, and we boys were hungry.

"This is my sister's revenge," said Ma bitterly.

After that, a strange thing happened. It happened gradually, so I can't say when Ma began to change toward the sleeping Katie, and became so tender and caring, washing her, feeding her. Always she would put the spices Katie loved in Katie's puree.

"But Ma, we don't have taste buds down there where Auntie Katie gets her food."

"Don't be cheeky young man. Katie herself said we must give spices to the sick. I'm only doing what she always said."

Sometimes I wonder if it wasn't the forced removals that made my mother kind. You see, Auntie Katie fell asleep in the middle of it all, in the midst of the weeping, tearing and destruction. Ma sat next to Katie's bedside and told her what was happening. When Katie was "awake," that is, when her eyes were open and staring, Ma propped her up on the pillows and they'd have a regular chat, except Katie never answered or showed what she thought of it all but only occasionally drooled, which can't be called a reaction.

"Listen, Katie, they are sending us away from here. They say this place is a slum, but actually they just don't like brown people so near their precious city. We have to go to the Flats. There's no shops, no schools, no nothing there. Don't wake up now, Katie, rather just sleep."

Inevitably neighbours and visitors heard about these strange conversations between Ma and her *non compos mentis* sister. Nobody accused Ma of being *mal* though. Instead, word got round that Katie Fortuin had gone to sleep because of Group Areas, in resistance to it. Then, because people always talk and dream and imagine, it was circulated that Katie wasn't going to wake up till justice returned. Our cottage became something of a shrine to a woman who had turned herself into a barometer of oppression, who refused to be moved.

But of course we had to move Katie, and she came with us first to Elsie's River and then to Mitchell's Plain, where last year I bought Ma a big double-storey house. Now Katie has her own room. All this became possible when I was promoted, in the sense that I stopped being a non-government organiser and became a government organiser. It's the same job but a whole lot better paid. I could've bought Ma a house in Plumstead, but she wanted to stay near the kind of people she's always known, who don't think green plastic curlers are a strange hairdo. In a way, I have Katie to thank for this—the promotion, I mean. If it hadn't been for her I'd probably have died in detention, slipped on a bar of soap, you know.

I spent most of 1986 inside Katie's brushed nylon nightie. Sometimes the electricity created beneath the mountain of bedclothes by that skin-warmed garment as my hair rubbed against it, was terrifying. The Security Branch were after me and climbing into bed with Katie was a spur of the moment decision.

"I've got nothing here but an invalid. Search my house, with pleasure," Ma told the police, and they did.

Their boots on the linoleum made an ominous crunching sound. I lay perfectly still between Katie's thighs, my head on her large cotton bloomers, inside her nightie, under the blankets, under the eiderdown. They said nothing. The linoleum creaked from their weight. It was very hot inside our pink nylon tent, but it smelt good, like fresh laundry. It was only then, when my nose was pressed against Katie's underwear, that I fully understood how well Ma looked after her sister. A stupid thought when you're on the verge of arrest.

When they'd left, I asked Ma what had happened.

"They looked and looked at the bed. The big blonde one was reaching his hand out to touch the bedclothes when Katie opened her eyes and stared at him, you know the way she does sometimes. Only this time I think she had a glint of accusation in her eye. Anyway, he drew his hand back."

For the rest of the year, I was in and out of Katie's nightie, as the occasion demanded. Only the closest family members knew I was home. Eventually the State dropped their case against me and I came out from Katie's nightie.

I worked for various anti-apartheid and non-government organisations and even got a bursary to study further. I met my wife Sandra at a postgraduate seminar. She shares the same ideals as me and was also involved in NGOs and the struggle. We fell in love not over candlelit dinners but at candlelit memorial services and meetings and workshops and late night arguments in Observatory communes. The Mixed Marriages and Immorality Acts have been repealed and there are lots of couples like us so we don't cause much of a stir. It was today, at our wedding celebration, that Auntie Katie first showed signs that she'd like to wake up.

Sandra's mother wanted us to get married at her club.

"You coloureds are very welcome these days," she said. Sandra was outraged, and said we'd rather get married in Mitchell's Plain. Which we did: today.

Ma has been cooking for days. There's *bredie* for 40 guests, stir-fried rice with vegetables (Sandra is a vegetarian), cucumber mousse from the back of a greengage jelly packet, potato salad, rice salad (for people who don't get enough potato salad and stir-fried rice), tomato and onion sambal, little iced cakes, four-tiered trifles, milk tarts galore and I don't know what all besides. Busy as she's been, Ma never forgot Auntie Katie.

Earlier today Ma gave Katie her share of the feast. She propped Katie up on the pillows even though Katie isn't fed through the mouth. Ma feels it's not respectable to eat lying down. As usual, she gave Katie the low down.

"Now, Katie, today is a great day. What would you say if I told you your nephew was getting married today? To a beautiful girl, and you know what Katie, she's white! How things have changed, Katie, since your day. You should see our guests. They are of every colour. They are all enjoying your spicy recipes, so what I'm giving you today is extra special."

Then she fed Katie and went back out to our guests. A little while later Sandra and I went in to pay our respects to Auntie.

"Katie," I said, "this is Sandra."

Sandra reached out to take Auntie's limp hand into her own. Imagine her surprise when Katie's hand grasped hers. My aunt, who'd been asleep for over two decades, began to speak.

"Pleased to meet you ma'am," said Katie.

"Auntie!" I cried, "you're awake! It's a miracle! Ma, come look! Katie's awake!"

I clutched Sandra to me. I was so excited and dying to share Katie's awakening with the rest of the family. But the guests outside were making such a racket no one heard my shouts. I looked at my aunt in wonder. She narrowed her eyes, trying to place me.

"It's me, Ricky," I said. "Auntie, you've been asleep for twenty-four years. So much has happened, so much has changed."

"You do look like Ricky. And now you've brought your madam to meet me. Are you doing garden work? I always thought they'd apprentice you to learn some trade."

"No, no," I laughed. "It's not like that anymore. That's all over now. I've got a good job. Sandra and I are married. You woke up on our wedding day!"

"Married? Then you're in big trouble my boy. Don't tell anyone. Just don't tell anyone. You could get locked up."

Then she closed her eyes and went back to sleep. I don't know if it was the shock or the joy of discovering that apartheid was dead. We tried to rouse her again, but to no avail. Ma was very cross to have missed this historic occasion. Immediately she resurrected the old myths about Auntie Katie, who had chosen to be comatose rather than witness the humiliation of her people.

"Why don't you phone that Professor who treats her? I'm sure he should know," said Sandra, who always makes practical suggestions.

"No, wait a moment. I'm thinking."

When Ma thinks you can be sure that a scheme is coming soon. I was right.

"Auntie woke up. On which day did she wake up? On the day Sandra and Ricky got married. What was so special about this day apart from wedding bliss? The food is what's different. Spicy food. I gave her nice spicy food in that stoma thing. Katie always said spice was medicinal. Now which spice had this miraculous effect?"

"Don't be ridiculous, Ma," I said, "Professor Powell tested her for everything. He's tried everything."

"He never tried nutmeg," announced Ma, and went straight to her kitchen cupboard. Sandra helped her heat milk in a saucepan and Ma stirred a whole teaspoonful of nutmeg into it.

"You'll probably kill the old girl," I said.

"Just watch," said Ma. Carefully she poured the mixture into Katie's gastric button, speaking soothingly to her sister as she did so. Then we all sat on the bed and waited.

Katie woke up. She looked at me and Sandra and shook her head. She turned around and squinted through the window where our last guests were saying their goodbyes.

"What are all those blacks doing here?" Katie asked. "Find Desiree and tell her someone left the gate open."

"I'm here, Katie. Me. Your sister, Desiree." Katie looked Ma up and down disbelievingly.

"If you're Desiree then I'm Jesus Christ," she replied, and went back to sleep.

That's when we gathered the whole family together to witness the official awakening of Katie Fortuin. Ma carefully packed nutmeg into two slow-release capsules she'd emptied. She placed these ceremonially in Katie's tummy opening and stood back to wait for the miracle.

Katie woke up and asked for tea.

As I already described, Ma and Katie have got reacquainted. Katie's met new members of the family as well as old members of the family with new appearances. Professor Powell, who has monitored Katie over the years, has been given the great news. Moments ago he arrived in a state of jubilation, not gingery anymore but peppery, only slightly disappointed to hear how Katie drifted off to sleep again after the tea. We've been sitting in the lounge waiting for Ma's latest dose of nutmeg to take effect.

In between taking these notes, I'm entertaining Professor Powell. Actually, he's so excited he hardly needs entertainment.

"I've been thinking in the car on the way over here, Ricky. Why would nutmeg do the trick? I'll have to take your aunt in for testing, of course, but I hypothesize that she was suffering from a chemical imbalance in the basal nuclei." Ma stares at the Professor as if he were speaking Cantonese.

"In the *substantia nigra*. The most uncanny thing, you won't believe."

"What's so uncanny?" I ask.

"Well, the *substantia nigra* is black. *Nigra*, you know, means black."

I'm not following, but Ma suddenly nods her head sagely.

"Aah," she says. "Katie was so offended by the Group Areas Act that she actually got sick in her negro substance. The part of her brain that contains her blackness, that part got ill."

"Something like that. Of course we're not talking medicine here. But I think it could make an ironic twist to my article on this amazing case. Coloured woman's anti-apartheid stance has intriguing medical parallel."

My brother Stan comes in from Katie's bedroom.

"She's awake," he says.

"Excellent. Now if I can correct that chemical imbalance, she'll stay awake like you or I."

Since her first reawakening, Katie has gotten used to seeing people aged. She's very pleased to see Professor Powell.

"Come close, Professor," she says, "I don't want them to hear this." Katie looks suspiciously at us over her shoulder. She whispers into his ear, but still I can hear her startling words.

"These people are all mad. They think I'm their relative. They believe that apartheid is no more. You know what, Professor Powell? I think you should get your nice young men in their white jackets and have this lot taken away."

Thus speaks Katie Fortuin. Her message has been delivered; she has settled back into a sleep Professor Powell promises to cure forever. Ma has summoned the press. There's a gathering expectancy in the house, with neighbours and prominent community members arriving to witness my aunt rise from her bed and greet this new world free of injustice and prejudice.

But I fear the reawakening of Katie Fortuin.

PART TWO

The Puddle

IMMANUEL SUTTNER ▼▼▼▼▼▼▼▼▼▼▼▼▼▼▼▼▼▼▼▼▼▼▼▼▼▼▼▼▼▼

Some friends of mine had been house-sitting in Randburg, and decided in the middle they wanted to go off to Malawi.

"It's a cinch," they told me, "the fridge is full of food, there's a great collection of videos and CDs, and besides, you need the change."

I willingly agreed, glad at the chance to get out of my stuffy little flat. The first night in my new home I got down the wok and made myself a sumptuous stir fry, then sat with my feet up on the Chippendale watching "Pretty Woman." After several glasses of carrot juice, a long conversation with Australia, and a night swim in the buff, I began to feel sleepy. I locked the Rottweiler and the house cat up in the laundry, and climbed into my hosts' double bed, content with only a cursory examination of their wardrobes.

As soon as I lay down I became aware of a steady dripping emanating from the bathroom. I got up, lit a candle, and went to seek out the source of the trouble. It was the cold tap in the bath, and I tightened it. The dripping didn't stop, so I figured the washer must be gone. I loosened the tap and the whole thing came off. Water gushed all over me, and onto the floor. I tried to force the cover back on, but the thread had rusted away, and wouldn't hold.

I would have to get the Swedish wrench out of the car. I unlocked the back door, but the security gate refused to open. When I tried to force the key, it snapped off. I therefore went out through the front door, and walked around to the garage. It was surprisingly chilly, and the flimsy negligee I had borrowed gave no warmth. I took the wrench from under the front seat, where I keep it for protection.

I tiptoed back through the rose garden, one hand holding the wrench, the other modestly holding the nightie from blowing up above my erection. I don't know why—cold air on my flesh always does that to me. Even before I got to the front door I knew something else had gone wrong. And indeed it had. The door had blown shut. My warm bed called to me, but I was locked out, with no way in. The windows all had burglar bars, and the Rottweiler, who had somehow gotten loose, stuck his head out and growled at me. I could hear the water in the bathroom. Soon it would begin to soak the bedroom carpet. If I tried to climb in, I faced getting stuck, being shot by a passing patrol of Eagle Security, or savaged by the dog. The only other person who had a set of keys was Salamina, the maid, who stayed in Dobsonville.

I got into the car and raced for Soweto. In White City I was abducted by an APLA cell, painted black, and coerced into joining them in a raid on a sperm bank. They were all very disappointed when they saw the giant cold rooms filled with little plastic jars.

"I thought they kept ambergris here," explained their leader, who sounded a little like old Opperman from Military Intelligence.

They tied me to a policeman, and after driving my car into a wall, went off. I woke up the officer.

"We value feedback from the public," he said, "and certainly if any members of the force have been amiss then we will spare no effort to bring them to brook. However, unsubstantiated allegations are. . . ."

I silenced him with a fifty and continued on foot, arriving at Salamina's house at three a.m. It took some time to explain to the terrified woman that I was not a supernatural winged apparition, but rather a middle aged bachelor with a shredded nightie and a thick layer of black paint. I took a taxi back, looking at my watch every two minutes and cursing the driver at each unscheduled stop. None of the constant stream of passengers getting in and out commented on my rather foreign appearance. Their gaze might rest upon me for a moment, but was then averted rapidly, as if they were very used to seeing strange sights and had become inured to them. I didn't have too much time to reflect on this because I was busy worrying about the house. The wooden floors and carpets were probably knee-deep in water by now.

In Louis Botha, my head was flung sideways into the large bosom of the lady beside me. After two of the drivers had swopped details (the third one just drove off), a gun battle broke out between rival tow truck drivers who had magically arrived on the scene seconds after the accident occurred. I hid under a pile of bodies until the shooting was over. The taxi driver, whistling softly to himself, stretched some plastic across the shattered glass of his Hi-Ace, and then we limped on to Republic road where I disembarked.

Empty suburban streets with their greenery and high walls make a very pretty sight in the pearly morning-glow. I vaulted the garden wall just as the sun was rising. Strangely enough, I couldn't hear the gushing of water within. Only the gentle throbbing of the automatic pool cleaner disturbed the silence.

Even stranger was that there was no water seeping out under the front door. I unlocked it, but it wouldn't open. Looking through the lounge window I saw that someone had pushed the grand piano against the door. Eventually I managed to push it back, and enter. The house seemed empty. Absolutely empty. They had even unscrewed the light bulbs and plug covers and taken them. In the kitchen little marks on the tiles indicated where the melamine units had once stood. Someone had scratched "Thlokomelo Nja" on the side of the piano. The Rottweiler was snoozing on the bare lounge floor, and cuddled up next to it was the cat.

Inexplicably angered by this graphic explosion of yet another myth, I did for them both with an AK47 I had taken from the taxi by mistake, and then went to see if the thieves had at least left the lady of the house's underwear for me to try on.

"What incredible monsters" I thought to myself when I discovered the bedroom cupboard had vanished. But my worst fears were confirmed when I walked into the bathroom.

They had even taken the puddle.

Mind-Reader

Maureen Isaacson ▼▼▼▼▼▼▼▼▼▼▼▼▼▼▼▼▼▼▼▼▼▼▼▼▼▼▼▼▼▼▼

It is exactly twelve months since forty billion fire rockets detonated their light into the heat of a darkened Cape sky, as Daniel opened his mouth in an arc of pleasure, as Sienna shuddered, as outside people screamed their joy. The new order was born.

Baby Karl still refuses to emerge. He can smell the air in his parents' house, Number Seventeen, Block Seven. It is weighted with the smell of morogo and pap; it is pendulous with waiting. Sienna has refused induction. Karl's will, like his mother's, is of wrought iron. He rides her ebb, feels the dark currents of his dad, snuggles deeper. Daniel is yesterday's hero, a sad playwright who defied the censors of the old order and who has now been overlooked for promotion at the State Theatre.

Today is Independence Day. New BlockSun X scarcely protects the fried egg nipples of Sienna and comrade Thuli. The sun beams a ferocious radiance onto the beach where they have escaped the celebrations. "When Karl does eventually arrive, I will need someone to continue the work of the Organization," Sienna is saying, as the contractions begin.

Five hours later, Thuli puts to use the knife she has brought along to slice the watermelon. Snip goes the umbilical cord. Splash goes the seawater. Two teeth glimmer like milk in the uncertain twilight. Eyes open and something is communicated. Take me to my father. Daniel's heart releases its burden but he does not understand how the baby's telepathic powers will further the ends of the Organization, as Sienna has prophesied. More lotion on my left buttock, more mashed apple, pass my rattle, please. Agoo. As there is nobody to continue her work, Sienna leaves it to Daniel to warm Karl's milk in the early hours of the morning and later, to prepare his sandwiches for school. There is no need to ask what Karl wants. Karl knows too much. He knows before his teachers do what they will say and why. They declare him a genius. Yes, perhaps he can discern dissidence and espionage and help the country to achieve true liberation, says his father.

Nobody must ever know of his gift.

He is a remote child, detached yet obedient. He delivers the information requested by his parents but is unable to penetrate minds that have locked their knowledge away. Also, he fails to discover what has happened to the fifty comrades who went missing on the night of his conception. "I tried," he says, after each new mission, and returns to his room.

He spends a great deal of time looking into the mirror. His eyes, vague with the desperation of searching for a young woman, any young woman, do not register a true reflection. He does not see that lying too long in Sienna's womb has left his face as flat as a compass. He attempts to slick back the hair that grows like khakibos on his oversized head but he does nothing to soften the glow of his nose. Obsessive clothes-pressing and finger nail-paring offer no guarantee against rejection. His voice rises like high tide when he speaks to girls. He knows too well what is going on behind their pleasant ways and cunning smiles. Loneliness turns his interest to the aero-dynamic construction of water towers and the interior workings of space craft. He delves into the mysteries of time and brings forth information from a future where men are unable to speak without musical accompaniment.

He meditates on a small black spot on the ceiling of his bedroom. Large pustules fight for dominion over his forehead. He spills gobs of spunk into handkerchiefs, which he washes and dries near the river. His school results make the newspaper headlines and at fourteen, he matriculates with twelve distinctions.

On his fifteenth birthday, before the Independence Day celebrations begin, he is called to the Freedom Mental Hospital. Here he is told he will train as a psychiatrist under Dr Motau. "It will take a mind such as yours to help us restore the sanity that was shattered by the old order," says the doctor.

"Memory is the map. Through memory we can learn to understand and control the threat to democracy," he is saying when a man in torn pyjamas shouts to him, "Hey boy! I thought I told you to come in through the tradesman's entrance!"

"Here is an example of an excess of memory which is unable to integrate with the present," says Dr. Motau. He force-feeds these patients with video-tapes of the events that led up to the Independence. Treatment is more severe for amnesiacs, the old regime supporters who now claim always to have possessed a spirit of liberalism. Dental drilling and hair waxing jolt the memory. "For the severe cases, and there are many, the perpetrators of human rights abuses who believe they were freedom fighters, we have more specialized treatments." Doctor Motau does not elaborate.

After a week, Karl will be expected to suggest a cure for all of these ills. His proposal will be passed on to Dr. Garcia, the hospital head, later to government. Doctor Motau refers to his superiors as "the powers that be." Karl senses a nagging dissonance in this doctor's excessive willingness to please but the man's mind is shut tight, like a security gate. How can he tell that this is Karl's first encounter with people such as these patients, people who live in the memories of his parents? Theirs was a different fight, the fight that is still unmentionable in the new country. Karl studies books about the mechanism of the mind. He tries to think of "solutions" that will aid the hospital in its research, with no success. He waits for time to pass.

One day a radiance bursts through the gloom of his vision. It emanates from a young nurse with milky hands. He follows her, careful to remain well out of sight. Her perfume reminds him of the garden where he played as a child. Now he smells the sweetness of the roses, now he scrabbles on his knees under the loquat tree. It is afternoon and soon his mother will call him in for tea.

Down three flights of stairs and then another, down a long corridor and into a darkened wing, he treads lightly, borne on hope. His destination turns out to be a ward, where people sit on chairs arranged in a circle and stare into space. "Vitamin time!" says the nurse. He hides behind a screen and watches her inject an orange liquid into the bruised veins of her patients. He counts fifty needles. Karl looks into the minds of the patients. Like overexposed film, their stories are imprinted there. These are the fifty missing members of the Organization! He must leave at once. A floorboard creaks and the nurse catches his eye. A letter of dismissal arrives on his desk. Doctor Garcia has signed it. He is not surprised, but he does not expect what he gets: incarceration in a rage red room and worst of all the waiting, in between the ultra violet lights and the standing after the feet flogging. When his mind is "clear," Karl is regressed to a prenatal state. Back in his mother's ebb again, he recalls the history of the Organization. He remembers its revival, its plans for the future, but the censor encoded in his early years is still operative. He does not talk, nor does he whine.

Six weeks later, Karl's mind is empty; it is like a blank in a pistol where there should be a bullet. When he is released he has forgotten everything he knew, which means he has forgotten who he is. Now that he is nobody, he has nowhere to stay and nothing to do. His home is a tall oak tree surrounded by veld, which is skirted by a low, threatening sky. His hair is matted, as if woven into a nest for the birds who are his fellow tenants. He thinks their thoughts, which are largely about worms. He flaps his arms and fancies that he is made of feathers. His shadow bites him. He pecks at the fetid waters of the nearby river. The days are as bland as porridge. Hunger twists his colon. How long can he continue to live this way? Once, when Karl was still able to think, he believed that there were no coincidences. Now a stranger sits beside him under his tree. "Don't do it! Don't leave your job," he tells the man. "You are about to receive a promotion."

"You are a mind-reader!" shouts the man; "I must take you to meet my uncle." The impact of sudden kindness shocks Karl back into memory, then out of it.

The man's uncle is head of an unnamed committee. He allows Karl to live in his disused coal shed. Karl paints an oak tree on the wall. He executes simple tasks in the uncle's office: floor scrubbing, boot polishing, tea making. The Organization is a danger to the country. Dusting, shining, onion peeling. Destroy the Organization. Clothing, washing, ironing, mending. Who are you, Karl? He does not know the names of these people. He is sent to another office where things are no different. Fetching, carrying, more cleaning. The Organization must die. Root out its members. Karl is now able to extract information from the area of his cortex that was damaged by his captors. He is able to receive messages. Congratulations, Karl, you have earned the title, New Freedom Fighter. Here is your weapon.

Back at Number Seventeen, Block Seven, the cracked white horse that once rocked Karl's small body stands to attention in his old room. It is late July. Icy winds freeze the eyes. Rain has soaked up the colour of the fields outlying the megalopolis. The mirror that once showed him how far he was from handsome now reflects a bitter rural scene beyond the rain-bloated garden. It is 8:30 p.m. Daniel is in the kitchen, warming his feet before the stove where the hot chocolate has begun to boil. Sienna climbs into bed at the same time as the steel of the AK 47 presses its coldness on Daniel's temple.

Now Daniel is marching, his hands beat the air above his head like angel's wings, as he moves to join his wife in the bedroom. Daniel and Sienna look into each other's eyes. Together they choke on their son's name. Finally it escapes into the air with desperation, announcing its liberation with an ugly double squawk: "K-a-a-a-a-r-l!" Would it make any difference if he knew that their grief over his disappearance has terminated the work they do for the Organization? Destroy the Organization. Pull out its roots. The boy ushers them into the afterlife. First Daniel. Then Sienna. It is 10:55. At precisely 11:00 p.m., his dying will begin. "Mother! Father!" will be his involuntary cry. In the morning, the park-keepers will find his body. When they dump it into the small vacant box into Number 7X69616@Death in the New Freedom Fighter section of the ever-expanding cemetery, the thud will scarcely be heard. Perhaps a gull will swoop overhead; perhaps the silence will be unrelieved. There can be no assurances.

SEITLHAMO MOTSAPI ▼▼▼▼▼▼▼▼▼▼▼▼▼▼▼▼▼▼▼▼▼▼▼▼▼▼▼▼▼▼▼

& so the new blackses arrive
all scent & drape to their clamour
head & heart the liquid odour
of roads that defy oceans

from the fiery splash of pool
pits they preach us redamp
shun from the dust
of the old ways

their kisses bite
like the deep bellies of conputers
the gravy of their songs
smells like the slow piss of calculatahs

& so
the new blackses arrive
& promise us life beyond the bleed
of the common yell
they promise us new spring
for the slow limp
of our heads

meanwhile
the ladder finds the sky at last
heart or herd slinks to the waters
mbira grows into a synthesiser
the songs ask for more sugar
& my salt sets sail for babylon

At the Commission

INGRID DE KOK ▼▼▼▼▼▼▼▼▼▼▼▼▼▼▼▼▼▼▼▼▼▼▼▼▼▼▼▼▼▼▼▼▼

In the retelling
no one remembers
whether he was carrying a grenade
or if his pent up body
exploded on contact with
horrors to come.

Would it matter to know
the detail called truth
since, fast forwarded,
the ending is the same,
over and over?

The questions, however intended,
all lead away from him
alone there, running for his life.

Mending

INGRID DE KOK ▾▾▾▾▾▾▾▾▾▾▾▾▾▾▾▾▾▾▾▾▾▾▾▾▾▾▾▾▾▾▾▾▾▾▾▾

In and out, behind, across.
The formal gesture binds the cloth.
The stitchery's a surgeon's rhyme,
a Chinese stamp, a pantomime

of print. Then spoor. Then trail of red.
Scabs rise, stigmata from the thread.
A cotton chronicle congealed.
A histogram of welts and weals.

The woman plies her ancient art.
Her needle sutures as it darts,
scoring, scripting, scarring, stitching,
the invisible mending of the heart.

TRC Stories:
It Gets under the Skin

HEIDI GRUNEBAUM-RALPH ▼▼▼▼▼▼▼▼▼▼▼▼▼▼▼▼▼▼▼▼▼▼▼▼▼

(In my dream)
it was a light-bulb
crushed in his bare hands.
He laughed and said
—This is what we do.
Scream because no one can hear—
Then he rubbed the gritty shards
inside
and there
in her soft pinkness
he carved his power
for posterity.

Truth Commission

JOAN METELERKAMP ▼▼▼▼▼▼▼▼▼▼▼▼▼▼▼▼▼▼▼▼▼▼▼▼▼▼▼▼▼▼

Out in the outside room,
sifting through
thoughts, papers,
looking for something,

looking for something like
Elizabeth Bishop's Sandpiper—
I look up;
look up to the fall of the rain,

half-halt: a hadidah, lame-footed,
heading her way
up the lawn
through the mist—

there flies her mate
freighting sticks to their nest
beak closed against his cry

(viva-a-a
a-a-a-amandla . . .)

looking for some sign I can hold to—

a woman feeling her way forward—arms
firm enough for limbs
of warm children—
hearing through the questions

of Granny's death, or how the red
and white cells fight
in a school friend's
leukemia, or the city's

dysentery: how do we live with this (how
the albizia's
new leaves dip down
with the rain, like old ladies' dewlaps);

sift through the riddles the child asks, asks,
unanswerable,
comfortless,
with the necessary

wonders of a search: take the simplest things—
what you may or may
not do, like wash hands
when you've been to the loo,

and never point a gun at anyone
even if it is
only pretend—
the easy answers

to the teasing questions; like if you can't
take the truth they
feed you at school
how to seek it, given that

if it blinds you on the road to Damascus
you must get up
for God's sake
and make your way, woman, yourself. . . .

Move in, then, across the wet grass to the kitchen,
switch on the news:

and when the truth comes
brazen, searing
across the airwaves
do you think I can face it—

the truth cuts me off again; this is
the truth: black out
black out the sight
of the killers in their ill-fitting

suits and shitty ties reeking
of craven
cowardice crouched
before the commission—

this is the truth: mothers who will not
forgive never
forget never
re-member the limbs they bore for murder;

o who can bring this stiff truth home to us
who will breathe it
into our warm kitchens—
or are we out, out in the cold, alone?

(Goya lined them up for us, against the wall
of his mind the
more clearly to
see them; in all the detail

their lives had made them before they were shot.)

From the radio
I dare not hear
from the TV I dare not look at

where I stand, in my kitchen: the vaalpens
Vlakplaas men
drugged their men
the more easily to shoot them.

O close my eyes—all night the mind feels for
the cold comfort of a worry bead—
turns over—the slump,
slump of the bodies
against the weak wall of the will.

The Devil

ACHMAT DANGOR ▼▼▼▼▼▼▼▼▼▼▼▼▼▼▼▼▼▼▼▼▼▼▼▼▼▼▼▼▼▼▼▼

Sharman was a devil. No, he did not have pointed ears or wicked eyebrows. Nor even unduly devious eyes. Devils are not that obvious. And, of course, Sharman did not know that be was a devil. In the beginning that is. A "sleeper" sent to wait in dormant darkness among unsuspecting citizens. Until he was called on to perform tasks that in his heart he would have dreaded doing had the call come too early. But immense patience was exercised in controlling Sharman's destiny and he was allowed the innocence of his youth, a virtue that was as fleeting in him as in any young person.

And so Sharman lived a quiet life in one of the leafy northern suburbs of Johannesburg, where he went to school and joined the tennis club and, when he was old enough to want to do such solitary things, went jogging along a quiet path in the nearby Zoo Lake park. Sharman had the placid appearance typical of the many thousands of his kind who had learned to insulate themselves from the strife and tumult of the country. Here, in the unhurried pace of the tree-lined streets, the most violent thing that young kids did was to be cruel to stray cats and crush underfoot the jacaranda blossoms that fell like snow from the branches of trees after a storm. Once, Sharman came home and showed off to his mother the lilac stains on the soles of his shoes, after he and other neighbourhood children had rampaged through the streets, dancing on the fallen flowers.

"Sharman," his mother said, "don't ever bring blood into my house again!"

He had turned away confused and angry, feeling alien in his own home, and a stranger to his mother. The next day she found a dark stain on the living-room carpet where Sharman had crushed a mound of blossoms into an oozing pulp. She complained to her husband, who observed the stain congealing with the phosphorescent glow of blood, and sadly remarked that "there was nothing to be done for this boy."

He was not Sharman's real father. A man with a strained and tremulous voice, he, through his silences, never let Sharman's mother forget that he had saved her from the sin of becoming an unwed mother, although in his mind the murky and unexplored mist of his wife's ancient infidelity was reduced to an indistinct "that."

"No," he told her, "I don't want to know who his father is. I don't want to talk about *that* at all."

Sharman, as he grew older, listened to their subdued conversations, the lisping of their lowered voices, and knew immediately that they were discussing him. Even when he became aware of his bastardhood, he continued to address very formally as "Father" this man who was not his biological father. Over time, *this man,* as Sharman began to think of his mother's husband, pushed into a fog of forgetfulness the memory of the shame and pain he had felt when he discovered that his newly-wed bride was carrying another man's child.

Her pregnancy had been well concealed, her tearful silence forced upon her by equally ashamed parents. "The baker always thinks that the bread in the oven is his," her father had urged her. "Say nothing!"

But Sharman's mother was unable to carry on with the deception for very long and confessed to her husband after only a few days. She wept for many hours, while he sat in the darkness of their room with his head in his hands. He never touched her again, and she never again shed any tears after that, no matter how great a cause for grief she had. Sharman, when he was old enough to know what the word celibacy meant, understood that the twin beds in his parents' bedroom symbolised not a chasteness but a bitter separation, like branches in a dying tree growing apart so as not to witness the inner shrivelling that each would suffer. Their moments of leisure, she knitting and he reading while the television flickered mindlessly, were filled with such emptiness that Sharman often wanted to weep. Their distracted lives, the inability of their minds and hearts to concentrate on anything for very long—like the fingers of badly bruised hands that were afraid to touch anything for fear of the pain it would bring—caused him immense sadness.

Finally, Sharman himself was unable to cry or feel remorse. Sadness at the things in life that go wrong turned to indifference. He no longer even felt any bitterness towards his mother and her husband for the tedious air of tragedy that they had established in their house. And he forgot his hatred of the sombre authority of their dark furniture, the cheap trinkets that filled glassed cabinets and the dull paintings of brushed landscapes which hung in neatly measured rows upon the fading floral wallpaper. He accepted as necessary the way in which they had carefully created a world designed to avoid pain.

Sharman's own innate character, though, began to reveal itself much earlier. The subtle smile when a dog was run down and other children cried, his refusal to bury birds or wish away with God-chase-the-devil chants the little dervish winds that interrupted their cricket games in the park. The hidden and unspoken anguish of his mother's life with a man so anonymous that Sharman often forgot his name could not be entirely to blame for what Sharman would one day become.

When they died, suddenly and within days of each other, worn out by the terrible and silent struggle they had waged inside of themselves for so long, Sharman displayed an almost shy lack of grief. He neither wept out loud nor suffered the surreptitious leakage of tears that men endure despite themselves. Nor did he smile or show any lack of respect as their bodies were driven away in a hearse and buried in an appropriate, subdued Christian manner.

The neighbours were not really surprised by Sharman's maturity, the polite way in which he declined help and accepted condolences. He had always seemed that kind of boy, somehow older in his conduct and in his eyes than the other kids in the neighbourhood. That he had arranged a Christian burial took them aback a little, as they had never thought of the old couple as belonging to any religion. A few suspected that they were Jewish, but could not think why this fact had to be concealed. Still, it was decent enough to have a prayer said when your body was lowered into the ground.

However, the speed and the manner in which Sharman courted and married Mabel Daniels, a local girl whose beauty was marred by a squint in her left eye, did astonish his neighbours. He visited Mr. and Mrs. Daniels, sat with them on their veranda. Dressed in a neat and unostentatious suit, it seemed as if he was busy negotiating to purchase something from them. Their house perhaps, which was the oldest in the area and had two quaint turrets that caused people to stop their cars and stare, or the antique furniture which Mr. Daniels in his senility had thrown into the backyard. Maybe Sharman was a businessman, an entrepreneur who would make something of himself after all. Heaven knows he deserved it. Such a sullen couple he had been reared by. Surely they were not his natural parents!

Sharman and Mabel strolled down the street on Sunday afternoons, though they never joined the throngs who ate ice-cream and promenaded around the lake in the park. Within months, they were married and had moved into the house that was now Sharman's.

It was not long afterwards that a double tragedy struck Mabel: her mother and father died in a car crash. This caused some discussion, especially among those who thought Sharman strange. No one knew what he did for a living. He went off in the morning in the neat old Peugeot that his stepfather had left behind and returned in the afternoon. Like any businessman or clerk. Yet nothing about him revealed his occupation, whatever that was. He carried neither briefcase nor tool-box and never seemed in any real hurry. There was an air of confidence about him that indicated he was in some powerful position. A man so young.

Sharman and Mabel buried her parents and sold the turreted house. For the next ten years they lived a comfortable life that set their neighbours at ease. Sharman's "strangeness" evoked no more than a cursory curiosity among people. Even those who made it their life's business to observe the lives of others and who noticed that birds eventually fled the thorny refuge of a much admired lemon tree in Sharman's garden to nest apprehensively in less secure trees elsewhere in the neighbourhood, regarded Sharman's quiet, brooding manner as no more than an idiosyncrasy brought about by his unhappy childhood.

Until Mabel grew tired of Sharman's solitary habits and secretive nature. It wasn't something that she suddenly noticed, but a slow moulting, his character taking on a shadowy skin, impenetrable and indifferent. Only she, it seemed, saw this side of him, this infuriating refusal to be a part of her life, a quiet rebellion against participating in the everyday events that constituted "living." Sharman never decided what they would have for dinner, or contributed to the lists of provisions to be purchased, very rarely bothered himself with the quality of the meat or the colour of the cloth that camouflaged the worn-through back of his mother's old horsehair sofa.

"But all husbands are like that," Betty Stuhler said. She and her husband Mark were the only friends that Sharman and Mabel had. They were more Mabel's friends than Sharman's. Betty noted that what she had always found strange in a man so lacking in humour, that ironic gleam in Sharman's eyes, was somehow quite frightening. Mark agreed, it had changed, that gleam, to some thing hard and forbidding. Soon the Stuhlers stopped inviting Mabel along to the garden market or the mall on a Saturday morning.

"Sharman has changed," Betty said, "it's the way he smiles. Something wrong with it."

"He doesn't smile any more, he smirks," Mark answered.

And so it was left to Sharman to accompany Mabel and wheel the trolley around in supermarkets, trotting behind her rapid and purposeful stride. But even this seemingly energetic participation was passive and trancelike. He was like an escort or a servant, and tolerated the menial task of dumbly pushing a grocery cart around only because he was indifferent to its indignity.

This slavish, dull-minded partnership that Sharman offered was not enough for Mabel. She wanted a man who shared with her the burdens of life and took seriously those important little details that made cohabitation bearable. She was infuriated most of all by his docile way of agreeing to all her suggestions, and then simply ignoring all the pacts that she so conscientiously thought out beforehand and offered at the dinner table or in bed when he had nowhere to escape to. Even then, he looked at her with distant and sympathetic eyes, as if listening to a child who needed to tell someone of the many and minor concerns that children have. They'll pass, everything will work itself out, Sharman's eyes seemed to say. He never spoke on such occasions, merely nodded while he ate or lay back on his pillow, his face composed into a smooth mask of inattention. Mabel trembled with fury and was tempted to lash out at him.

Once she had actually taken up a heavy silver candelabra in her hand, ready to strike at his mechanically assenting head across the table from her. An inexplicable feeling of dread overcame her, as if Sharman, behind his pliant mask, was a menacing stranger whom she had in all innocence invited into her home. This excited her for a moment, the thought that there was someone else hidden inside this effigy-husband, his ill-fitting clothes and scarecrow gauntness. But Sharman refused to let her get any closer to him, bristling like one of those house-dogs that become treacherous without warning and snarl at people they've known all their lives. Mabel replaced the heavy ornament, noting, despite the pain caused by the hot wax that dripped onto her hand, that it was made of solid silver.

Finally, Mabel ran off with an estate agent's assistant named Stewart who was at least ten years younger than herself. Stewart had been sent to assess the value of Sharman and Mabel's house, which they wished to sell, she told him, because they wanted to move away from this neighbourhood where everything was sinking into quiet decay, where people grew old without noticing, until they were about to die and it was too late to do anything about it. There must be more to life than dying.

At first, Stewart was startled by the candour with which Mabel spoke about life and death and the lack of joy in people's lives. Her husband Sharman appeared to agree, casually moving his head up and down as if suffering from some nervous condition. Stewart sensed in Mabel a great unhappiness, a melancholy that made her seem more exciting than she really was. He had heard stories of older women who enticed young estate agents into their homes and into their beds. Because of their boredom, because of the dull lives they shared with husbands such as Sharman.

It was a month or so since Sharman had first agreed to sell the house and move to a much younger suburb; after all, they were only in their mid-thirties and needed to be among younger people. Here everybody seemed to be of pensionable age, people who retired to the dismal comforts of their small and smooth lawns or walked stiffly in the park each day because there was nothing better to do. He had agreed, probably, to silence Mabel, to calm her tirade and make her wipe the tears of her hysteria from her eyes. But of course he reneged on the agreement. He did nothing to advertise the house for sale or engage the services of an estate agent, even though he had promised to do so as a sign of his commitment to saving their youth.

Mabel took the initiative and chose an agent from the business directory, attracted by the name Hercules Estate Agents & Removal Services. She was not sure why this name seemed so enticing. Certainly not the thought that they would send around men with wiry muscles who would bask unashamedly in the warmth of her admiration. It was more that the name had the ring of destiny to it, though she had no idea who "Hercules" was.

When Stewart arrived she was certain that she had made a mistake. He seemed too young and too eager to make a sale of any significance. But she persevered because of her desperation to get out of this deathly suburb, and was disturbed and flattered by the attention Stewart paid her, his subtle compliments, the way he smiled when he looked at her, his long staring appraisal of her knees when she sat down making her feel naked and exposed.

Stewart began taking them through his ritual presentation, facts and fig-ures and quick little selling phrases in bold-lettered pamphlets that he kept in a plastic folder. Sharman's silent discourtesy, the smile-turned-to-smirk aloofness that had driven away their friends, on this occasion gave way to blatant rudeness. He scarcely suppressed his yawns as Stewart eagerly ex-tolled the virtues of some or other property that they could swap this neat but ageing cottage for. "Isn't that superb? A steal at the price! You'll even make a profit," Stewart said while Sharman, more distracted than usual, kept peering out of the window at the rustling trees. The wind rattled the windows and the sky darkened. A ferocious thunderstorm was about to strike the city, it seemed, but this was not so unusual during summer, and was in Mabel's opinion no excuse for Sharman's bad behaviour.

Then, without warning, Sharman fell asleep. His head slumped forward onto his chest and he began to snore.

So angry and ashamed was Mabel that she burst into tears. Stewart reached out to comfort her, and she slid into the temptation of this unexpected gesture—one that Sharman would never have offered—and pressed herself up against him. Her angular body had a peculiarly hungry quality, a hard-ness of flesh melted down by a yearning for tenderness that caused Stewart to sweep her into his arms. She led him to her sewing room, and there, upon a settee strewn with bits of cloth and stared at by dummies of perverse anorexic loveliness, she guided the young man's entry, and rejoiced at his quick climax. His flood of premature passion was more satisfying than Sharman's slow but detached lovemaking.

When Sharman awoke the sky had cleared and the wind had settled down. Mabel was gone with the savings book and the jewellery she had collected over the years. Gone too was all the silver, those precious objects his mother had cleaned and cared for as if they were more than just expen-sive heirlooms. Mabel had left a note saying that she could no longer live with a man who cared nothing for her and was so blatant in his disrespect for her individuality and her womanhood. Sharman was surprised by the venom in the note, by the fact that she had such a terminology harboured bitterly within her.

With a characteristic lack of public sorrow, he soon went about his life as if Mabel had never existed. He knew, however, that whenever the wind blew with a certain cold tone and the leaves of the trees rustled as if shaken by a giant hand, he would be overcome by a great drowsiness. As if something was being born inside of him and he needed all his energy for this birth. He did not know what this thing was that periodically threatened to be formed, but sensed that it asserted itself when he was faced by a decisive moment, whether brought about by pain or grief or even the prospect of something joyful.

Sharman was a man not given to fervent enquiry and did not pay much attention to these disturbing events. Then on a bright and sunny Sunday he woke from his afternoon nap and felt compelled to switch on the television, something he had done very rarely since Mabel's departure. He saw Nelson Mandela walk out of prison into the sunlight, saw the crowds, the black-green-and-gold flags, the banners waved by supporters hailing the release of their famous leader after twenty-six years in prison. Suddenly the sky grew dark and a fierce storm descended on the city of Johannesburg. A thousand miles away Nelson Mandela was about to enter the white heat of the streets of Cape Town. Sharman's city, in the meantime, was engulfed by a brief but terrifying deluge. He sat transfixed on the creaking sofa, and fell into a trancelike sleep.

When Sharman awoke, Mandela was gone. Cleaners and workmen were restoring order to the city of Cape Town. Sharman felt an inexplicable sense of satisfaction when the announcer described the chaos that had occurred as the crowds waiting for Mandela to appear became impatient. Outside Sharman's house a great smell of fecund damp arose and seemed to seep into his body. Things grow in wetness like that, he thought, and it has been very dry for a long time. He felt inside of him a certitude, heavy yet comfortable, a dark and glowing presence.

Flinging the door wide, Sharman went out into the garden. The birds immediately fell silent, filling him with a peculiar feeling of solitary pleasure. But just then a group of black people came toyi-toying up the street, their joy at Mandela's release defiantly evident, as they danced at a measured pace past suburban residents lined up to watch from the safety of fenced-in properties. Many of those in the procession worked in the neighbourhood as domestics or gardeners. Some lived there in back rooms, or even inside the homes of more liberal employers.

Sharman recognised Zeph, one of the leaders of the parade, which he guessed must have started in the park where working people from the area relaxed on Sunday afternoons. Somebody would have stood up and pranced about drunkenly, shouting "Mandela's free!" Others would have joined in, until an impromptu column was formed and one of them, pointing an upraised finger towards the houses on the other side of the lake, shouted "Phambili!"

Sharman, surprised by his own awareness of "those" people and his unexpected insight into how such marches began, observed Zeph more closely. He was a tall, powerfully built man with a face that beamed disarmingly when he was spoken to. The husband of some domestic worker or other, Zeph earned a precarious living as an odd-job man. After reading a strange, handwritten advert pinned to a tree—Reliable Man Mirakulous Fixing Leacking Roofs—Sharman had hired him to work on their roof. The misspelling and the incorrect grammar were deliberate, Sharman remembered thinking. There was more to Zeph than just his clever ability to market himself.

The fact that this same entrepreneur now led an animated bunch of people in an open demonstration of allegiance to Mandela, whom many whites still thought of as a terrorist and therefore mistrusted, did not bother Sharman. He was in fact drawn to Zeph's sense of rhythm, his ability to change step in midstride and give new momentum to those behind him. Sharman noted how these changes were passed down to the rear in rippling, unspoken commands.

He closed his eyes and imagined himself inside that lithe body, bathed in sweat, feeling the exertion of stamping to some inner martial beat, at once vigorous and disciplined. He experienced a moment of terrifying lightness, as if he had been robbed of his gravity. Then he heard another heart beating close to his own, felt its horror at this invasion, and realised that he *was* inside Zeph's shuddering body. Zeph's mind began to panic, and transmitted convulsive messages to his suddenly immobile, shivering limbs.

With a skill that he seemed to have practised somewhere, Sharman calmed the man's brain and relaxed the stiff muscles in his neck, stretched the taut fingers and rigid toes, until Zeph's fluid tempo was restored. No one had noticed his momentary paralysis. Sharman was elated. He knew he could will Zeph to do anything he wanted, to attack onlookers, smash a window, set a car alight, then turn and incite others behind him to do the same. He could whirl Zeph around and get him to strike one of the marchers, provoking them to fight among themselves, so that this little freedom jog degenerated into just another drunken brawl. This, however, seemed too crude a use of the man whose mind and body he now directed.

Sharman led them along for a while, constantly having to resist the temptation to lunge mockingly at some frightened old couple out for a stroll, until he was satisfied with his ability to control this power he had so unexpectedly acquired.

When he returned home, Sharman went directly to the garden shed, where he found a metal box. He prised it open to reveal the metallic gleam of pistols and rifles, and neatly stacked boxes of ammunition.

Over the next few days Sharman went about with immense confidence. He called at the bank, where a large sum of money was deposited in his name, and withdrew ten thousand rand in crisp notes. He hired cars with a brusque certainty that would have startled Mabel. But he no longer thought about Mabel, or the Stuhlers, or any of the people he had known. He was still astonished by his ability to enter the bodies and minds of other people, and he trembled with pleasure at each prospect.

Sharman spoke the language of the people whom he inhabited, copied the inflections and peculiarities of their tongues very quickly. Soon he changed their characters, without anyone noticing any outward alteration in the habits and demeanours of men and women they had known all their lives. Suddenly these familiar people would disappear for a while and then come back exhausted. They would always have on them more money than they or their families had ever known. At times Sharman's "victims" betrayed strange new quirks, uttering hoarse laughs and nodding their heads in a nervous but agreeable manner.

In the bodies of others, Sharman travelled the country. On board speeding trains carrying migrant workers from Natal, smelling their powerful smells and loving the odour of their fears, their resentments, their fierce clannishness. Sometimes he had to enter the bodies of taciturn Afrikaner miners, who drank brandy and went underground with a bravado that he immediately recognised as a form of inner terror. He developed a kinship with misfits of all sorts whose explosive tempers he transformed into calculated bravery and daring.

He saw many massacres during his travels, from Boipatong to Bambayi, Sharpeville to Everton, Bekkersdal, Katlehong, Vosloorus, the names of townships and squatter camps that most people in the country knew as places of death. He loved above all the sound of the suburban trains, the catlack-catlack of their speeding wheels on the steel track moments before the shooting began and screaming people jumped from windows to their crushing deaths below. Sharman never pulled a trigger himself, nor did he allow the bodies of the people whom he entered to do so. They were the quiet ones at the edge of the crowd whose subtle glance provoked the enemy into raising a weapon to shoot, or the voice whose whisper planted in young men with angelic faces the horrific courage to pour petrol upon passers-by and set them alight.

The most difficult of Sharman's inhabitings were women. He could not sense the rhythms of their bodies or feel the shape of their imaginations, and consequently found it difficult to anticipate their responses. He made the few women who had been his vehicles seem awkward and without grace. It was as if they were indeed possessed. He had to flee the body of a woman whose family had begun to beat her in order to rid her of the demon they swore they could "feel" inside of her mind and spirit. But on the whole, he was successful. He had nudged into brilliant and murderous goading more sane people than any other devil he knew.

The thought that he may not be alone in this mission to keep the country on the precipice of its own death startled him. He searched the faces in crowds, sought out the unobtrusive ones, those who seemed to recede into the shadows of their own bodies. He became certain that there were others like himself, that something compelled them to compete with each other, and that their performances were being judged.

Sharman began to work harder, fighting the tiredness of his body with the luminous darkness in his mind, until his whole being became light and insubstantial and he was able to do without sleep or even food and drink. His inhabitings became more frequent and more frenetic, his victims chosen at random, without the customary detailed investigation and forethought. His work lost its subtlety and his mayhem became too obvious. On two occasions his "bodies" were caught in compromising places, lingering at the scene of a massacre for no other reason than to stare at the faces of murdered people. One of them Sharman had to abandon in prison; the other—a fine specimen of fierce body and fevered mind—was left to die a bewildered and bleeding death in the veld. Sharman had somehow eased his grip on their minds, for a few seconds only, but enough to allow them fleeting recollections of their real lives, and they stood staring at the butchery they themselves had been responsible for—whether sickened or exulted, none of the witnesses who observed them could tell.

In the end though, it was boredom and not exhaustion that forced Sharman to reconsider his tactics. He had seen how the violence brought the spirits of ordinary people to seemingly overwhelming depths . . . only for them to recover their ability to forgive and laugh and continue living. He realised that all the endless killing had been foolish. People wearied of it, turned away from the beauty of its horror precisely because it numbed them. Their deadened senses no longer experienced that sweet, irresistible terror at the anticipation of savagery. The very randomness of the violence diminished its drama, made it ordinary and everyday.

No, something much bolder was needed, a demonstration of the precise power of evil. The destruction of a symbol, someone who embodied all those vague virtues of optimism and compassion. He had to find an icon to strike down.

Suddenly Sharman's memory returned to the day Mandela was released, to the brightness of his own spirit the following morning. Kill Mandela and everyone would feel a sense of loss. Better, that loss would not be a mindless one, its rage would have purpose, it would engulf friend and brother, and destroy the nobility among enemies who believed that even war had to be fought with justice. The conflict would be given a vengeful shape, would make mothers less vulnerable to the death cries of children, to the silence of dead brothers and husbands. Sharman would strike at the very sense of honour of the country. He would arrange the slaying of Nelson Mandela.

On a fine summer's morning, the heat in the city having been cooled by a night of soft rain, Sharman entered the being of Veli Maluleke, a sixteen-year-old schoolboy who lived with his mother on the grounds of Mandela's gracious home in Houghton. Miriam Maluleke had worked for the previous owner of the house, which had been sold with all that it contained—furniture from the New York of the sixties, brigand carpets from mujahedin Afghanistan, Greek statuettes bought at the tourist kiosks in Athens, fake Bushman rock paintings. All of these things Mandela had cleared out, together with the wrecks of vintage cars which counterfeit parts had failed to bring back to life.

Somewhere in Australia a rich and tasteless man was collecting again all the bargain refinements that money can buy, while Miriam waited with sad expectation. Once more she would have to move, first to Sibasa in the north of the country and the home abandoned by her Mozambican husband when he abandoned her, then back to the cities to seek work in the kitchens. But Mandela allowed her to stay, found money—because it was said that he had none of his own—to rebuild the servant cottage in which she lived. And best of all, paid for her son Veli to return to school.

And so it was that Veli was inhabited on his way to Sacred Heart College. As Sharman entered him, the perfect blue of the boy's blazer seemed to burn for a radiant moment, his heart raced, then returned to normal once Sharman had settled in.

Sharman had done his homework, his colleagues would be forced to say. Veli was perfect. Innocent and young, almost beautiful, although Sharman found it a bit distasteful to think of a male body as "beautiful." But it would help, this angelic sensuousness. Mandela's murderer would be a guiltless youth. Surely, people would think, there had to be something amiss with Mandela for so lovely a child to want to kill him. And there was Veli's sad childhood and his mother's tragic story. Miriam, married at seventeen, a child herself, to a Mozambican refugee, who, the moment there was hope that the civil war in his country would end, at the first sniff of peace in the air, had deserted her and his ten-year-old son. Sainted Miriam and "orphaned" Veli had to come to ugly Johannesburg to seek survival and forgetfulness. What a human interest story. Think of the tears the *Sunday Times* would wring from this.

And death would come in the morning, amidst the flowers on the smooth patio floors, beside the pool with its cascading terraces, blood against the cool white walls that Mandela's decorators had rescued from the aubergines and lilacs of the rich man who took the "chicken run" to Australia. Poignant and pointed the act would be. Young Veli, with his head bowed, an automatic weapon hanging from his limp hand. But Sharman had to be patient. He could not let the perfection of the plot lull him into complacency. For the moment, he had to go where Veli went, discover the subtleties that lurked in people like Veli, those secret shades of thought that threatened to redeem these normally passive and pliant minds. Sharman had bitter knowledge of this. Don't trust them, their minds and their hearts. Sharman would let Veli live his life for now. And test him, soon.

Veli lived a young life, full of energy and innocence. He was completely ingenuous in his relationships with others. He laughed much too easily, and was too generous in his warmth for Sharman's liking. And far too sensuous. Veli loved his own body, not with the shallow narcissism that the first awakening of the senses in young people brings about, not merely with the insolent self-glorification that comes from the far-too-early acknowledgement of one's own bright plumage, but with an instinctive and wholly spontaneous joy in the beauty endowed to him. A gift from nature, Veli's smooth face and slim body had been fashioned by the bastard accident of his mother's refined blackness and his father's more distant and dusky Africanness.

The boy touched himself with guileless pleasure whenever he bathed, running the softness of his gently opened palms over the equal softness of his body. Sharman shuddered with distaste, not so much at this excessive self-love, but at the effect it had on himself. In the past he had remained inside the beings of people as they raped or even when they made love. Their brutal shuddering, their indifference afterwards, or their gentle intimacies, had had no effect on him. He would yawn with boredom and even fatherly indulgence at their antics, secure in the dispassionate shadows of their minds. It was like being in the celibate bedroom of his mother and her husband, a child suspended in the balm of an uncarnal womb. Now he was overcome by a restlessness that made him seek out the sensory corners of Veli's mind, where this aberrant self-indulgence was surely born, and try to stop it or divert its messages into other, duller impulses. But Sharman was always confronted by an impenetrable serenity, a barrier of warm hues that blended with each other to create a luminous rainbow which reflected and made harmless his own intrusive energy. Soon, he would have to decode the secretive messages that flashed from Veli's mind to the beacons of his flesh. He would have to subvert and distort their meaning. Or else he would never control and guide his young missile of death.

Veli lied with a sweetness that pleased Sharman and made him envious. He was off to his extra maths lessons, he told his mother smilingly, and plucked an apple from the basket in the kitchen with a boyish gesture so natural it made Sharman think that the art of pure deception died as youth faded. As you got older you had to rely on artifice and elaborate construction. Even as Veli flung the half-eaten apple thoughtlessly into the immaculate bed of roses and hastened his step as he left the Mandela home, there was an air of ease about him that worried Sharman.

Sharman's plans for the assassination were at a crucial stage. He knew that the timing had to be right, that Veli should not have to gain access to Mandela through any subterfuge. There had to be a chance encounter, an everyday passage into the fateful space that brings together victim and murderer. Everyone had a "private hour." Sharman forgot where he had heard this term, but he thought it an appropriate way of describing the vanity of famous people, the conceited idea that they had two kinds of lives, and that the pleasure they took in the personal and private was more special than even the intoxication of power granted them by their public lives. Those moments when self-importance transcended even importance, and the rich and the famous and the revered were able to dispense with the defences that their power allowed them.

Friday morning was Mandela's private hour. With a lumbering but elegant saunter, he walked barefoot to breakfast on the patio, cooling his huge feet on the tiles. This was a habit he had learned in prison. Sunlight without dusty shadows to ignite lay crisply on the uncut offerings of fruit, juice in a jug and mugs of coffee. There was always a guest at this simple repast, a daughter or a close friend not directly associated with his being the first black president of his country. A famous writer perhaps, sparrowlike in her chair, or the saried Indian woman and her bent husband, all bringing with them a practised air of respectful connivance in Mandela's desire to spend this hour away from his politics or his fame. Without guards or scurrying aides. Veli would approach this gathering of bright people, their perched heads exchanging mundane chit-chat, the visitors trying very hard to be as casual and relaxed as Mandela. He would rise to greet Veli, a patriarchal boom of laughter catching everyone's attention, Mandela the father about to embrace lost youth. And Veli, in his school uniform, his resplendent innocence, would open his school satchel and shoot Mandela with the government-issue Uzi it contained. A simple act by a simple boy. No one else would be harmed, even if they tried to interfere. They had to live to bear bewildered witness to this tragic, incomprehensible act.

It was a Thursday. After his usual private hour the next morning, Mandela would be leaving on an extended trip abroad. Sharman had to bring Veli under control today, still the quickened pace of the boy's heartbeat, reduce his pulse to the measured level that would allow easy manipulation of his unpractised arms, steady his young, innocent eyes as the weapon was raised and focused on the target. To dispel any momentary fear or shock when Mandela would be in his sights, he would have to appear like any other target, just another old man.

But Veli's pulse was racing, excited by an anticipation that Sharman could not identify, for it was without the thrill of terror foretold. A gate scraped open, Veli entered a garden, a young girl waited in a doorway, he sauntered towards her without outward haste although his penis was already erect, she smiled, they embraced for a quick moment. Sharman smelled the acrid incense of her young skin. The door closed, they walked arm in arm down a corridor of shadows, footsteps muffled by a deep carpet. Up a flight of stairs, and already their desire broke through its rather-too-adult containment. Another door was opened and quickly shut. Light from a distant window framed the typical teenage litter on a desk. A gilt-framed portrait of Veli, of another curly-haired boy, his skin the colour of dirty honey.

"Where's Michael?" Veli asked.

"Later," the girl answered.

Already they were whispering. She undressed, staring up at his face. He was slightly taller than her.

"Ah, Alice," Veli said, as she stood naked before him.

Veli bent down and kissed her breasts, breathed in the excessive heat that new ripening brings, and began to take off his own clothes. Sharman found the ritual awkward, Veli contorting his body in order to remove his shirt and trousers, all without interrupting the passage of his tongue across the softly downed surface of Alice's skin. Not once did he pause at any particular spot or delve into folds of skin even as they offered themselves to his mouth. When they fell onto the bed, Sharman sensed the lack of youthful hesitation, the inept pauses that brought giggles to couples as young as they. Their awkwardness was adult, his gentle, moaning entry into her body and her comfortable response were accomplished with a grown-up lack of triumph. And their labour, a balletic set-piece almost, of arched backs and closed eyes. His strong arms pressed against the bed to raise himself away from her, her arms clutched at the tenseness of his buttocks.

Sharman had an irresistible urge to intervene, to let his weightlessness in Veli dissipate, to crush this young woman—for that was what she had become in the thrust of her flesh—and smother her beauty, its ruthless blossoming, all gleaming sweat and daring pulsation that he had thought only murderers were capable of. But he was unable to break the rhythm of their senses, their harmonic moans and synchronised sighs. Though for a second he caused Veli to thrust viciously into Alice so that she opened her eyes, startled by the pain, this intrusion was overwhelmed by the height of their passion, smoothed by their gradual descent into a peaceful abyss.

They slept while Sharman raged inside Veli until he was exhausted, and considered dispiritedly, then dismissed, the thought that he could easily slip out of Veli's being and murder them both. What petty vengeance that would be for a wrong he could not yet identify. No, he would wait for Mandela to die. But Sharman's patience, his stoic thoughtlessness, was shattered by a new shuddering in Veli's body. Yes, he was having sex, and with the same fervour as before, but this had a different, rougher quality. From honey to dirty honey. Veli was lying on his stomach and someone was on his back. The curly-headed boy was—and Sharman could only think of the word "fucking"—fucking Veli from behind.

Sharman recoiled, and with the volition of a horror he could not resist, attempted to leave Veli's being. He struck the barrier of rainbow colours and fell back. He was unable to leave. As Michael's penis increased its passionate exploration of Veli's body, a gentle but gnawing search at the walls of sensitive membrane, Sharman increased his frantic efforts to escape. Veli experienced a shrill agony inside himself, not in his anus where Michael joyously moved about, but somewhere deeper. He screamed out loud, and with a twist of his powerful back flung Michael away.

"Veli, what is it?"

Veli turned to face Michael.

"Oh my God, it hurt, for some reason, it hurt so badly."

Michael embraced Veli, and then Alice was there, and gentle hands wove their different texture of comfort over Veli's body, his weeping face, until they fell asleep like that, Veli in the soothing nakedness of Alice and her brother Michael. Sharman felt tired, near to death with weariness, he thought. The realisation that they were accustomed to falling asleep like this, or that they coupled—no, no, that was inappropriate—a trio, Veli inside of Alice and Michael inside of Veli, moving about with grotesque rhythm, what practised decadence that required! It was not he who performed "these acts," Sharman rationalised, he was apart from his prey, superior to them, aloof from their many sordid weaknesses.

"These acts," the naive experiments in untried and yet already aged sensuality that Veli and Alice and Michael dabbled in, were but a small part of the cosmic entwining and disentwining of limbs that Sharman had seen. People making love in the midst of battle, fornicating, copulating even as war chants rose from the darkness beyond the hill. Such warnings of an implacable enemy on the march did not stop them. Indeed, it seemed that impending death increased their frenzy, that the picture of a spear about to plunge into a breast or the mechanical roar of a firearm shattering a face that had been kissed and caressed only moments before, drove those mortal bodies to physical feats which those who survived would later recall with disquiet, like the involuntary remorse after too much rich food and drink.

The three young people awoke from their sleep when it was already dark. It was Alice, disturbed by Veli's incessant murmuring, who roused them. With the tense alertness of experienced thieves they smuggled Veli down dark corridors, through hidden doors and out through the garden gate. They walked side by side in the quiet street, not speaking, until the Mandela home was in sight. Alice and Michael watched as Veli negotiated his way past the guards at the gate, and then the two turned away, hand in hand. Sharman's distant vision of their intertwining fingers made him suspect that they would make secret journeys to each other's beds later, and invoking Veli's image, a dark and ghostly aphrodisiac presence, they would—who knows what? The word "fuck" now seemed so repulsive that he thought of his mother's enforced celibacy as a virtue he had not understood.

There burned in him all night a hatred, a fevered disgust, that caused Veli to shiver and shout out loud. Sharman's anger allowed no respite and he raged within the fragile walls of Veli's sanity until the boy began to vomit, blobs of hissing blood that blocked the toilet bowl and forced his mother to drag him outside where he continued spewing up a foul-smelling substance, yellow and dirty, at times effulgently dark. Miriam prayed to all the Gods she could recall, Christian, ancestral, to the voices of night birds in the trees, to the cold stars and even the humming darkness of the suburban night.

Until Veli fell asleep and the tinder-dry heat in his body began to subside. The next morning, his exhausted mother still asleep. Veli rose and dressed himself. A morning of bright voices. On the patio a group of people at breakfast, a ritual he had seen before. There in their midst, the old man whom everyone called Baba. He saw Veli and rose from his seat, a smile upon his face. Veli smiled shyly and lowered his head. He hurried past the gaily chatting group. He had left his satchel at Alice and Michael's. He would need it for school.

Emotions and the Delegates

Jonathan Grossman ▼▼▼▼▼▼▼▼▼▼▼▼▼▼▼▼▼▼▼▼▼▼▼▼▼▼▼▼

The easiest way to tell that she was foreign would have been to ask her. But you don't always ask people about themselves even when it is the easiest way to find out. And anyway, I had my own way from as soon as I saw her. It was not just that she was one of the few white faces. My face is also white. Or that she had a tell-tale blazing red suntan. She was actually burnt quite brown. It was because she wore little white socks with her sandals. Only foreigners do that.

She was terribly progressive.

So the points of identification followed. She had marched for South Africa in the streets governed by a Danish Thatcher and sacrificed South African apples and oranges and deprived herself of South African wine. She could have added that like millions of people all over the world, she had not bought South African gold or South African diamonds. But much more. She knew someone who had been in exile. She had mixed with exiles and drunk with them and marched with them. She had felt. She had been one with the struggle. She had sent telegrams demanding the release of political prisoners. Now she was here. Sitting in a meeting in Retreat. She had come to take her place and join the celebrations.

"How do you feel about the future?" But it was not really the question she wanted to ask. And I was not really the person she wanted to answer. I didn't answer. "What has brought you here?" It was not what I wanted to say or ask. She probably didn't really want to answer. She was a psychologist. She was a delegate at a conference on the trauma of people who had been tortured. She knew the language that we were still being taught about reconciliation and healing. Now was the time to shift from adversarialism. She would even make that shift for the struggle. She was part of the future.

She reminded me of the time I had sat on a plane coming from _____ and listened to a conversation between the two people next to me. One was visiting South Africa for the first time. The other was a new South African. He thought Mandela was wonderful but he was worried about standards. Would Mandela be able to maintain standards— I suppose against those wild people who were determined to lower them? He was talking rubbish, I thought. I said so. When he went to the lavatory the person in the middle visiting South Africa prepared to say something to me. He put his hand in front of his mouth as if to amplify the already enormous announcement he was going to make, but hide from the consequences if things got awkward. "I am part of an official delegation visiting South Africa from the _____ Anti-Apartheid Movement." I knew that already. I had seen the itinerary that he was reading. I had heard them talking in the airport. I had seen the middle ranking famous former political prisoner amongst them. They were going to be met by a cabinet minister. They were going to visit parliament.

We were coming in to land over False Bay. We flew over Seal Island. The delegate got very excited. It was a moment in history. "Is that Robben Island?" he asked me. Should I have given him his moment in history? I was tired and brutal. "No. It is Seal Island." Then I watched as he wrote in his diary. "SA for the first time. The emotions of flying over Robben Island with _____" (the middle ranking famous political prisoner who had actually been in Pretoria Central).

I remember when I saw the veterans of the civil war at the front of the May Day march in Madrid. Something without a name crawled up my spine and into my heart when they shouted "Viva!" for the workers of South Africa. I remember the red flags and the beating drums at the end of the May Day march in Paris. The pamphlets said: "More workers and youth have marched and boycotted and been on strike in solidarity with the struggle in South Africa than with any other struggle in history."

It was all different then. The emotions of May Day in Madrid. The emotions of seeing Seal Island. Better to murder a baby in its cradle than harbour an unspoken desire. Easier to turn Seal Island into Robben Island than believe that workers made history. One Island into another Island. The arithmetic works. One for one. Not nonsense about cutting the cake into so many pieces when the cake is not big enough. It's all there, in the diary of the delegate.

One time I visited Jackson in his shack because there was another crisis. I found him sitting on a grand dining room chair with frayed upholstery at a table which sloped with the floor. In front of him was a diary also. It was a diary from 1993. The year was 1996. There were newspapers and magazines all over the table. We finished talking about the crisis. Then he showed me the main entry in the diary of 1993 that he was working on in 1996. On the table that sloped with the floor, sitting on the grand chair with the frayed upholstery. It was a list of telephone numbers of prominent leaders: Joe Slovo—who was dead. Jay Naidoo, who is now the Minister of Posts. Cyril Ramaphosa, now in big business. More names. More numbers. Jackson was putting them all in his diary. He showed me that he had them all, there in _____ squatters camp where there was no telephone. Even their cell-phone numbers.

I wanted to ask him: "Why are you making this list? What are you going to do with it? Why have you got a duck in your yard? I can understand a hen. But a duck? Why have you got daisies? I can understand vegetables. But daisies?" But I didn't ask.

Jackson liked to tell a story. Before he came to _____ squatters camp, he worked nearby in _____. He had literature of the struggle. He used to sit and read it to other workers and discuss the future. The time when the struggle would bring jobs and houses and money.

"What are you doing Jackson?"

"Nothing!"

"What are you discussing Jackson?"

"Nothing!"

"Don't tell us 'nothing'. We know it's politics."

Jackson laughed at this point of the story, each time.

"They called me the mayor."

Don't tell us nothing. We know it's politics. The fear called by its name. Politics in the backyard. Poison in the water.

He was one of the first in _____ squatters camp. It is not an easy place. The wind comes. The rain comes. The sand is always there. But he built his shack there. Like many others. In his diary he could have written of how they came to destroy the shacks and remove the people. About bodies in front of bulldozers, and shacks destroyed in the light and rebuilt in the dark. He talks about the blue flash that came and burnt many shacks and killed four people. And he is still sitting there, making his list of phone numbers. When they told him to move he said no.

"These are our shacks. This is our place. You say we must go. We say no. We go when we say. We stay when we say. They must put proper houses for us here." More politics from the backyard. Clear the backyards, and the politics comes from the shacks.

"One thing you must know about us," said Jackson. "We had unity and we had hope. No one was sitting with folded hands. Each one was turning to the one next to him."

"That time," he said, "it was the time of the struggle for the new South Africa. That time we were ready to die."

And now it was 1996. And I was sitting next to the woman with the little white socks and sandals who wanted to celebrate so that she could record her emotions. It was her entitlement, after everything. But something was wrong. Now she had one burning question. Eventually it came out. "Why is there so much dirt where people are living?"

I wonder. Did the delegate write the same question in his diary? Or did he go on from one moment in history to another? His entitlements. The emotions of flying over Robben Island with _____; the emotions of being met by a cabinet minister. The emotions of going to parliament. And then a new paragraph. The emotions of seeing the filth in _____? Doesn't fit. Not neat arithmetic. Like swapping one island for another island. Or distributing the slices according to the size of the cake.

"I'm sorry," she said, "if it is not the right question to ask. But I must ask you. It makes me so sad to see all this dirt. Don't people want to do something themselves to make things better?" The emotions of being so sad.

I have seen Jackson with blazing eyes. But he is not in his own diary. What is there is a list of telephone numbers and Jackson has not got a telephone because there are no telephones in _____ squatters camp.

What's in a Name?

BERNADETTE MUTHIEN ▼▼▼▼▼▼▼▼▼▼▼▼▼▼▼▼▼▼▼▼▼▼▼▼▼▼▼

call me coolie
call me coloured
call me Anything You Like
but in the mirror
my reflections're fractured
still me

crystal and plastic
have rims
but I don't verb too well

so
don't fuck
with my ancestors
generations of walking
in shit's
luck

sticks & stones
broke our bones
& names'll
always
hurt us
but
we're still
a round
& f**king
angry

Je To Mozny

EDWARD LURIE ▼▼▼▼▼▼▼▼▼▼▼▼▼▼▼▼▼▼▼▼▼▼▼▼▼▼▼▼▼▼▼▼

Yes, I agree with you, that is indeed a strange title for a story. Those are Czech words meaning "it is possible."

Now how does a young man like myself from Gleemoor Township come to know anything as Eurocentric as that? Well, I happened to be bred and raised in a back-of-beyond Moravian Mission village tucked away in a fold of the Cape mountains and that's the language spoken in Moravia.

No doubt you are wondering where on the earth is Moravia. It's right next door to Bohemia which for a long time I thought existed on the left bank of Paris about a hundred years ago, peopled by men with thick black beards who argued in pavement cafés and starved in garret studios where they painted pictures that now are sold to Japanese electronics manufacturers for millions and millions. You see, it is possible, *je to mozny*, for the underrated to move up-market because values do change with time.

But not in our village; there nothing changed from the time our black-robed founding fathers decided it was their holy duty to improve the indigenous Khoi-San species by crossing it with their own fertile Central European seed and teaching the succeeding crops of hybrids, including myself, not to speak in clicks but rather to learn a civilised language like Czech. Morally strict, soundly conservative, right from the year dot they insisted Czech be a compulsory subject in the little school they built, and it still is. At eight-fifteen every morning you can hear the children greet their teachers with a chorus of "*dobry den*"; heaven help any sleep-befuddled youngster who mumbled "good morning" or "goeie môre"; his backside would be left looking like the inflamed rump steak of a zebra or a tiger.

Except in the class of Mister du Plessis, who taught us Czech, there it was different. He never needed to punish us; with him no child ever misbehaved; we simply didn't; he was that kind of man.

So it was obvious that I should study Slavic languages through Unisa when my parents died and I left the mission village to stay with my Uncle Ben and Auntie Annie in Gleemoor. In a home like theirs, with embroidered samplers on the wall, "God Bless This House" and "Patience Is A Virtue," one simply did not, I repeat "not," experiment with sex and strong drink amongst the bright lights of Klipfontein Road in Athlone, only a stone's-throw away. And certainly no throwing of stones at Caspirs, no ways. Yes, they rendered unto Caesar et cetera, were almost indecently decent, a childless couple who smothered me with affection and hand-knitted bedspreads, practically force-feeding me with eat-up-it's-good-for-you food. They fussed, spoilt me rotten, more so than my own parents ever had. Uncle, a retired carpenter, spent weeks making me a desk with the tools he kept still sharpened and oiled in a shed at the back, so I could study "more proper," make something of myself, so they could be proud of me.

When at last I could put B.A. after my name they cried and praised the good Lord as though He had written the exams and not I. Uncle made an elaborate frame for the certificate and hung it above the ball-and-claw display cabinet.

In the new South Africa, here I come. These days, nothing to hold me back, no discrimination, no anything to stop me becoming whatever I choose to be.

I don't want to boast but the letter I wrote to Foreign Affairs was just perfect. "*Pienkny*"—that's the Polish for "beautiful." All right, I do admit it, I am showing off a little.

All the Slavic languages are pretty similar; I could make myself understood in Warsaw or Prague or Moscow, even Bulgaria; I was tailor-made for the job, they needed me, they'd create a place especially for me. Impeccably groomed, I'd dash from some reception in a palace, black briefcase with silver bands in one hand, inside it folders marked "Highly Confidential," to a conference in some panelled boardroom, where I'd negotiate, firmly but fairly, for reduced import tariffs on Outspan naartjies and sour figs, moskonfyt and mebos. Then at night a candle-lit dinner with some beauty oozing continental charm who possibly, excitingly, might be a spy. I'd stroll with her, arm around waist, feeling her hip-bones gyrate with each step, along the banks of the Vltava or the Wisla or the Mockba, the lilt of gypsy violins magical as the lights reflected on the water. A diplomat, I'd be diplomatic, persuasive.

No "possible" about my appointment, no *je to mozny*, it was only a matter of time before I'd be flying, business class of course, to Pretoria for briefing.

Six months later I got a postcard. "The matter is receiving attention." As long as I hadn't been pigeon-holed and simply forgotten. But till confirmation arrived I needed a temporary job, to fill in time and to help me scrape together enough cash for the down-payment on a pin-stripe suit, so I could make a really with-it impression at the initial interview though surely later I'd be given a clothing allowance. Surely.

The supermarket strike gave me my chance. Yes, they could fit me in. The young lady recited her speech with the conviction of a tired time-share salesman. Why they don't use a recorded message beats me. I'd have to start at the bottom but. . . .

"I'll have you know that I am a university graduate," I protested.

"You're a what?" She screwed up her eyebrows into the shape of question marks and began again from the beginning. I'd have to start at the bottom but with hard work and loyalty to the Chairman and support for his sporting sponsorships it is possible I could rise to become. . . .

I felt a bubble bursting from the side of my head, connected by a string of blobs. On it was a ladder, me with a foot on the bottom rung, half-way up was written "Branch Manager" and at the very top "'Managing Director."

Nothing could stop me. I'd use my skill in Slavic languages to arrange the import of . . . well, say caviar for example, create a market for it in Kenilworth Centre or why not right here in Athlone?

When I reported for duty I was shown my work-place, a claustrophobic cubicle at the back of the reserve store. My job consisted in switching off the thumping on the shop's loudspeakers every two minutes, then screeching "storff eennoussmin" into a microphone, followed by any one of half-a-dozen standard messages selected at random, then switch the public-address back on again. It was meant to show customers how on-the-ball we were.

For hour after hour, week after week. Each month I wrote another letter to Foreign Affairs till I got laryngitis from all the shouting I had to do, and that got me the sack.

So now what? For how much longer could I go on presuming on my uncle's and aunt's charity? The nights weren't too bad; I spent them composing letters to the Department, beautifully phrased, carefully drafted, in English, Afrikaans, Russian, Polish, Czech, Bulgarian. As for a reply—*nyet*. You see, I do know how to say it in Russian.

The days were awful; they made of me a drifter, a parasite of society, a sponger on a thoroughly loveable pair of pensioners who allowed themselves no luxuries so that I could spend my time awaiting my turn to stare at the Situations Vacant columns in the Athlone Municipal Library's copy of last night's Argus.

We were a band of regulars, the discards, the hopeless. We sat there, slumped as though our backbones had been broken, our eyes blind to the stacks of books that mocked us with their adventures and their knowledge. Any newcomer was a morsel of interest that we sucked dry with stares of inspection. He seemed vaguely familiar. It possibly could be, it definitely was Mister du Plessis, an older, greyer, shrunken version of my former teacher, with that dried-out biltong look that so many old men acquire.

Still polite, as kindly as I remembered him to be, I think he pretended to recognise me, returned my greeting of "*dobry den*" with a repetition but seemed a bit puzzled when I continued in Czech. Only then did I realise with the shock of an adult truth, that poor old Mister du Plessis knew no more of the language than what he had got us to learn off by heart from a dog-eared text-book.

We chatted, in English, in whispers, above the bowed heads of the unemployed, the bored pensioners, under the frowning eyebrows of the librarian, past her finger pointing to the "Silence Please Stilte Asseblief" notice.

Yes, well, he would be retiring shortly, not to spend his remaining years in the village as he had hoped, "Ach no, what," things weren't any longer what they used to be because. . . . He leaned forward to clutch my lapel and hiss into my ear, "They've opened something called a disco right next door to my cottage and true as I'm standing here I'm telling you it's impossible. Impossible. So I thought it is possible, maybe there's chance of picking up some part-time like a job here where there's more scope because the pension. . . . Young man like you, you'd know about discos, things like that, all the goings-on in those sort places."

Again I felt a bubble burst from my over-active, larger than average brain. On it was written "teacher," then "headmaster." Yes, I had a brain all right. "If you're staying here for any time why not drop in for tea one day. Tomorrow suit you? About four, say. It's not far from here."

Uncle and Auntie were delighted into a panic. Soon the house reeked of furniture polish and baking.

Next day, at a quarter to four, Uncle in his suit, choked by a tie tight as a garotte, spotted a finger-print on the glass over my certificate. Auntie untied her apron-strings and congratulated herself with "They come out only but real good this time. He'll lick his fingers just like that fried chicken with the bokbaard."

A ring on the door-bell, introductions, "No, you sit here, it's more like comfortable." Seventeen seconds is a long time when it's silent.

Uncle, as host, cleared his throat to place an exclamation mark at the beginning of his sentence. "Du Plessis you said. Nowa thatsa likea foreign name hey."

I felt myself blush. "Uncle, it's Italians who talk like that. Du Plessis actually is a French name, originally that is, but Mister du Plessis, he's one of us."

"Ach what," said Uncle, "French, Italian, what's the odds. Same difference. All from that part the world."

"Did you say French?" asked Auntie. "Tell me, it's true they really eat snails over there? Sies. Wait a bit, you'll see just now I've made for you something much more nicer."

"Mister du Plessis taught us Czech in the mission school."

"You don't say." Auntie seemed impressed although I had explained it all the day before. "Now in that other sort-of-like a language of yours how for example you'd say 'koeksisters'? They know about things like that over there?"

Mister du Plessis perched uncomfortably on the edge of his comfortable chair, his knees squeezed together as he squeezed out "Well, a word-for-word translation . . . and to tell you the honest truth I've never actually so much as set foot there, in person that is, only read about. . . ."

Uncle and Auntie both nodded, waiting for him to continue. It's rude to interrupt a visitor and they were politeness incarnate. They went on waiting.

Mister du Plessis had to say something. "Matter of fact I've never travelled further than Pietersburg. That's way way past Jo'burg. Teachers' conference. I'd prepared a paper only there wasn't time but I did take part in the discussion."

Nineteen seconds can seem a lot longer than seventeen.

Till Uncle rescued us by leaning forward in interest and nodding a few times. "Places over there, not like Pietersburg, I mean where they talk funny, you know where I mean, they're very old I suppose."

I could tell from the sing-song way he spoke that Mister du Plessis was quoting. "Many of the finest buildings date from the Habsburg dynasty."

"Don't even talk to me about Dynasty." Auntie flapped a palm in dismissal. "What I say is, actually, far as I'm concerned, for my part give me Dallas rather any day."

The visitor cocked his head to one side and raised an eyebrow in interest. "Yes, one does form attachments to places and there's no accounting for tastes. You manage to get there quite often I take it."

"You can say that again. What's called a regular. Comes every Thursday night eight-thirty and I'm right there. What you mean 'attached'? Man, I could of had eyes and ears glued to the set with some of that quick-set sticky stuff comes in a tube."

It's possible, *je to mozny*, that Foreign Affairs would still save me because suddenly I remembered the Serbs too spoke a Slavic language. It is possible I'd be posted to Sarajevo where it is possible I'd be lucky enough to get blown into a shell-hole for the earth to swallow me.

"Tea with koeksisters," announced Auntie, with three words jerking me back ten thousand kilometres from Bosnia to Gleemoor.

Tea-time was sticky with syrup and the stretched seconds of social strain. Minutes are sixty times as long as seconds and still not a word about a teacher to replace him.

Mister du Plessis sighed. "Looks lovely for sure except . . . just a touch of sugar. It's the diabetes."

"Ach, come on," coaxed Auntie, "be a devil, just for once."

"Man, but it's sad." He sighed again. "You know what, in the village nobody bakes their own things any more. I'm telling you it's a changed place, I feel there like one of those singises they find in stones you see in a museum. They're even going to stop teaching Czech when I retire end of next term. Can you believe it? After all those years."

The balloon at the side of my head deflated to lumpy wrinkles so like those on the faces of the three others in the room. Another took its place.

Why wait to be sent officially to some romantic city, say like St. Ex-Leningrad? Not possibly but definitely I'd find work there. With the Russians becoming hooked on hamburgers and supermarkets I'd be able to shriek slooshahytyeh pahzhahloostah into a microphone better than any local. After all, I had the experience.

Then hand-in-hand with a Tanya or an Anastasia I'd stroll through snow along the banks of the Neva while she fluttered the lashes of her otchy chornyeh at me. Freezing air, fevered blood. . . . I felt myself shiver.

"You're cold," said Auntie. "Go put on that pink jersey with the yellow stripes I knitted for you. Come on, show your teacher."

Mister du Plessis, a faint grey figure, gradually faded out of the house rather than left it, faded as had my hopes of becoming the headmaster of a mission school.

Now what? If patience really was a virtue it meant that day after day I must drag myself down the garden path to lift the flap of the letter-box and fish out special offers from the Readers Digest. At my age could I go on accepting pocket-money from a pair of hard-up elderly relatives? Or ask to borrow a hefty sum which I'd then use to leave them, after all they'd done for me? If only they'd been awful.

Somehow I had to start scraping together the price of a ticket that lay as far beyond my empty pockets as the Kremlin is from the Tuynhuis.

Strange, but it was the supermarket which inspired me to fly, not by Aeroflot from Jan Smuts but from the family nest, and not by offering me back my job but by providing an abandoned trolley tilted at a drunken angle in a ditch.

So now when you see a healthy young man staggering down the street don't be disgusted by the way he lurches; it's not from downing a kannetjie of Chateau Cardboard but because the soles of his shoes have worn through. And don't presume he's been driven so crazy by meths strained through a hunk of stale white bread begged at some madam's back door that he mutters *"praznie butilki"* to himself. You'd refuse to believe that any such unwashed ragged outcast of polite society would know better than you do how to say in Bulgarian what he yells at each front gate—"empty bottles." Be careful; you could be sneering at one who some day might still come to be addressed as His Excellency the Ambassador. Be very careful, because it is possible, *je to mozny*.

The Day of the Boycott

FELICITY WOOD ▼▼▼▼▼▼▼▼▼▼▼▼▼▼▼▼▼▼▼▼▼▼▼▼▼▼▼▼▼▼▼▼

I drove up the hill, past the suicidal cows and goats and thorn trees festooned with plastic bags and through the gates of the university. As soon as I entered, I knew something had happened. I felt as if I were standing in a swimming pool that had been drained of all its water. The essential item had vanished: there were no students.

I wandered into the Arts Block, which had been plonked like a giant brick on the rolling brown hilltop on which the university was situated. The upper level of the Arts Block consisted of a long windowless corridor, with offices on one side and lecture theatres on the other. Below, in semi-subterranean gloom, were tutorial and seminar rooms, one of which had been converted into two small cramped offices. One was mine, the other belonged to a colleague currently on leave. Without the students, the long corridors had an eerily empty quality. There were no workers to be glimpsed either, since there had been a workers' stayaway for the past week.

I was due to lecture the English 3 class on George Eliot's *Middlemarch*. In the lecture theatre, however, I surveyed rows of empty seats. Without looking behind me, I placed my book and notes on the table below the blackboard. My hand touched something cold. I turned around. There, lying stiff and straight on the table was Professor Van Rooyen, the Head of the Department of Sociology, who had died five days ago and had been buried—or so I had believed—yesterday. Van Rooyen's face seemed frozen into a nasty, supercilious sneer. He looked as if he'd been struck dead while confronting a group of first-year students who'd come to ask why he'd failed their assignments. I let out a long low wail of pure terror. The book and lecture notes went flying.

"Heh, heh, heh, heh."

The sound came from somewhere in the middle of the lecture theatre. A closely cropped head, a sardonic bearded face and a pair of skinny shoulders rose slowly into view.

"Gave you a fright, didn't he, Rosemary?"

It was Jake September, lecturer in the Department of Sociology. Disreputable, eccentric and cynical, he drifted around campus offending members of staff, and entertaining and alarming students. And I'd been responsible for bringing him to the university.

Several years ago, Hilary, an acquaintance of mine in Cape Town, had contacted me about a Sociology post at the university that a friend of hers had just applied for. There were no other contenders for the post apart from

Jake, because Personnel had lost all the applications. They did this on a regular basis, whether out of deliberate malevolence or simple incompetence, for personal gain or a combination of all three. There was no way of telling. But I had suggested to Hilary that Jake send an additional application to me, which I could forward to the Selection Committee, thus bypassing the treacherous bog of Personnel. So Jake got the post. When he arrived at the university, he came to thank me for my help. After that, I saw him quite often. I soon discovered several important facts about Jake.

The first thing I discovered was that he did not have a Master's degree in Sociology from a university in the American Midwest (as stated on his curriculum vitae). He had instead Sociology 2 from the University of Cape Town.

"Well, they didn't ask for any certificates, Rosie," he said, when I expressed my shock at this act of deceit. "And if they don't check up, it's their own fault. Anyway, I put a lot of time and effort into inventing Arcadia University, so when the Selection Committee asked me about the Master's degree I'd done and the university I'd got it at, they certainly got their money's worth."

I hate being called Rosie. It conjures up images of jolly, fat barpersons or apple-cheeked women in idyllic rustic settings. But by the time I felt I knew Jake well enough to tell him this, he'd been calling me Rosie so often that pointing it out would look silly, I felt.

The next thing I found out was that Jake had been keen to obtain a post at a homeland university because he had been supplying Hilary and a number of others with LSD, and someone had tipped off the police.

The last important fact about Jake was that his great passion in life was his artworks. They consisted of metal and wire twisted into various shapes, along with conglomerations of objects, placed together in incongruous, disturbing (and messy) combinations. Jake's theory was that a teaching job at a homeland university would give him enough spare time and money to pursue his passion relatively undisturbed, beyond the grasp of the South African legal system.

Now I gawped at Jake and Professor Van Rooyen in the gloom of the lecture theatre.

"B . . . but they buried him yesterday. How can he be here?"

Jake grinned, exposing his missing front tooth. "I don't know what they buried yesterday, but it certainly wasn't him. I got him from the funeral parlour the night before last."

I didn't ask Jake how he had got Van Rooyen out of the funeral parlour. Jake had, as I had discovered from the occasions I'd locked my keys in my office or in my car, a remarkable talent for picking locks.

"Jake, you've got to return him! They must have called the police! They must be looking for him right now!"

"Probably not. Imagine what it'd do to business if they admitted that the corpse they were supposed to be looking after had vanished. And luckily none of Van Rooyen's nearest and dearest wanted to gaze into his face to bid him a last farewell. Whatever they shoved into that coffin—possibly a sack of mealie meal, for all I know—I'm sure it was of more service to humanity than old Van Rooyen ever was."

"But Jake—*why?* What did you do it for?"

Jake leaned back in his seat, and put his feet up on the desk in front of him.

"I've always hated old Van Rooyen's guts. He sucked up to the Broederbond when they controlled this place, and then he sucked up to the new management in exactly the same way. He behaved as if he'd got some top parliamentary position, just because he sat on all those university committees. And he was a complete dictator. He ran the Sociology Department like it was his own private homeland. He. . . ."

"OK, OK, Jake, but you still haven't said what you're going to do with him."

Jake grinned. "All those Transformation Committees he's sat on for the last four years are going to have some effect on him at last. I'm going to *transform* him into a work of art. I'm going to preserve him and make him the focal point of one of my pieces. He could have a frilly pink showercap on, and green plastic Ninja Turtles. . . ."

"Jake, for heaven's sake!" I snapped. "You call that art?"

Jake sat up, and leaned towards me.

"Look at yourself, Rosemary! Here you are, teaching George Eliot. And what did you do your M.A. on—the poetry of Keats? Get with contemporary culture! A lot's happened since those eighteenth century wankers!"

"Eliot and Keats wrote in the nineteenth century," I interrupted coldly.

"Sixteenth, seventeenth, eighteenth, nineteenth—who cares? They're all dead and gone. Like Van Rooyen here," Jake paused to smile fondly at the figure stretched out before him. "Well, dead, but definitely not yet gone."

"You can't use someone's body like a piece of scrap metal!"

"Why not?"

"There'll be an outcry! His family will sue you. . . ."

Jake's eyes took on a dreamy expression. "This is contemporary art, Rosie. It's about going beyond where anyone else has gone before. All the better if there's an outcry. It'll put me on the map. And as for his family suing me, well"—his eyes gleamed—"when I'm finished with the old bugger, he'll be unrecognizable."

"Er, Jake, but how are you going to preserve him? He must have started decaying already."

Jake smiled at me. "Good old Rosie, as practical as ever. Don't worry, I've got that all worked out. You remember my friend Eddie?"

"That friend of yours in Jo'burg who preserves peoples' dead pets for them?"

"The very same! Eddie's really excited—he says he's never had an opportunity to do a human body before. He's coming down today with his equipment, and we're going to get to work on Van Rooyen."

"But this isn't a hamster or a guinea-pig! Is Eddie going to manage to preserve something as large as a human being?"

"Look, Rosie, Eddie's preserved someone's Great Dane. If he can do a Great Dane, he can do Van Rooyen."

"And why are you carting Van Rooyen around campus like this? Shouldn't he be in a fridge somewhere?"

Jake nodded. "Good question, Rosie. And so he has been, in a nice big fridge that no one seemed to be using in the basement of the Science Building. And he still would be there if there hadn't been a power failure on that part of campus this morning. After I got Van Rooyen out of the fridge, I remembered that you had a lecture, so I thought I'd bring him over here, so that you could say good morning to him. With the boycott on, I knew that there wouldn't be any students around."

The swing doors at the top of the lecture theatre were pushed apart, and in strode Drusilla Nkosi, my most glamorous third-year student.

Today Drusilla was wearing a tight fitting short black leather skirt and a padded leather jacket with a deep pink shirt underneath. Her lips and fingernails were painted the same shade of pink, and her hair swung just below her firm jawline in rows of beaded plaits. In my faded Whole Earth Centre sundress and flat leather sandals, I felt myself shrink into the shadows. Drusilla had once mentioned that she usually succeeded in getting four or five bursaries a year so that she could spend the proceeds of at least two of them on her clothes. (No one checked up, so students who were skilled in applying for bursaries could accumulate any number of them.)

I hastily stepped in front of Van Rooyen, obscuring as much of his face as I could.

"I was walking past the Arts Block, and I thought that I'd come and see if you were waiting here for all of us. I must just tell you that some of the students have threatened to disrupt any lectures that take place today. So I don't think you should wait around here too long. Oh hullo, Mr. September, I didn't notice you. And who's this?"

"Oh, um, this is . . . this is a visitor from another English Department. . . . We were, well . . . we were going to enact a scene out of *Middlemarch* for you—you know, when Causabon's dying and Dorothea's ministering to him."

Drusilla's deep pink lips curved in a smile. "What a nice idea, Ms. Martin. I do hope you can do it for us some other time. But as I was saying, perhaps you'd better move on."

"Thanks, thanks, Drusilla, we will," I hastily interrupted. "And I really do appreciate your coming to tell me this."

Drusilla smiled again, waved airily, flashing five perfect bright pink fingernails at us, then sashayed out of a side door. In the distance, we could hear singing.

"Jake, both of you must get out of here! NOW!"

"Couldn't agree with you more," said Jake springing to his feet and producing several sheets sewn together in a makeshift shroud.

"Here, help me get him into this."

"No ways, Jake. You handle him on your own!"

"Look, Rosie, what if someone came in now and found him? We've got to get him out of sight. No, not that way—feet first!"

After some manoeuvring, we managed to encase Van Rooyen in his shroud. It was a highly unpleasant business, and ice-cold and shrunken in death as he was, I half expected him to wake up suddenly and ask me what I thought I was doing with him.

"What are you going to do now?" I said.

"Stash him in another fridge until Eddie arrives," said Jake. "You've got a fridge in the Arts Faculty, haven't you, Rosie?"

"Yes, we do, and it's used for refrigerating the milk for midmorning tea, not deceased professors," I retorted. "With no classes today, there'll be nothing for everyone to do except sit around and drink tea. And that will probably be the case for all the Faculty fridges on campus."

Jake frowned, then snapped his fingers. "Got it!" he announced. "The Staff Centre hasn't been open for the last few days because of the workers' stayaway. Let's pop Van Rooyen in one of the fridges in there! No one's going to be wandering around there today. The workers are only going to be returning to work the day after tomorrow."

"Jake, you can do that on your own! I don't see why you have to rope me in!"

"Ah come on, Rosie, be a sport," said Jake in what was intended to be a persuasive tone. "Van Rooyen's very awkward to lug around. I've been wheeling him around on a trolley. He's frozen stiff, so I can prop him upright. But it was really tricky and I kept worrying that he might fall off. With you to help me, we could get him into the Staff Centre in no time. Please?"

"All right Jake, I'll help you," I said. "Then I don't want to have *anything* more to do with this. Do you understand?"

Jake grinned. "Sure, sure Rosie—but you'll get a special invitation to the opening of the exhibition. You wouldn't want to miss that."

We made our way down to the Staff Centre, Jake pushing the trolley with Van Rooyen propped on it, and me holding Van Rooyen in place. He was extremely heavy and utterly stiff, and we might well have been carting a log of wood around. A seam had opened at the bottom of the shroud, and Van Rooyen's feet, long, white and knobbly, with yellowish toenails, were poking through. It looked as if he was beginning to claw his way out of his shroud. I was terrified that someone might suddenly stop us to take a closer look at Van Rooyen's toes. However, the only people I could see were distant groups of students (probably the source of the singing we'd been hearing) hurrying towards the administration building.

Jake led me towards the back of the Staff Centre. A gate led into a courtyard. The gate was bolted on the inside, but not locked. Jake clambered over the gate, unbolted it, wheeled Van Rooyen into the courtyard, then managed to haul himself up through a half-open toilet window. He leaned out.

"Here we go, Rosie. Help me get him through the window."

Jake grabbed hold of Van Rooyen, and with me lifting as much as I was able, he began pulling him through. There was a ripping noise and, like a ghastly butterfly emerging from a chrysalis, Van Rooyen parted company with his covering.

"Oh shit, there goes the shroud," Jake remarked. "Oh well, the main thing is just to get him stowed away for the time being. I'll wrap him in my office curtains when Eddie comes along. Don't look so shocked, Rosemary. He's just a big piece of frozen meat, that's all. Let's find a fridge."

Jake helped pull me through the window and we lugged Van Rooyen through the Staff Centre. I tried to avoid looking at Van Rooyen, but I had to help carry him, and it sent shivers down my spine. Without his shroud, I was more aware of the chilly quality of his body, reminiscent of the flesh of a dead frog. We carried him through the deserted rooms to a fridge just next to the lounge. Jake glared at the fridge in exasperation.

"Dammit, this is just too small. We'll never get him in here! Where the hell are we going to find a big enough fridge?"

A brilliant idea occurred to me. "Jake, what about the VIP dining room upstairs? It only gets used by the Vice Chancellor and the people in the very top management positions. They sometimes have their meals or entertain really important guests up there. And drinks are stored in this massive fridge next to the dining room. I'm sure it'd be big enough."

Jake nearly dropped his end of Van Rooyen in his excitement.

"You're brilliant, Rosie! Let's get him there right away!"

"The door to that section of the Staff Centre's usually locked though. Management like to keep that area to themselves. Not even the workers can go there unless they're let in. But you'd probably find a way of getting in."

Once outside the VIP area, Jake tinkered with the locked door for a short while, then there was a click and the door swung open, revealing the inner sanctum, which, with its plush carpets, wood panelling and expensive pictures and furniture, contrasted strikingly with the rest of the Staff Centre. Next to the dining area stood a huge fridge.

Jake opened it and pulled out trays and bottles and cans. We positioned Van Rooyen inside, like a modern-day pharaoh in an electric sarcophagus. For the first time, I was able to muster up enough courage to look at Van Rooyen properly, and I didn't like what I saw. In the bright glare of the refrigerator lights, his skin had a yellowish-white sheen reminiscent of Emmenthaler cheese. Combined with the sneer, the total effect resembled a jaundiced mummy from a third-rate horror movie.

Jake piled cool drinks back around Van Rooyen's feet and surveyed his handiwork.

"Perhaps I could even exhibit him like this, Rosemary. He looks quite intriguing, up to his knees in cool drinks."

"Just close the fridge door and let's get out of here. I don't want to have any more to do with this, OK?"

Jake grinned at me. "Don't worry, Rosie, Eddie and I will sort the rest out. But thanks for all your help. Especially that suggestion about the fridge."

I hurried Jake out of the Staff Centre, locking the door of the VIP area behind us. We clambered out of the toilet window again. Everything seemed deserted, but singing and shouting was coming from the direction of the administration building. I began making my way back to my office, when I heard the sound of running footsteps, and someone collided with me.

"Oh Miss Martin, Miss Martin, I'm so sorry. I was hurrying down to Admin, and I wasn't looking where I was going."

It was Shakespeare Mqamelo, an English 3 student. By some strange quirk, Shakespeare, one of the most militant and radical members of the student body during his first two years on campus, had been blessed with a name that epitomised Eurocentric literary culture. However, it was now Shakespeare's fourth year and he was on the Student Representative Council and, from some points of view, had sold out to the Establishment.

"It's quite all right, Shakespeare, don't worry."

"I won't be able to make that consultation I arranged with you for today, Miss Martin, now that all this is happening."

"That's OK, you must be very busy, being on the SRC at a time like this. Come back and see me when all this is over."

Shakespeare's expressive face immediately became despondent. "I really don't know when all this is going to get sorted out. The student body won't return to classes until the university management undertakes to improve the condition of the residences. But management just says that they simply can't afford to carry out all the repairs we're demanding."

The students had been expressing a great deal of unhappiness about the state of the residences for some time. Shabby and dilapidated, with a derelict air, they did indeed need extensive repairs. Shakespeare sighed.

"It was certainly a lot easier when I was in my first year. The students complain that the SRC doesn't deliver the goods. The SRC elections are coming up soon, and some of us are standing for a second term, but we're really worried that most of the students aren't even going to bother to show up to vote. But anyway, I better get down to Admin now. See you around, Miss Martin."

I waved goodbye and hurried back to the Arts Faculty. I heaved a sigh of relief. At least it was all over.

As I was making myself tea in the kitchen, Hilton and Sarah, two other members of the department, came bursting in. Behind his small round glasses, Hilton's eyes bulged with excitement and paranoia. Sarah's black beret was tilted at an unstable angle above her left eye and her large, brightly lipsticked mouth opened dramatically wide as soon as she saw me.

"The kitchen's a lot safer than the offices," she announced. "Do you know that the students have said the lecturers must vacate their offices, else they'll forcibly evict them and flood their offices with the fire extinguishers?"

"No," interrupted Hilton breathlessly, "they're going to burn the offices down. Most of the fire extinguishers don't work, anyway."

Sarah glared at him briefly. "Whatever they do, they're going to raid the departments first," she said. "In departments like ours, where the failure rate is so high, they're going to make off with all the departmental records, so that there'll be no mark lists."

"But aren't such things usually kept on the computers?" I asked.

"They're going to carry off all the computers too," said Sarah. "And they're most likely to start right here with this department. Students have been behaving in a very menacing way towards us. I think some very garbled assignments I got recently may actually have contained veiled death threats. We've moved all our important books and papers into the storeroom downstairs, and we're going to lock ourselves in the kitchen."

"And Rosemary, they're burning down the administration building right now," said Hilton. "Come to my office and see."

We all trooped into Hilton's office. We could only see the back of the administration building, but huge billowing clouds of black smoke were rising from the front of it.

"It's just lots and lots of tyres, you know," drawled a languid voice behind us. Palesa was a member of our department who sat on a wide range of university committees and seemed to spend most of her life at meetings. In fact, seeing her in the department at all was such an uncommon spectacle that I sometimes felt that her main purpose behind putting in an appearance was simply to inform students she was supposed to be teaching and staff about top-level meetings she'd recently attended.

"It can't just be tyres," said Sarah. "Look at all that smoke."

"I've just been in Admin, at a meeting about the crisis on campus. It was with the Vice-Chancellor and representatives of all the key university groupings," replied Palesa. "So I could see all the burning tyres. In fact, we had to adjourn the meeting, because all the smoke got sucked into the air-conditioning. We're going to have to meet again elsewhere on campus. Afterwards, management'll meet with the student representatives. The situation needs to get resolved soon because the VC's going overseas the day after tomorrow."

"I'd also want to get away from this mess if I could," muttered Hilton. "Where's he off to this time?"

"He's going to be meeting crucially important potential funders in the States," said Palesa, looking at Hilton disapprovingly. "However, they're very concerned that the institution they're funding should be reputable and stable, with no major scandals or disruptions. The workers' stayaway is about to end, but we'd like the problem with the students to be resolved before the VC leaves for America."

"So he can do a quick whitewash job so that the cash can be handed over before the next crisis erupts, I suppose," said Hilton. "By the way, where're you going to be meeting, if not Admin?"

"Oh, most probably the dining room in the VIP area of the Staff Centre," responded Palesa. "The students are likely to mill around outside while we meet, but that can't be helped. Rosemary, what. . . ?"

I raced out of Hilton's office and down the corridor, and went crashing into Jake.

"Rosemary, Rosemary, the students are barricading the gates of campus," he gasped. Grabbing me by the wrist, he dragged me into an empty office with a view of the main entrance.

"Jake, I've got something even more important. . . ."

"Look there—they've completely blocked the main entrance!" Burning tyres had been laid across the road and a crowd of students surrounded the gate, shouting and jeering at approaching cars and forcing them to turn back. People trying to walk through the gate or clamber over the fence were being chased away.

"God, how's Eddie going to get through?" wailed Jake. "He might even have arrived by now."

A large pale blue panelled van was parked on the other side of the road at a safe distance from the mob. A heavily built man was standing next to the van and surveying the scene at the gate. Jake leaned dangerously far out of the window, and began frantically windmilling his arms.

"Eddie, Eddie!" he screeched. "Hey, Eddie, can you hear me?"

A few students wandering below the window looked up with interest, but Eddie seemed to be more concerned with the action at the gate. Then he clambered into his van and drove away.

Jake let his head and torso hang limply down, and began beating on the wall below the windowsill with his fists.

"Jake, you're going to fall out if you lean out like this," I said, tugging at his T-shirt. "Look, he's probably just gone to have a drink at the Royal Hotel. I'm sure he'll be back later. But I've got something else to tell you. Come down to my office."

In the seclusion of my office, I broke the news. Jake sat with his head in his hands.

"You don't think that they're liable to delay the meeting until things have quietened down a bit, do you?" he eventually asked, clutching at straws.

"Not a chance, Jake," I said grimly, and quickly explained the situation with the funders. We stared at one another in silence, and suddenly a pounding started up on my door.

"Mr. September!" a deep voice called. "Are you there?"

Jake leaped across the room and flung himself into a cupboard. I pushed the cupboard closed, then opened my door, to see two large and dignified men standing in the corridor. One of them held out his hand to me.

"Good morning, Miss Martin. May we come in? I'm Zola Makalima. And this is my partner, Ian de Vries."

I wished that I was inside the cupboard as well.

Zola Makalima had graduated from the university years ago with a degree in Biblical Studies and English. He had taken over a run-down funeral parlour, which he had called *Death Be Not Proud, Though Some Have Called Thee Mighty and Dreadful, Thou Art Not So* (as a concession to his literary background). However, he lacked the necessary financial backing. Then Ian de Vries arrived in town to take over his family's hardware shop. To his family's horror, he sold the business and, with the proceeds, joined forces with Makalima. Now Makalima and De Vries's funeral parlour (simply called *Death Be Not Proud*) outclassed all the local competitors.

The two men made their way into my office and sat down. "We think you can help us, Miss Martin," said de Vries. "We're looking for Mr. Jake September. We went to his office, and we saw a note on the door, addressed to someone called Eddie. In it Mr September stated that he was with you. So here we are."

"I'm afraid I haven't seen Mr. September all morning." I tried, unsuccessfully, to adopt the tone I used on students who came to complain about being failed for plagiarism. "You haven't come to the right place."

"But we trust that we will be able to avail ourselves of your assistance, Miss Martin," said Makalima. "We have discourse of deep significance to convey to Mr. September, which perhaps you could relay to him, when next you see him."

"I don't . . ." I began, but Makalima continued as if he hadn't heard me speaking.

"Shakespeare has said, 'The sceptre, learning, physic must / All follow this and come to dust.' While not disputing this unquestionable truth, we do do everything within our humble powers to ensure that our clients' loved ones depart from this earth in a solemn and dignified manner. However, the body of a leading member of this noble institution, a Professor Van Rooyen, was removed from our establishment the night before last."

"Today we heard," De Vries went on, "that late that night Mr. September's car was seen near our funeral parlour. Mr. September is an eccentric personality. It's quite possible that he has some very unpleasant personal tastes. I am sure you get my meaning."

"But why are you coming after Mr. September like this? Surely it would be easier to let the police decide who's responsible?" (I had complete confidence in the local police force's ability to do nothing whatsoever.)

"It has been said that a good name is worth more than rubies and pearls," said Makalima, "and we would certainly concur with that. Should word ever get out that a body had been stolen from our funeral parlour, the effect that it would have on our reputation would be disastrous."

"Mr. September knew he would be seeing you this morning, Miss Martin," De Vries went on. "The note on his door states that clearly. Tell him that, should Professor Van Rooyen's body be returned to us within the next two hours, we will take no further action."

"But you really don't think Mr. September has the body. . . ."

"If Professor Van Rooyen is not returned within the next two hours," De Vries interrupted, "we will have to call in our own people to deal with this.

I hope for Mr. September's sake—and your own, Miss Martin—that it will not be necessary. And for both your sakes, we also hope that no one else discovers that Professor Van Rooyen's body was stolen from our establishment."

Both men rose to their feet. "Thank you for allowing us so much of your time," said Makalima. "We trust that the seeds we have sown have not fallen on stony ground. Those who have ears to hear, let them hear."

They shook hands with me and departed. When the sound of their footsteps had died away, I yanked the door of the cupboard open. Out tumbled Jake, choking with fury.

"How dare they! How DARE they!" he spluttered. "To suggest that I practice necrophilia! On Van Rooyen! In the old South Africa, someone like De Vries would have ended up in Security Branch!"

"Frankly Jake," I retorted, "I think some type of performance art involving you doing that to Van Rooyen is far more likely to cause a stir in the art world than including him in any of those pieces of yours. After all, you were talking about pushing over boundaries and social taboos."

"Look, look here Rosie, this is no time to argue. What we need now is to sit down and think fast about how we can get ourselves out of this mess we've landed ourselves in, Rosie."

Something inside me snapped. "We!" I shrieked at him. "We! I like that! You stole Van Rooyen in the first place! You planted him in my lecture theatre and made me lug him around campus! And now Makalima and De Vries are threatening me as well as you with their heavies! How dare you suggest I'm in any way responsible for this disaster! And I fucking HATE being called Rosie!"

Jake's mouth dropped completely open. Before he could close it, there was a gentle knocking on the door.

Jake was halfway back into the cupboard when we heard Drusilla's voice.

"Ms. Martin? May I come in?"

"Drusilla! Where. . . ."

"I've been next door in Room 82." (Room 82 was used only for departmental meetings and seminars.) "Dr. Badi, who's my tutor, said I could work there, and unlocked it for me. But, Ms. Martin, I just felt I should say that perhaps you shouldn't shout quite so loudly. I don't think Mr. Makalima and Mr. De Vries are still around, but it's probably best to be safe, don't you think?"

"Drusilla! Have you been next door all this time? How much have you heard?"

"Well, all of it, Ms. Martin," said Drusilla. She did not look in the slightest bit embarrassed.

"You must have had your ear glued to the wall for quite a while," snapped Jake. "I thought you wanted to work. Haven't you got anything better to do than to listen in on other peoples' problems?"

Drusilla was unperturbed. "I'd hardly say that my ear was glued to the wall, Mr. September. These walls are extremely thin, so I couldn't help hearing what was going on. But I can't help feeling that you might perhaps be taking too gloomy a view of the situation."

Jake rolled his eyes heavenwards. "I'm really comforted to hear that! Now, Ms. Nkosi, we'd both really appreciate it if you went back next door and went on with whatever you were supposed to be doing in there, and tried to forget about everything that you couldn't help hearing through the wall."

"But Mr. September, I do think that it's quite interesting that Professor Van Rooyen should have ended up in the VIP area of the Staff Centre. As we all know, it's the only place on campus that no one can get into except the university management. And, with the workers' stayaway, not even the workers have been let in there to clean it recently."

"Drusilla," I interrupted as sternly as possible. "What exactly are you driving at?"

"And it's also interesting," Drusilla continued sweetly, "that the Vice-Chancellor should be about to go on a very important fund-raising mission to funders who are likely to be put off should any scandal arise concerning the university."

"Wait a moment," said Jake. "Do you have some idea how we can get out of this situation?"

"Perhaps I should go back to Room 82 now," said Drusilla. "After all, as you suggested a few moments ago, Mr. September, I really should get back there and go on with my work."

"Wait! Wait!" I shouted as Drusilla rose to go. "Don't go away! Please help us!"

Drusilla sighed, sat down and fixed her large dark eyes upon me. "Actually, I think that you, Ms. Martin—and you, Mr. September—could help me even more."

"What do you mean?"

"Well, it's quite a fortunate coincidence that my two majors happen to be English and Sociology, isn't it? I wrote my Sociology 3 long essay for you, Mr. September. I think I deserve distinction for that essay. I know you only gave me 52% for it, but you might like to read over it again, and think about that mark a bit more carefully. And you're the English 3 coordinator, Ms. Martin. I really would appreciate it if you could add fifteen percent onto my year mark."

"Drusilla," I gasped, "how dare you even think for a moment that we'd be prepared to stoop to that kind of academic dishonesty! What sort of people do you think we are?"

"Well, two fairly desperate people, I'd say," responded Drusilla. "What's a little bit of academic dishonesty compared to what's going to happen if that body doesn't get back to the funeral parlour soon? But, if you'd rather not. . . ."

"Rosemary, are you crazy!" yelled Jake. "Don't go, don't go, Ms. Nkosi! Of course you can have your distinction if you can help us out! Rosemary, can't you see it's our only hope!"

"But what Drusilla's asking of me goes against every. . . ."

"I can just see the headlines in the Sunday *Times*," interrupted Jake. "'*'I never meant to do it'* says blonde body-snatching academic Rosemary Martin, recently sacked from her job and awaiting trial.' And no one will ever want to publish that article on the early poetry of Wordsworth that you've been working so hard on."

"Drusilla, I'd find it morally unacceptable to raise your year mark higher than eight percent. You just aren't C-grade material."

"Fifteen percent, or nothing, Ms. Martin."

There was a moment of silence. I sighed. "OK, then, Drusilla," I said. "I'll do it if you're really able to sort things out."

Drusilla smiled. "I'm so glad that we're all in agreement. Well, I had better be going now, I guess."

"But what exactly are you going to do?"

"I'm going to suggest to my classmate and SRC member Shakespeare Mqamelo that he help himself to a cool drink from the fridge next to the dining room."

With that, she was gone.

Several things happened within the next few weeks. The very first thing was that one hour after our conversation with Drusilla, Professor Van Rooyen was returned to Makalima and De Vries by two highly apologetic SRC members. They explained that a particularly nasty student prank had taken place, but the university had apprehended the culprits. The SRC members requested that, for the sake of the reputations of both establishments concerned, disciplinary action should take place privately through university structures, so that the matter could be treated with complete confidentiality.

Shortly after that, Jake was visited by a representative of Makalima and De Vries, who expressed profuse apologies for the wrongful accusations that Jake had been subjected to. The representative expressed the hope that Jake did not feel so wounded that he was considering some kind of legal action, or was perhaps thinking of making public the unfortunate event that had triggered off the accusations. Mr. Makalima and Mr. De Vries, the representative concluded, wished to offer Jake something to make amends for the upsetting time that he must have been through. He handed over an envelope containing a cheque for a large sum of money and departed.

Next, the university management agreed that, despite the university's financial crisis, extensive repairs needed to be done to the residences. The students returned to class, and within a week, the repairs to the residences were well underway.

The SRC elections took place and students, exhilarated by the radical improvements in their living conditions, turned up in huge numbers to vote for the people who had been responsible for forcing the university management to repair the residences. Word had got out that it had been Shakespeare Mqamelo who had played a central role in the negotiations with management, and Shakespeare was voted back in with the largest number of votes by far.

Drusilla Nkosi was awarded 82% for her Sociology 3 long essay. Her English 3 year mark of 66% was less spectacular, but nonetheless respectable. Shakespeare Mqamelo gave her an account of the meeting that took place between the SRC and the university management after he had, on behalf of the SRC, drawn the university management's attention to Professor Van Rooyen, knee deep in Diet Cokes and Fantas in the VIP area refrigerator. Drusilla relayed the details of the meeting to Jake and myself.

Shakespeare had stated that it was well known that only the most prominent members of the university administration had access to the VIP area, and to the fridge. Thus, if the matter were made public, it would be hard for the university to avoid the accusation that the corpse of Professor Van Rooyen had been stored in the fridge by some member of the top university management, for some extremely unpleasant purpose.

At this point, other SRC members had commented on the Vice Chancellor's forthcoming fund-raising mission, and the negative publicity that the university had recently been receiving in the press. Regrettably, they stated, the newspapers seemed most interested in printing negative things about the university. However, they continued, such was the loyalty of the student body towards their university, that the SRC were prepared to do everything in their power to protect its good name and they would give their word that nothing concerning this regrettable incident would ever be mentioned by any SRC member outside this room.

The SRC did hope, Shakespeare added, that the university administration felt the same love and respect for the students. The unfortunate situation involving the condition of the residences, he concluded, was surely a misunderstanding that could be resolved.

The meeting adjourned fairly soon after that. Unlike most meetings that took place, it did not take very long for all the parties present to reach a clear understanding.

The Vice Chancellor departed on his fund-raising expedition. The funders expressed a great deal of praise for the important work the university was doing and undertook to provide the university with the financial assistance it was seeking.

The only person for whom events did not turn out well was Jake's friend, Eddie. As I had suspected, when he was unable to enter the university, he had retired to the bar of the Royal Hotel. Weary after his long journey, he had ordered drink after drink, reasoning that it would be a very long time before the barricades on the gates were lifted. Several hours later, as the students were prancing around campus in a victory toyi-toyi, he emerged unsteadily from the bar, tripped over an uneven piece of pavement, fell into the road and was flattened by an oncoming taxi.

Jake arranged for Eddie's remains to be transported back to Johannesburg, and travelled up to Johannesburg himself to help organise the memorial service. This took the form of an extended pub crawl, as it was decided that Eddie's ashes should be sprinkled through his favourite bars at the Randburg Waterfront.

A week after Jake had departed for Johannesburg, he faxed a letter of resignation to the university. He wrote to me saying that he had met Richard, Eddie's partner, who needed someone to assist him in the business, now that Eddie was gone. Jake stated that he had had enough of university life and he felt that his new job would equip him with important skills he needed to develop his artistic career. In a postscript, he asked me to tell the Department of Sociology that he had taken four hundred first year assignments to Johannesburg with him. Unfortunately, he would be unable to return the scripts to the department, since they had all been destroyed in an accident.

I didn't hear from Jake for quite a while after that. However, recently I received an invitation to the opening of an art exhibition in the post. There was a note scrawled across the top of the invitation in Jake's large, tangled handwriting: "Dear Rosemary, I've finally managed to get it together. I hope you can come. Love, Jake."

My first thought was that I really couldn't afford to travel to Johannesburg at the moment. All the same, I felt curious. I wondered which of his pieces Jake would be presenting, and how the exhibition would be received. I remembered the last time Jake had talked about holding an exhibition, and how he'd been planning to make Van Rooyen the centre-piece. Well, he'd had to do without Van Rooyen. I found myself thinking of Jake's new job, which he'd said would provide him with the skills he needed to develop his artistic career. Did that mean he was going to exhibit stuffed hamsters and guinea-pigs? And then I suddenly thought of Eddie's demise, and how Jake had arranged for Eddie's body to be transported up to Johannesburg, and had played a major role in assisting with the funeral arrangements.

But Eddie had been cremated and his ashes had been scattered through the Randburg Waterfront's bars. Nonetheless, Van Rooyen hadn't been buried at his funeral, and none of his mourners had been any the wiser. It would be far easier to get away with it with an urn full of ashes. After all, they could be the ashes of simply anything. And then I remembered the four hundred missing Sociology 1 essays.

I sighed. It looked like I'd have to go to the opening of the exhibition after all. It was the only way I'd ever find out.

PART THREE

The WHITES ONLY Bench

IVAN VLADISLAVIĆ ▼▼▼▼▼▼▼▼▼▼▼▼▼▼▼▼▼▼▼▼▼▼▼▼▼▼▼▼▼▼▼▼▼

Yesterday our visitors' book, which Portia has covered in zebra-skin wrapping-paper and shiny plastic, recorded the name of another important person: Coretta King. When Mrs. King had finished her tour, with Strickland herself playing the guide, she was treated to tea and cakes in the cafeteria. The photographers, who had been trailing around after her trying to sniff out interesting angles and ironic juxtapositions against the exhibits, tucked in as well, I'm told, and made pigs of themselves.

After the snacks Mrs. King popped into the gift shop for a few mementoes, and bought generously—soapstone hippopotami with sly expressions, coffee-table catalogues, little wire bicycles and riot-control vehicles, garish place-mats and beaded fly-whisks, among other things. Her aide had to chip in to make up the cost of a set of mugs in the popular "Leaders Past and Present" range.

The honoured guests were making their way back to the bus when Mrs. King spotted the bench in the courtyard and suggested that she pose there for a few shots. I happened to be watching from the workshop window, and I had a feeling the photographs would be exceptional. A spring shower had just fallen, out of the blue, and the courtyard was a well of clear light. Tendrils of fragrant steam coiled up evocatively from a windfall of blossoms on the flagstones. The scene had been set by chance. Perhaps the photographers had something to prove, too, having failed to notice a photo opportunity so steeped in ironic significance.

The *Star* carried one of the pictures on its front page this morning. Charmaine picked up a copy on her way to work and she couldn't wait to show it to me.

The interest of the composition derives—if I may make the obvious analysis—from a lively dispute of horizontals and verticals. The bench is a syllogism of horizontal lines, flatly contradicted by the vertical bars of the legs at either end (these legs are shaped like h's, actually, but from the front they look like l's). Three other verticals assert their position: on the left—our left, that is—the concrete stalk of the Black Sash drinking-fountain; in the middle, thrusting up behind the bench, the trunk of the controversial kafferboom; and on the right, perched on the very end of her seat, our subject: Mrs. King.

Mrs. King has her left thigh crossed over her right, her left foot crooked around her right ankle, her left arm coiled to clutch one of our glossy brochures to her breast. The wooden slats are slickly varnished with sun-

light, and she sits upon them gingerly, as if the last coat's not quite dry. Yet
her right arm reposes along the backrest with the careless grace of a stem.
There's an odd ambiguity in her body, and it's reflected in her face too, in an
expression which superimposes the past upon the present: she looks both
timorous and audacious. The WHITES ONLY sign under her dangling thumb
in the very middle of the picture might be taken up the wrong way as an
irreverent reference to her eyes, which she opens wide in an expression of
mock alarm—or is it outrage? The rest of her features are more prudently
composed, the lips quilted with bitterness, but tucked in mockingly at one
corner.

The photographer was wise to choose black and white. These stark con-
trasts, coupled with Mrs. King's old-fashioned suit and hairdo, confound
the period entirely. The photograph might have been taken thirty years ago,
or yesterday.

Charmaine was tickled pink. She says her bench is finally avenged for
being upstaged by that impostor from the Municipal Bus Drivers' Association. I doubt that Strickland has even noticed.

There seems to be a tacit agreement around here that *Mrs.* King is an
acceptable form, although it won't do for anyone else. When I pointed this
out, Charmaine said it's a special case because Mr. King, rest his soul, is no
more. I fail to see what difference that makes, and I said so. Then Reddy,
whose ears were flapping, said that "Mrs. King" is tolerated precisely because
it preserves the memory of the absent Mr. King, like it or not. He said it's
like a dead metaphor.

I can't make up my mind. Aren't we reading too much into it?

Charmaine has sliced the photograph out of the unread newspaper with a
Stanley knife and pinned the cutting up on the notice-board in Reception.
She says her bench has been immortalized. "Immortality" is easy to bandy
about, but for a while it was touch and go whether Charmaine's bench
would make it to the end of the week.

We were working late one evening, as usual, when the little drama began.
The Museum was due to open in six weeks' time but the whole place was
still upside down. It wasn't clear yet who was in charge, if anyone, and we
were all in a state.

Charmaine was putting the finishing touches to her bench, I was knocking together a couple of rostra for the Congress of the People, when Strickland
came in. She had been with us for less than a week and it was the first time
she had set foot in the workshop. We weren't sure at all then what to make
of our new Director, and so we both greeted her politely and went on with
our work.

She waved a right hand as limp as a kid glove to show that we shouldn't mind her, and then clasped it behind her back. She began to wander around on tiptoe, even though I was hammering in nails, swivelling her head from side to side, peering into boxes, scanning the photographs and diagrams pinned to chipboard display stands, taking stock of the contents of tables and desks. She never touched a thing, but there was something grossly intrusive about the inspection. Strickland wears large, rimless spectacles, double glazed and tinted pink, and they sometimes make her look like a pair of television monitors.

After a soundless, interrogative circuit of the room she stopped behind Charmaine and looked over her shoulder. Charmaine had just finished the "I," and now she laid her brush across the top of the paint tin, peeled off the stencil and flourished it in the air to dry the excess paint.

I put down my hammer—the racket had become unbearable—and took up some sandpaper instead. The people here will tell you that I don't miss a thing.

Strickland looked at the half-formed word. Then she unclasped her hands and slid them smoothly into the pockets of her linen suit. The cloth was fresh cream with a dab of butter in it, richly textured, the pockets cool as arum lilies.

"What are you doing?" Strickland asked, in a tone that bristled like a new broom.

Charmaine stood back with the stencil in her hand and Strickland had to step hastily aside to preserve a decent distance between her suit and the grubby overall. Unnoticed by anyone but myself, a drop of white paint fell from the end of the brush resting across the tin onto the shapely beige toe of Strickland's shoe.

The answer to Strickland's question was so plain to see that it hardly needed voicing, but she blinked her enlarged eyes expectantly, and so Charmaine said, "It's the WHITES ONLY bench." When Strickland showed no sign of recognition, Charmaine added, "You remember the benches. For WHITES ONLY?"

Silence. What on earth did she want? My sandpaper was doing nothing to smooth the ragged edges of our nerves, and so I put it down. We all looked at the bench.

It was a beautiful bench—as a useful object, I mean, rather than a symbol of injustice. The wooden slats were tomato-sauce red. The arms and legs were made of iron, but cleverly moulded to resemble branches, and painted brown to enhance a rustic illusion. The bench looked well used, which is often a sign that a thing has been loved. But when you looked closer, as Strickland was doing now, you saw that all these signs of wear and tear were no more than skin-deep. Charmaine had applied all of them in the workshop. The bruised hollows on the seat, where the surface had been abraded by decades of white thighs and buttocks, were really patches of brown and purple paint. The flashes of raw metal on the armrests, where the paint had been worn away by countless white palms and elbows, turned out to be mere discs of silver paint themselves. Charmaine had even smeared the city's grimy shadows into the grain.

Strickland pored over these special effects with an expression of amazed distaste, and then stared for a minute on end at the letters WHI on the uppermost slat of the backrest. The silence congealed around us, slowing us down, making us slur our movements, until the absence of sound was as tangible as a crinkly skin on the surface of the air. "Forgive me," she said at last, with an awakening toss of her head. "You're manufacturing a WHITES ONLY bench?"

"Ja. For Room 27."

Strickland went to the floor plan taped to one of the walls and looked for Room 27: Petty Apartheid. Then she gazed at the calendar next to the plan, but whether she was mulling over the dates, or studying the photograph—children with stones in their hands, riot policemen with rifles, between the lines a misplaced reporter with a camera—or simply lost in thought, I couldn't tell. Did she realize that the calendar was ten years old?

Charmaine and I exchanged glances behind her back.

"Surely we should have the real thing," Strickland said, turning.

"Of course—if only we could find it."

"You can't find a genuine WHITES ONLY bench?"

"No."

"That's very hard to believe."

"We've looked everywhere. It's not as easy as you'd think. This kind of thing was frowned upon, you know, in the end. Discrimination I mean. The municipalities were given instructions to paint them over. There wasn't much point in hunting for something that doesn't exist, so we decided at our last meeting—this was before your time, I'm afraid—that it would be better if I recreated one."

"Recreated one," Strickland echoed.

"Faithfully. I researched it and everything. I've got the sources here somewhere." Charmaine scratched together some photocopies splattered with paint and dusted with fingerprints and tread-marks from her running-shoes. "The bench itself is a genuine 1960s one, I'm glad to say, from the darkest decade of repression. Donated by Reddy's father-in-law, who stole it from a bus-stop for use in the garden. It was a long time ago, mind you, the family is very respectable. From a black bus-stop—for Indians. Interestingly, the

Indian benches didn't have I‌NDIANS O‌NLY on them—not in Natal anyway, according to Mr. Mookadam. Or even A‌SIATICS. Not that it matters."

"It matters to me," Strickland said curtly—Charmaine does go on sometimes—and pushed her glasses up on her nose so that her eyes were doubly magnified. "This is a museum, not some high-school operetta. It is our historical duty to be authentic."

I must say that made me feel bad, when I thought about all the effort Charmaine and I had put into everything from the Sharpeville Massacre to the Soweto Uprising, trying to get the details right, every abandoned shoe, every spent cartridge, every bloodied stitch of clothing, only to have this jenny-come-lately (as Charmaine puts it) give us a lecture about authenticity. What about our professional duty? (Charmaine again.)

"Have we advertised?" Strickland asked, and I could tell by her voice that she meant to argue the issue out. But at that moment she glanced down and saw the blob of paint on the toe of her shoe.

I had the fantastic notion to venture an excuse on Charmaine's behalf: to tell Strickland that she had dripped ice-cream on her shoe. Vanilla ice-cream! I actually saw her hand grasping the cone, her sharp tongue curling around the white cupola, the droplet plummeting. Fortunately I came to my senses before I opened my big mouth.

It was the first proper meeting of the Steering Committee with the new Director. We hadn't had a meeting for a month. When Charlie Sibeko left in a huff after the fiasco with the wooden AK47s, we all heaved a sigh of relief. We were sick to death of meetings: the man's appetite for circular discussion was insatiable.

Strickland sat down at the head of the table, and having captured that coveted chair laid claim to another by declaring the meeting open. She seemed to assume that this was her prerogative as Director, and no one had the nerve to challenge her.

The report-backs were straightforward: we were all behind schedule and over budget. I might add that we were almost past caring. It seemed impossible that we'd be finished in time for the official opening. The builders were still knocking down walls left, right and centre, and establishing piles of rubble in every room. Pincus joked that the only exhibit sure to be ready on time was the row of concrete bunks—they were part of the original compound in which the Museum is housed and we had decided to leave them exactly as we found them. He suggested that we think seriously about delaying the opening, which was Portia's cue to produce the invitations, just back from the printers. Everyone groaned (excluding Strickland and me) and breathed in the chastening scent of fresh ink.

"As far as we're concerned, this date is written in stone," Strickland said, snapping one of the copperplate cards shut. "We will be ready on time. People will have to learn to take their deadlines seriously." At that point Charmaine began to doodle on her agenda—a hand with a stiff index finger, emerging from a lacy cuff, pointing at Item 4: Bench.

Item 2: Posters, which followed the reports, was an interesting one. Pincus had had a letter from a man in Bethlehem, a former town clerk and electoral officer, who had collected copies of every election poster displayed in the town since it was founded. He was prepared to entrust the collection to us if it was kept intact. Barbara said she could probably use a couple in the Birth of Apartheid exhibit. We agreed that Pincus would write to the donor, care of the Bethlehem Old-Age Home, offering to house the entire collection and display selected items on a rotating basis.

Item 3: Poetry, was Portia's. Ernest Dladla, she informed us, had declined our invitation to read a poem at the opening ceremony, on the perfectly reasonable grounds that he was not a poet. "I have poetic impulses," he said in his charming note, "but I do not act upon them." Should she go ahead, Portia wanted to know, and approach Alfred Qabula instead, as Ernie suggested?

Then Strickland asked in an acerbic tone whether an issue this trivial needed to be tabled at an important meeting. But Portia responded magnificently, pointing out that she knew nothing about poetry, not having had the benefit of a decent education, had embarrassed herself once in the performance of her duties and did not wish to do so again. All she wanted was an answer to a simple question: Is Alfred Qabula a poet? Yes or no?

No sooner was that settled, than Strickland announced Item 4: Bench, and stood up. Perhaps this was a technique she had read about in the business pages somewhere, calculated to intimidate the opposition. "It has come to my attention," she said, "that our workshop personnel are busily recreating beautiful replicas of apartheid memorabilia, when the ugly originals could be ours for the asking. I do not know what Mr. Sibeko's policy on this question was, although the saga of the wooden AK47s is full of suggestion, but as far as I'm concerned it's an appalling waste of time and money. It's also dishonest. This is a museum, not an amusement arcade.

"My immediate concern is the WHITES ONLY bench, which is taking up so much of Charmaine's time and talent. I find it hard to believe that there is not a genuine example of a bench of this nature somewhere in the country."

"Petty apartheid went out ages ago," said Charmaine, "even in the Free State."

"The first Indian townships in the Orange Free State were established way back in October 1986," said Reddy, who had been unusually quiet so far, "in Harrismith, Virginia and Odendaalsrus. Not many people know that. I remember hearing the glad tidings from my father-in-law, Mr. Mookadam, who confessed that ever since he was a boy it had been a dream of his to visit that forbidden province."

"I'll wager that there are at least a dozen real WHITES ONLY benches in this city alone, in private collections," Strickland insisted, erasing Reddy's tangent with the back of her hand. "People are fascinated by the bizarre."

"We asked everyone we know," said Charmaine. "And we asked them to ask everyone they know, and so on. Like a chain-letter—except that we didn't say they would have a terrible accident if they broke the chain. And we couldn't find a single bench. Not one."

"Have we advertised?"

"No commercials," said Reddy, and there was a murmur of assenting voices.

"Why ever not?"

"It just causes more headache."

"Oh nonsense!"

Reddy held up his right hand, with the palm out, and batted the air with it, as if he was bouncing a ball off Strickland's forehead. This gesture had a peculiarly mollifying effect on her, and she put her hand over her eyes and sat down. Reddy stood up in his ponderous way and padded out of the room.

Pincus, who has a very low tolerance for silence, said, "Wouldn't it be funny if Charmaine's bench turned out to be the whites' only bench?"

No one laughed, so he said "whites' only" again, and drew the apostrophe in the air with his forefinger.

Reddy came back, carrying a photograph, a Tupperware lunch-box and a paper-knife. He put the photograph in the middle of the table, facing Strickland. She had to lean forward in her chair to see what it was. I wondered whether she fully appreciated the havoc her outsize spectacles wreaked on her face, how they disjointed her features. She looked like a composite portrait in a magazine competition, in which some cartoon character's eyes had been mismatched with the jaw of a real-life heroine.

Everyone at the table, with the exception of our Director, had seen this routine before. Some of us had sat through it half a dozen times, with a range of donors, do-gooders, interest groups. For some reason, it never failed to involve me. I also leant forward to view the eight-by-ten. No one else moved.

I looked first at the pinprick stigmata in the four corners.

Then I looked, as I always did, at the girl's out-flung hand. Her hand is a jagged speech-bubble filled with disbelief. It casts a shadow shaped like a howling mouth on her body, and that mouth takes up the cry of outrage. The palm Reddy had waved in Strickland's face was a much more distant echo.

I looked next at the right hand of the boy who is carrying Hector Peterson. His fingers press into the flesh of a thigh that is still warm, willing it to live, prompting the muscle, animating it. Hector Peterson's right hand, by contrast, lolling numbly on his belly, knows that it is dead, and it expresses that certainty in dark tones of shadow and blood.

These hands are still moving, they still speak to me.

Reddy jabbed the photograph with the point of his paper-knife. "This is a photograph of Hector Peterson, in the hour of his death," he said. Strickland nodded her head impatiently. "The day was 16 June 1976." She nodded again, urging him to skip the common knowledge and come to the point. "A Wednesday. As it happened, it was fine and mild. The sun rose that morning at 6:53 and set that evening at 5:25. The shot was taken at 10:15 on the dot. It was the third in a series of six. Hector Peterson was the first fatality of what we would come to call the Soweto Riots—the first in a series of seven hundred odd. The photographer was Sam Nzima, then in the employ of the *World*. The subject, according to the tombstone that now marks his grave, was Zolile Hector Pietersen, P-I-E-T-E-R-S-E-N, but the newspapers called him Hector Peterson and it stuck. We struck out the "I," we put it to rout in the alphabet of the oppressor. We bore the hero's body from the uneven field of battle and anointed it with English. According to the tombstone he was thirteen years old, but as you can see he looked no more than half that age. . . . Or is it just the angle? If only we had some other pictures of the subject to compare this one with, we might feel able to speak with more authority."

This welter of detail, and the offhand tone of the delivery, produced in Strickland the usual baffled silence.

"Not many people know these things." Reddy slid the point of the knife onto the girl. "This is Hector's sister Margot, a.k.a. Tiny, now living in Soweto." The knife slid again. "And this is Mbuyisa Makhubu, whereabouts your guess is as good as mine. Not many people know them either. We have come to the conclusion, here at the Museum, that the living are seldom as famous as the dead."

The knife moved again. It creased Mbuyisa Makhubu's lips, which are bent into a bow of pain, like the grimace of a tragic mask, it rasped the brick wall of the matchbox house which we see over his shoulder, skipped along the top of a wire gate, and came to rest on the small figure of a woman in the background. "And who on earth do you suppose this is?"

Strickland gazed at the little figure as if it was someone famous she should be able to recognize in an instant, some household name. In fact, the features of this woman—she is wearing a skirt and doek—are no more than a grey smudge, continuous with the shadowed wall behind her.

I looked at Hector Peterson's left arm, floating on air, and the shadow of his hand on Mbuyisa Makhubu's knee, a shadow so hard-edged and muscular it could trip the bearer up.

The child is dead. With his rumpled sock around his ankle, his grazed knee, his jersey stuck with dry grass, you would think he had taken a tumble in the playground, if it were not for the gout of blood from his mouth. The jersey is a bit too big for him: it was meant to last another year at least. Or is it just that he was small for his age? Or is it the angle? In his hair is a stalk of grass shaped like a praying mantis.

"Nobody knows."

Strickland sat back with a sigh, but Reddy went on relentlessly.

Nevertheless, theories were advanced: some people said that this woman, this apparent bystander, was holding Hector Peterson in her arms when he died. She was a mother herself. She cradled him in her lap—you can see the bloodstains here—and when Makhubu took the body from her and carried it away, she found a bullet caught in the folds of her skirt. She is holding that fatal bullet in her right hand, here.

"Other people said that it didn't happen like that at all. Lies and fantasies. When Nzima took this photograph, Hector Peterson was still alive! What you see here, according to one reliable caption, is a critically wounded youth. The police open fire, Hector falls at Mbuyisa's feet. The boy picks him up and runs towards the nearest car, which happens to belong to Sam Nzima and Sophie Tema, a journalist on the *World*, Nzima's partner that day. Sam takes his photographs. Then Mbuyisa and Tiny pile into the back of the Volkswagen—did I mention that it was a Volkswagen?—they pile into the back with Hector; Sam and Sophie pile into the front with their driver, Thomas Khoza. They rush to the Orlando Clinic, but Hector Peterson is certified dead on arrival. And that's the real story. You can look it up for yourself.

"But the theories persisted. So we thought we would try to lay the ghost—we have a duty after all to tell the truth. This is a museum, not a paperback novel. We advertised. We called on this woman to come forward and tell her story. We said it would be nice—although it wasn't essential—if she brought the bullet with her."

"Anyone respond?"

"I'll say."

   Reddy opened his lunch-box and pushed it over to Strickland with the edge of his palm, like a croupier. She looked at the contents: there were .38 Magnum slugs, 9 mm and AK cartridges, shiny .22 bullets, a .357 hollow-point that had blossomed on impact into a perfect corolla. There were even a couple of doppies and a misshapen ball from an old voorlaaier. Strickland zoomed in for a close-up. She still didn't get it.

   "If you'll allow me a poetic licence," Reddy said, as if poetic licence was a certificate you could stick on a page in your Book of Life, "this is the bullet that killed Hector Peterson."

So we didn't advertise. But Strickland stuck to her guns about the WHITES ONLY bench: we would have the real thing or nothing at all. She made a few inquiries of her own, and wouldn't you know it, before the week was out she turned up the genuine article.

   The chosen bench belonged to the Municipal Bus Drivers' Association, and in exchange for a small contribution to their coffers—the replacement costs plus 10 per cent—they were happy to part with it. The honour of fetching the trophy from their clubhouse in Marshall Street fell to Pincus. Unbeknown to us, the Treasurer of the MBDA had decided that there was a bit of publicity to be gained from his Association's public-spirited gesture, and when our representative arrived he found a photographer ready to record the event for posterity. Pincus was never the most politic member of our Committee. With his enthusiastic co-operation the photographer was able to produce an entire essay, which subsequently appeared, without a by-line, in the *Saturday Star*. It showed the bench in its original quarters (weighed down by a squad of bus drivers of all races, pin-up girls—WHITES ONLY—looking over the drivers' shoulders, all of them, whether flesh and blood or paper, saying cheese); the bench on its way out of the door (Pincus steering, the Treasurer pushing); being loaded onto the back of our bakkie (Pincus and the Treasurer shaking hands and stretching the cheque between them like a Christmas cracker); and finally driven away (Pincus hanging out of the window to give us a thumbs-up, the Treasurer waving goodbye, the Trea-surer waving back at himself from the rear-view mirror). These pictures caused exactly the kind of headache Reddy had tried so hard to avoid. Offers of benches poured in from far and wide. Pincus was made to write the polite letters of thanks but no thanks. For our purposes, one bench is quite enough, thank you.

   You can see the WHITES ONLY bench now, if you like, in Room 27. Just follow the arrows. I may as well warn you that it says EUROPEANS ONLY, to be precise. There's a second prohibition too, an entirely non-racial one, strung on a chain between the armrests: PLEASE DO NOT SIT ON THIS BENCH. That little sign is Charmaine's work, and making her paint it was Strickland's way of rubbing turpentine in her wounds.

When the genuine bench came to light, Charmaine received instructions to get rid of "the fake." But she refused to part with it. I was persuaded to help her carry it into the storeroom, where it remained for a month or so. As the deadline for the opening neared, Charmaine would take refuge in there from time to time, whenever things got too much for her, and put the finishing touches to her creation. At first, she was furious about all the publicity given to the impostor. But once the offers began to roll in, and it became apparent that Whites Only benches were not nearly as scarce as we'd thought, she saw an opportunity to bring her own bench out of the closet. The night before the grand opening, in the early hours, when the sky was already going grey behind the mine-dump on the far side of the parking-lot, we carried her bench outside and put it in the arbour under the controversial kafferboom.

"When Strickland asks about it," said Charmaine, "you can tell her it was a foundling, left on our doorstep, and we just had to take it in." Funny thing is, Strickland never made a peep.

I can see Charmaine's Whites Only bench now, from my window. The kafferboom, relocated here fully grown from a Nelspruit nursery, has acclimatized wonderfully well. "*Erythrina caffra*, a sensible choice," said Reddy, "deciduous, patulous, and umbrageous." And he was quite right, it casts a welcome shade. Charmaine's faithful copy reclines in the dapple below, and its ability to attract and repel our visitors never ceases to impress me.

Take Mrs. King. And talking about Mrs. King, *Mr.* King is a total misnomer, of course. I must point it out to Reddy. The Rev. King, yes, and Dr. King, yes, and possibly even the Rev. Dr. King. But Mr. King? No ways.

It seems unfair, but Charmaine's bench has the edge on that old museum piece in Room 27. Occasionally I look up from my workbench, and see a white man sitting there, a history teacher say. While the schoolchildren he has brought here on an outing hunt in the grass for lucky beans, he sits down on our bench to rest his back. And after a while he pulls up his long socks, crosses one pink leg over the other, laces his fingers behind his head and closes his eyes.

Then again, I'll look up to see a black woman shuffling resolutely past, casting a resentful eye on the bench and muttering a protest under her breath, while the flame-red blossoms of the kafferboom detonate beneath her aching feet.

land

ANTJIE KROG ▼▼▼▼▼▼▼▼▼▼▼▼▼▼▼▼▼▼▼▼▼▼▼▼▼▼▼▼▼▼▼▼▼▼▼▼

under orders from my ancestors you were occupied
had I language I could write for you were land my land
but me you never wanted
no matter how I stretched to lie down
in rustling blue gums
in cattle lowering horns into Diepvlei
rippling the quivering jowls drink
in silky tassels in dripping gum
in thorn trees that have slid down into emptiness

me you never wanted
me you could never endure
time and again you shook me off
you rolled me out
land, slowly I became nameless in my mouth

now you are fought over negotiated divided padlocked sold stolen mortgaged
I want to go underground with you land
land that would not have me
land that never belonged to me

land that I love more fruitlessly than before

(Translated by Karen Press)

Recognition

David Medalie ▼▼▼▼▼▼▼▼▼▼▼▼▼▼▼▼▼▼▼▼▼▼▼▼▼▼▼▼▼▼▼▼▼▼▼▼▼▼

When I saw the envelope in which the invitation came, I thought it might be a request for an interview. I still get those occasionally, although fewer and fewer as time goes by. People nowadays don't want to ask me about Kobus and about those years as they did after he died. They think he belongs too much to the past. And I too have become something left over from the past. Let me tell you, that is a sad fate. This has become a young country now, and whether people are pleased about it or fighting against it, that is where their energies lie. Those who do try to recall the past want it to be tough and aggressive. That is certainly not my style. Besides, I am an old lady. I lead a quiet life and would not have it otherwise, but there is still a part of me that does not like to be forgotten; and because I have a responsibility towards Kobus's memory, I would not like him and what he accomplished to be forgotten either. That is understandable. There is a kind of loyalty that must be suspicious of things that are new.

I thought also that it might be an invitation to attend a political rally of the Party. Sometimes I am invited to participate in those sorts of gatherings. I find it hard to refuse, because I know that they want me there to represent Kobus and I suppose they are the last people who still cherish all that he fought for. Yet it is difficult for me to know what to do, for I feel that the Party is no longer the one that he represented so loyally, and that he would not approve of some of the directions it has chosen. Also, I am not a political person in myself, even though I was the wife of the Prime Minister for a number of years. Politics was Kobus's life and, of course, I supported him in every way that I could. But if he had remained a lawyer or I had married a schoolteacher like myself, I would have been quite contented. Politics is a rough business and I am not a rough person. As a child, I did not even like competitive games. Then I found myself having to support Kobus in the most competitive game of all. But I did what was needed and perhaps even more than was needed. I shirked nothing, no matter how unpleasant. I do not say this because I expect praise or gratitude. I say it simply because that is how it was. I must insist on the truth of what was. People are not satisfied with changing the present nowadays, they want to change the past too. I feel I have to protect what I know. I have become strangely jealous of my own life.

Anyway, I tore the envelope open. At first I thought it must be a joke or a trick that someone was playing on me, for I really was never so astonished in my life. I had been so isolated and so removed from what is happening in politics, despite the courtesies extended to me by the Party, that I didn't know that such a gathering was even being planned. And it is the last thing I would ever have imagined likely. The present government could not possibly be favourably disposed towards me—that is, if they ever gave me a thought. Yet, if this was not a hoax, I was being invited to a luncheon at the residence of the President.

I was distrustful. I didn't want to do anything that would make me feel regret afterwards. I didn't want to be used by any group of people for their own political ends, except by the Party, who usually use me very respectfully; and even then I am not entirely happy about it. I am cautious by nature and being married to Kobus for all those years has made me even more so, for he was a careful and scrupulous man, and he taught me a great deal. He taught me more as a father teaches his child than as a man teaches his wife. And I knew so little, even though I had been to the Teacher's Training College. But what I learned I have kept with me all my life, for where else does stability lie?

The only way I could establish whether or not it was a joke was to phone up Magdalena. If I received an invitation, then she must have received one too, I thought; and she is more in touch with what is happening politically at the moment than I am. I worked out that there were six widows of former prime ministers or presidents still living. But Magdalena was the only one I could speak to. The husbands of two of them were bitter rivals of Kobus. The third one's husband betrayed him terribly, even though they studied together at the University of the Orange Free State and were allies for many years after that. Kobus never forgave him and the quarrel went on until the day Kobus died. The fourth widow has Alzheimer's disease—they say she doesn't even recognise her own children.

Magdalena said that it was a genuine invitation. The President wishes to make peace with the past, she said; this is his way of showing that reconciliation can take place. She sounded very excited about it. She was certainly going to attend the luncheon and she urged me to attend it too. I said that I would think about it. Magdalena always loved feeling important; that is one of her little failings. Her husband died in office and so she lost him and the public attention at the same time. I do not condemn her for being that way, but I am different. Even when Kobus was Prime Minister, I did not exploit the powerful position that circumstances had given me, although I worked hard and carried out my duties conscientiously. I like to think that, as a result, I was a dignified and thoughtful presence and a good role model for women generally, not only for those whose husbands were in politics.

Magdalena said that she had already established that the other widows, except for poor Mrs. Havenga, were willing to accept the President's invitation. She told me that Mrs. Havenga just sits and stares blankly. It was pitiful to see. Her husband had the largest majority in parliament ever achieved in the history of the Party and she remembered nothing of it. All those triumphs were lost to her. She also told me that Mrs. Groenewald had not been well, she had had a hip replacement last year and other health problems, but she was very excited about the invitation and determined to attend the luncheon. I said politely that I was glad she was feeling up to it; I didn't think it was necessary to remind Magdalena about the great quarrel between Kobus and Jan Groenewald.

Was Magdalena sure that accepting the invitation was the right thing to do, I asked? Was it *politically* the right thing to do? Of course, she said. The President was recognising our importance and the importance of our late husbands. It would be good for the morale of the people who still believed in the old values to see the President extending such recognition and courtesy to us. We owed it to those people. They were in such despair. Their culture was under attack. They struggled to get jobs because of Affirmative Action. They had become outcasts in their own land. Before I put the phone down I said that I would accept the invitation. I still had some reservations, but I kept them from Magdalena. She was thrilled. Every widow would now be coming, she said; except, of course, for poor Mrs. Havenga.

You cannot imagine how strange it felt to enter the official residence again after all those years. People feel uncomfortable even when they have cause to enter a house which they once lived in; imagine, then, how disconcerting it was for me to enter the residence where I once, as the Prime Minister's wife, entertained important people from all over the world— Taiwan, Chile, Paraguay. Now I entered as the guest of a man whom my husband fought to keep out of it. It was so difficult for me that I had to think deliberately about my pride before I went in—how much pride I would wear, how I would wear it. It was almost like deciding how to arrange a scarf. The taxi dropped me off and I walked slowly and deliberately, carrying myself without haughtiness but rather as I felt a woman should who is conscious all the time of a solemn duty. I wanted to be worthy of that important thing that had been entrusted to me and that others, despite their own importance, were prepared to recognise in me.

Magdalena was ahead of me and I could already see that she was not behaving in a dignified manner. The President himself was receiving her at the door and she was gushing over him, not permitting him even to complete his words of welcome. There was something cringing about her, I thought; a smallness in her gratitude. I felt ashamed of her behaviour. I was determined that there would be nothing to be ashamed of in my behaviour. Someone who was standing near the President approached me and I told him who I was. He returned to the President with the information and then the President came towards me, smiling and greeting me. I shook his hand firmly. I said I was pleased to be there. I thanked him for the invitation. That was all. I was ushered into the dining hall.

It looked very different from the room that I had known, the room that I had redecorated myself a few months after Kobus became Prime Minister. The colours were bolder. We had painted the walls a light salmon colour, but now they were reddish brown with a white border. Not one work of art that we had chosen was still there, not even the Pierneef or the Van Wouw sculpture. Why was it necessary to remove those? The Pierneef was a landscape, the Van Wouw was a torso—there was nothing political about them. In a strange way, the sight of this redecorated room affected me more than all the other changes I had seen, such as watching the President being sworn in or the generals from the army and the air force saluting a black man.

Of course, I showed none of the emotion that I felt. I looked around to see where I had been seated. Before I could find the card with my name on it, Magdalena was pointing it out to me and waving at me. It was not too near to her, thankfully, nor too near to Mrs. Groenewald, who was making a point of ignoring my presence. The seats on either side of me were still empty. A waiter stepped forward immediately to offer me a drink. I chose soda water, as I always do.

Gradually the table began to fill up. There were a number of black women, whom I was surprised to see there. Then I realised that it was a gathering of political widows of all sorts, including the widows of people who had fought against the previous government. Black women and white women were being seated next to one another. The woman on my left was an Indian woman. She introduced herself, but her name was not familiar to me. The one on my right greeted me, but did not introduce herself, so I did not tell her who I was either. I tried to glance at her name card, but it was angled towards her and I could not read it. After that she sat quietly, making no attempt to speak to me or anyone else. She was a young woman, much younger than most of the other women there. She was perhaps less than forty years old.

When the President came into the room, we stood up. He asked us all to sit down. Then he made a short speech. He was honoured to receive us all; he was delighted that we had come. This was a time of reconciliation and dialogue, and we were all participating in that by sitting down to dine together, some of us bitter foes in the past, and showing the country that such things were possible. Then he spoke of those few who were not there, whose health had prevented them from coming. He named them all and said that he would call on them soon. He even mentioned Mrs. Havenga, and I wondered whether he knew what condition she was in. He named two women who had managed to come despite recent health problems of a serious nature, and thanked them in particular. One of them was Mrs. Groenewald.

Then the President sat down and they began to serve the meal. There was a cold cucumber soup, followed by saddle of venison. Television cameras had been set up and it was strange to think that we were being filmed as we ate. The Indian lady turned to me repeatedly, happy to make small talk, and we spoke about the food and about the President's speech. She pointed out some of the women and told me who they were and I did the same for her, pointing out and identifying each of the widows from the former government. The black woman on the other side remained very uncommunicative. If I spoke to her, she answered briefly, but made no effort to contribute to the conversation of her own accord, so I gave up and spoke to the Indian lady all the time. While the dessert was being served, the President got up and began to move around the table, speaking to each of the women. I could see Magdalena clasping his hand and looking up at him, speaking at length while the television cameras and microphones were focused upon her. I was pleased that I could not hear what she was saying.

When the President got to our part of the table, the Indian lady sprang up and they hugged each other. They clearly knew each other well. The President enquired after members of her family, they spoke of mutual friends and acquaintances. Then he moved on to me. He spoke to me with great courtesy. He knew that I had two daughters and he enquired after them. He asked me about my health. He wished to know where I lived. Did I enjoy my retirement from the pressures of political life? Not particularly, I said; it was a duty that one assumed without question and gave up when the time was over.

It occurred to me, as we spoke, that he was two years older than I. He was kindly, polite, yet somehow distant in a way that I could not quite put my finger on. His eyes are more inscrutable than the photographs suggest. I was not very pleased with my responses; I felt they were a little ungracious. I wanted to do more than thank him for inviting me to the luncheon. I wanted to thank him for the gesture, for the symbolism. I know the importance of symbolism, for our own culture is full of symbols. But I didn't know how to do so without gushing like Magdalena, without yielding something up to him that I was supposed to keep from him. So I was formal, polite in my turn and controlled. He passed on.

When he greeted by name the black woman next to me, I felt startled. I drank some soda water to hide my reaction. Hearing that name again, the name that had vexed Kobus for so many years and even after he retired from political life, the name that had been linked to his throughout the world, was a shock to me. That name had first begun to inconvenience us before Kobus was Prime Minister—it was when he was still Minister of Justice. And when he became Prime Minister, journalists and other people hostile to the government referred whenever they could to those suicides and accidents that occurred while people were in police custody; and always they referred, in particular, to the death of this woman's husband. And perhaps, as Kobus admitted to me, some of them were caused by police exceeding their duties, for those were trying times, and in trying times people are not always at their best. But it didn't mean that Kobus had anything to do with it. He was a fair man, firm but always fair. And it grieved him that his name should be linked to such events and I grieved with him, for I was protective of his reputation as, indeed, I still am.

Yet here was the widow of the most notorious of all those detainees, the one whose death caused an international outcry. I had been sitting next to her throughout the luncheon and I had not known who she was. Now, after the President moved on from us to speak to another group of ladies, we looked at each other and were silent. Her silence made me very uncomfortable. I felt the need to say something, something appropriate to the occasion, but it was difficult to know what to say.

Finally I said, "I'm sorry, I didn't know who you were."

"I knew who you were," she said. We sat silently again. She bent her head to her dessert. It was clear that, if any gestures were to be made, they would have to come from me.

"The President has done a great thing," I said. "He has brought us together so that we can make peace with the past and recognise our common humanity. After all, we are all widows. Each of us has suffered a loss."

She looked up again and seemed to stare at something behind me, something in the far distance.

"Is that what you have come to do—to make peace with the past?" she asked.

I thought for a while before I answered. "No," I said. If there was one gesture I could make, it was to tell her the truth. It was a relief to do so. "I came to make sure that no one is going to take the past away from me."

When I said that, she blinked and looked directly at me. It was impossible to know what to make of the expression on her face. Only someone who knew her well could have interpreted it, and I didn't know her at all.

"Perhaps we have something in common after all," she said.

Excerpt from
Freedom Lament and Song

MONGANE WALLY SEROTE ▼▼▼▼▼▼▼▼▼▼▼▼▼▼▼▼▼▼▼▼▼▼▼▼▼▼▼

remember
the honesty of history is and can be cruel
it is also
it is also a song, it is footsteps
history is you and me
history is day and is night
history is how you fought to lift a hand
and how to put it down
history is history
in the heart of a worker
in the head of a worker
and a man
and a woman
history is the birth of a child
history is the death of a child
history is that which happens
that which is repeated
and done
and through time and
history
because it is like the seasons
it repeats itself like a reflection
in your eye
in my eye
when i see me in you
and you in me in my eyes
history makes and unmakes life and time
speaks
listens
it is the morning minute
which we push and must intervene
shift
which we witness
which changes you and me
as we know
it did

history is the heavy hour arm
history is the light minute arm
to the small second
is you and me
history is no similar minute
or hour or second
history is now when it's no more
history ends when it ends
if it ends
history is the old lady of the bolshoi
who intervenes
and the little girl learning ballet
it is the woman who dances
spins and swings
propels and flies
in a dance
in the air and space
it is the will
it is the altitude
it is you
history is a dance of the muscle
of the body on the air
on the heart
it is the body and the dance on the air
history flies like light
it is time
it flies like an eagle in the blue space
in the swift and smoke air
it pounds
it dances and flails
it flies, swings and spins
like time
like the earth
like day and night
history makes time and you and me
history is like science
is like technology which embraces knowledge to use it
it shapes things
it shapes the brains and faces
it is a story
history exists at the beginning of time

and enters at its end
history speaks and glides in speech
when time ends it starts
and when it ends time begins with human intervention
history i said
is hard like steel
is soft like the glide of a vulture
history
is my story and i speak of it
i tell my story
remember history
history is the Zairean dance
is the Ghanaian dance
history is the Angolan dance
and the township dance
history is the Mozambican dance troupe
no matter the size of war
no matter the size of the sound of the war
no matter the size of the explosive package
the dance troupes
the dancers are here to continue the dance and dance
they are the size of life they dance
here we go again, they survive life
the song and history, says
here
life says, we go again.

Fragments from
the Life of Norman Rubarto

PAUL MASON ▼▼▼▼▼▼▼▼▼▼▼▼▼▼▼▼▼▼▼▼▼▼▼▼▼▼▼▼▼▼▼▼▼

I

Pencils, crayons, charcoal sticks, paintbrushes, water colours and papers—each holds its place inside the drawers of Norman's bedside table. There is time spent alone in Oupa Rubarto's orchard in the summer light between evening and dark. Norman watches the trees patiently, awaiting the sounds of the fruits dropping to the dried leaves that cushion the ground. There are sounds from the garden—distant sounds felt as movements in the dark.

Yes, he has spent other evenings in Oupa's aviary, absorbing the whirring of birds' wings. Early one morning he had stood alone on the patio of Oupa's farmhouse. Holding his ball, he had seen Oupa chasing the man out of the maid's room with a knobkerrie in his hand. The knobkerrie had swung down in an arc, and it had hit the man. Norman had hidden behind the wicker chair on which Ouma always sat, and as the man ran past the patio he had seen a big patch of blood spilling its legs from the top of his head down his cheeks to his neck—like a huge baboon spider. The maid had screamed.

Oupa had not seen Norman seeing him. He had held the ball tight to his chest because he had been afraid Oupa would take it away from him for having watched him hitting the man with the knobkerrie. Nobody else had been awake then.

Evenings blunted the sharp aloneness. The aloneness is always with Norman. He holds it close. He feels it like the fruits dropping to the ground; the birds in the aviary; not like morning, which comes as a stick or a hard hand pulling his arms from his chest.

II

Overseers or guardians? It cannot be known, nor told. There are two of them.

The girls, picking jasmine, do not notice them. The flowers have to be picked quickly for there are only two hours each day. Thorns around the jasmine prick their fingers. Grandmamma had given them her old pair of woollen gloves with leather patches sewn to the finger-tips. But still the thorns prick through. Mama and Grandmamma had both picked jasmine, but Grandmamma is now too old, and mama's fingers can no longer move.

Grandmamma says, "But hands also weave and touch. They build and play and hold water."

Norman studies the picture closely. He keeps it in a secret place inside his bedside table, underneath the pencils and crayons. The girls' eyes do not leave the flowers as they move. They have large white pouches hanging to their bellies.

Now the two who seem to be overseers have both girls in their line of vision, though they do not look at them. Their eyes are dreamy—as if they are looking at something beyond the girls. It can never be seen what they are looking at; if anything is there. The sky is grey. It greys the girls picking jasmine. It greys the ground on which they stand. It greys the land which stretches behind them to the invisible horizon. The only white is the jasmine, the pouches, the cloaks and the head-scarves of the two who watch. One of the men holds a staff, which touches the ground. It too is white. Only their faces and their hands are bare.

In the evenings the girls pick the jasmine for their perfume.

III

Memories are seldom of events. The picture he has drawn of the three of them touches something else. It recalls something equally real; more so.

Yet now, looking at it, an event returns.

Foreground—trees; faces smiling; hands holding self-made flags of rebellion; naked feet in the shallow gutter; tattered jeans. Their brimming boy-zest.

Background—across the fields behind the school's fence a power station, uniform and monstrous. Behind the boys and to the left—the goal posts, then the centre-spot. . . . And it comes back.

It is an early morning in mid-June, windless; an hour before the bell rings for classes to begin. They place sixteen candles around the centre-spot, and sit. In long silence they watch the faint slighting dance of the flames.

IV

Norman has no choice but to stay here, where they will not find him. In the evenings from his chair at the window he follows her regular motions. The curtains at her window are of a fabric that presents her form clearly, but without radiance. He draws her in charcoal and pencil and in water colours of blue and grey. She sells her body. Her skin has the lustre of a screen upon which images from her memory move. The images are visible between the shadows that fall from the bedposts and the bodies that move on top of her. When she sits in front of her dressing table, or moves alone and naked about her room, the images lure Norman till he feels shamed and retreats.

She was on the streets, he sees. There was the time of petty thieving. Things are better for her now. She ceases to draw her curtains till her form blurs to fading. Norman feels elated—there has been enough of her lives in the semi-darkness. It is time to leave his staled name behind.

V

The hymns he sings to his new name are to no avail. They read like two hands held facing each other in front of his chest—in motion against each other without touching his chest or each other.

Shona has picked up the habit of using it, for it has to be used. Each voicing grates his ear and his mood grows foul. They drive bit by bit, stopping off frequently beside the straight and only road through the parched land.

It is late morning and the sun washes the land into white light. On the horizon an image is visible. In the heat waves it appears to move, mantis-like. As they draw nearer it is a little man, jacketed and motionless, with his arm raised and his forefinger pointing skyward.

The little man flaps his tongue against his gums as he watches the approaching car. He bundles his teeth into the inside pocket of his shabby jacket and points his forefinger at his destination.

He steps in, smiling, his lips sucked tight. He remains silent, for he is sapped. He has spent the night with the large lady at the shebeen. He spends a night of every week with her, and sets off for town in the mornings that follow, his mind still blurred, carrying the fullness of her scent and her room.

A few hundred metres from the town he splutters. Norman hears a phrase repeated—"stow muh teef."

Shona translates—"He says his name is Amos and he doesn't have teeth. Somebody stole them. He has come to the clinic in town to buy a new set of teeth, which are not very expensive. But he has no money unfortunately, and asks if we might be able to help him."

Amos has unusually liquid dreams. They start in his head during the nights and flow over into the days when he has less work to do. He stays alone in his room near the farm's windmill. He works on the crops, as a cowherd, and fixes the fences and the water pipes. It is hard work, and he is tired every night. But he never has dreams of his work. The dreams come from elsewhere to his head, and they flow from his head to join themselves to the things in his room. Every morning he looks around his room for them and brings them to the table where he sits for his breakfast. He puts them into words. The air and the land are dry and hard. Some nights he takes the words outside and uses them to speak his dreams into the air. These are also his rehearsals—because he takes them to the shebeen where he drinks beer with the big lady. She gives him pleasures for the dreams he gives her. He speaks only in dreams to her and takes out his teeth when he speaks to the white people. Stow muh teef.

A heavy cluster of clouds disperses the light. Details in the land can now be traced with ease, and Norman does so in pencil as Shona drives. In the rear-view mirror Norman's eyes meet the quaint toothless smile of the little man. His mood now altered, he finds himself sketching the old man's face and inventing words with which Amos speaks his life.

But the little man near the windmill is not saying such words, or anything like them when he enters the town and the people ask him why he is there and what he wants from them dressed like that, toothless and with his hands outstretched.

VI

He lays his pencil and drawing pad aside. From his table on the restaurant's terrace Norman sits opposite two couples—one elderly, the other young. The young man's voice booms its new knowledge of the local inhabitants. His large hands gesture at the street; his smile is large and satisfied as he leans back. The street is a-bustle with people wearing hats; with carts drawn by tick-sucked horses; and hawkers of cheeses and meats so fetid Norman maps their auras onto his memory for later pencilling.

On the other side of the street runs a high wall of roughly-hewn stones. Pinned to the wall is a billboard: the image of a gentleman in a fine shirt and bow tie; a monocle for his left eye; his arm in the sleeve of a jacket being placed over his shoulders. There is a carnation in the left lapel of his jacket. One might imagine him at a decisive moment: leaving the dinner, the opera or, perhaps, the dance.

Beneath the billboard, on the kerbside, sits a man with his back to the wall. His head is bowed. With his elbow on his knee, his hand rests on his brow. He wears torn pants and tattered sheepskin moccasins. The brow of his cap shadows his hand. Only blackness can be seen for his face.

Above his shoulders, in the sunlight, shine the two faces of the billboard. Next to the faces are four lines of verse. Norman has been watching the couples from his table. He replaces his spectacles to study the quatrain. It ends with the word "elegante."

The man has remained in the same position, as if frozen, through the two or so hours of lunch. The sun beats down on him, as it does in these parts. Their bill arrives. From his attaché case the young man removes his camera to photograph the scene before them. He gestures at the man and the billboard with an outstretched arm, and addresses his companions with passion—"Just think, if I hadn't . . . if I hadn't remembered to bring my camera this morning, what we see here would be . . . nothing. Nothing."

"That would be sad," replies the elder lady, "very sad."

Norman's eyes glaze. He looks down at the oak table and follows the patterns of its grain.

VII

Norman sits in the gallery with a full view of the people watching the moving images on the screen that encircles them. He has been commissioned to sketch pictures for a brochure promoting the newly-built 360 degree screen. From where he sits the sight is amusing—the spectators look up in every direction like a congregation of penguins between meals and matings. They stand transfixed, eyes glossed, paper-thin, as if the times attached to the events before them have not and never can be their own.

An action catches his eye: a tiny boy kicks a big man. The big man turns to scowl at the crown of the boy's head as the boy issues inaudible complaints. The big man returns his gaze to the screen. Again the boy kicks him. He snarls and says "Hey boy, what is it you think you're doing?"

When the interval arrives he scowls at the boy once more and contemptuously raises his eyes. They meet with Norman's in the gallery. He nods a greeting.

After the interval the doomed tussle continues. The big man's face grows tight with indignation. At the show's end Norman overhears him addressing his companion, "Did you see the little bugger kicking me?"

"Yes," replies his partner, "several times, in fact."

"He kept on kicking me on my ankle and the stupid little bugger could have looked at the screen anywhere else and he wouldn't have missed anything. It's because they're allowed to do exactly as they wish; exactly as they wish!"

It is a small story, perhaps even meagre, thinks Norman. It revolves around a single action. Or, rather, a singular action. He hears the big man's voice again, "That little bugger behind me kicked me on my ankle through the whole show and cried that he couldn't see because I was so big. His parents stood still next to him and said nothing. So I said nothing. He could have looked anywhere else!"

But we know he could not have looked anywhere else: the singular boy with no choice but to perform a singular motion, and to repeat that motion. He had to look exactly there where Big Man stood, and nowhere else.

VIII

He sits with Shona while she speaks to the scuba-diver. The man's profile is a delight to sketch: it is bent like a pincer. Norman remembers a day with Shona: they stood on a stretch of beach cluttered with crabs that did not move. They checked the crabs for signs of life, and the pincers of a large one shivered. Soon bodies of others tremoured faintly.

"They're stranded," she said—and so they used shells to push the crabs onto ribbons of kelp and carry them back to the rock pools. They watched them until bubbles, like restored dreams, rose from their heads, and their stalk-eyes bowed.

He listens as Shona speaks to the man. "We jumped in the water," he says, "and the sea was full of millions of some sort of crab larvae, but with big bright blue eyes—so that as you jumped into the water there were these millions of blue eyes, and they climbed all over us. And when you try to go under water they're all sort of clinging to your wetsuit. And wherever we went that day . . . they . . . we had these things on us."

Shona says, "Mm."

"And I've never seen it again," the man continues. "But it's something that . . . when I talk to other divers I can bring it up. So, you know, these things—I don't know what they're doing there, but . . . it . . . it's just an interesting observation."

She says, "Mm, mm."

Norman can see she is thinking in visions: visions rattling across the floors of silent seas; a million crazed big bright blue eyes waiting to dance on wetsuits.

"And I've dived down and found the crayfish all moving in across the sand—thousands of them. I'd only discovered it by accident, and for the next couple of weeks we went scuba-diving amongst them. It made a very interesting observation, and since then we've found that they do that every year, you know—the . . . the crayfish actually walk into the bay. . . . In their thousands."

Norman watches her: her eyes clocking visions now running rampant. She says, "Mm, mm. Mm."

IX

Beneath the loose cotton garment the huge buttocks jostle like playful bull-dogs. From where he sits Norman follows their motions discreetly. She rifles about in her sling-bag and a bunch of keys fall to the street. She bends to lift them. To contain it NOW, for it shall never come again! Norman lays out his crayons, pencils and sketch-pad.

Shona's lateness allows times such as these to gather himself—to draw out the auras. Some of them are sharp and clear casements for the bodies. Some are broken; others blurred. Some flare up, dim, and flare again. Her aura has a dullish and regular glow. He sighs, allows his pencil to slip from his fingers, and closes his eyes.

X

Norman sits in his father's garden, overlooking the bay.

"Say property, not garden. We own this land," father had said as he held out his hands and gestured dramatic semi-circles. Norman remembered Oupa Rubarto's arms. They used to move in exactly the same way when he drove them across his farm in the open Landrover.

Now, from the edge of father's property, his garden, Norman catches sight of the rising moon. He hears father's voice again, "Even when it's full the moon is never bigger than your thumbnail when you stretch out your hand and hold your thumb between your eyes and the moon." Words heard many times as a child, when they were together as the full moon rose.

Its fullness now, as it rises from the horizon at the other side of the bay, sparks little desire to raise his thumb to it: the significance of the gesture puzzled him. Instead, Norman obeys the urge to kneel, then sit cross-legged, for this makes sense. The moon is red because minutes before the sun has sunk behind him. The wire grating of the fence provides a frame for the moon.

"Just another way of looking at the moon," he thinks. He smiles at his father, for himself.

Looking out over the clear water of the bay, Norman remembers now the way father had instructed him to use the oars. "Like this," he would say, "lift them, skimming carefully just above the water as you push and lean forward, for the strength must come from your shoulders and your back and not from your arms. And as you dip them in, you lean back slowly. Like this—move your arms back, using the strength from your back and your shoulders."

He could never get it right, for father said every time, "No, wrong, wrong! You'll never row properly if you use only your arms. . . ."

The memory fades—eclipsed now by the memory of rowing with Shona, holding an oar each and rowing slowly, uncoordinatedly, moving ahead in curves and occasional circles; laughing.

Norman lingers on this memory as his eyes move from the sea back to the moon. Its redness fades. He begins to smell fertiliser from the vegetable garden. He holds up his hand to the sky and looks at the moon between two of his fingers, and through the mesh of the fence, "Doubly framed. Doubly my own."

He smiles grimly.

He lies on the ground and stretches his arms from his chest, fingers raised to the sky. Following the stars, he traces spiral patterns with his forefinger.

Spirals: in the time before he could read. He remembers a picture on the cover of a book: a spiral stairwell made of marble. It moves around a thin column up into the open sky. It is not attached to anything but a slab of dark stone at its base. Two steps lead from the base to the bare earth; and at the base lies a woman in an orange robe. Her head to its side, she lies on her back with her limbs splayed.

Why is the stairway the shape it is? Why isn't it inside a building? Why is the woman lying at its base? Father's response was abrupt—"It's a spiral stairway."

Why do her arms and legs lie as they do, as if they are broken? And her head as it is—as if she is dead? Has she fallen from the top of the stairway that fades into dark blue at the top of the picture. Why is she *there*?

"It's art boy, it doesn't matter why she's there," father had replied. "Enough questions now. It's art, like what you do with your crayons and pencils. You must be silent when you look at it."

Norman repeats the questions, reaching out to take the book from the desk. Father slaps him on the palm of his hand and places the book on a shelf too high for him to reach. The feeling is close. That night too—through the open window—he had smelled the fertiliser.

Supine, he draws a pencil from his breast pocket and uses the stars as points to draft his first design for a spiral stairway to his studio. He recalls father's incomprehension when he told him he had changed his name. He had said nothing, never asked for the reason. The motion of Norman's hand is loaded with natural intent.

The light breeze brings sharp odours to his nose, and returns his mind to father. The way he used fertiliser seemed always to have enraged father—"Spread it evenly, not in patches like you've done here. Its nutrients must feed all of the vegetables."

Once again he hears the echo of his lame defiance—"Well, I prefer the carrots to the cabbage . . . so, it's not so. . . ." Father had not let him finish, and was nervously scooping handfuls from the bag to distribute them, "Not like this, but like this. Like this."

His face was strangely shrivelled, as if struggling to conceal a vulnerability. Norman had seen that face once before: when father arrived at the exhibition that marked the completion of his art studies.

The instructions and their demonstrations had never ceased, until now. With predictable obstinacy he had refused to be admitted to a clinic—"I will not leave my home. There are always things to attend to here."

Norman recalls the night he had suggested to father that he needed the constant care a clinic would provide.

"You know I can't go," father had replied. "You, more than anyone. I can't be taken where I won't be useful. I won't be taken where I can't be useful."

He had not repeated the suggestion.

Sitting cross-legged again, Norman scans the lights at the other side of the bay. The sky is cloudless. Other words return—"Look, my boy, look how clearly the moonlight falls onto the sea, like a silver highway to the other side that invites you to walk on it. Like magic."

He had been taken to the clinic that morning. In the visiting hour his uncle had arrived. Outside the ward his uncle had said:

"He should have come here long ago. Such selfish stubbornness. Couldn't the man see how he was burdening you?"

The man's words echo as he stretches out his body and allows his head to rise and drop from side to side—putting the stars into a dizzy wheeling motion. Father had taught him the trick when he was a boy. He stops the motion of his head, and raises his finger again to trace the spiral patterns.

Selfishly stubborn, resolute, intractable, unmoveable. Words heard and overheard—speaking of, condemning, his father.

Throughout the illness he accepts assistance without asking for it.

XI

Near the end Norman visits him almost every day, and the instructions and demonstrations continue as ever. He complains of constantly feeling cold. One afternoon Norman helps him move to a room that receives the sunlight. While clearing a pile of papers from his bedside table Norman notices an architect's manual for the building of houses. Inside the book is a sheet of paper covered by father's illegible script. He opens the book to remove the paper and to reveal an essay on the construction of spiral stairways.

Father has been in Intensive Care for over a week, and breathes with difficulty. Norman decides—perversely perhaps, or for a reason he feels no need to fathom or explain—to show father the architect's designs for his stairway to the studio. Father asks for his reading glasses, and holds the designs to the light. Within seconds his face flushes and he coughs violently. Norman holds his shoulders firmly, and at last his head falls back to his pillow. He removes the designs from his limp hands, and places them in a compartment inside the bedside table before the nurse arrives.

She helps father into a sitting position again. After a minute or two the coughing ceases. He raises his hand to the nurse and gestures his need for pen and paper. When the equipment arrives he looks up at Norman and nods—"If you don't mind, boy, I've work to do."

He allots specific hours of each day to working on the staircase, to resting, and to seeing visitors. He organises with the matron for Norman to visit for an hour of each day, outside of the standard visiting hours.

In the five days that remain Norman arrives a little early each time—to discover him at work with pen and paper. He stands still in the doorway, unnoticed, and watches his father. He reflects upon the words of his uncle, from the night he lay on the ground. Selfishly stubborn. Resolute. Intractable. Unmoveable. Alive.

Norman watches him until his eyes rise from the page.

This Carting Life

RUSTUM KOZAIN ▼▼▼▼▼▼▼▼▼▼▼▼▼▼▼▼▼▼▼▼▼▼▼▼▼▼▼▼▼▼▼▼▼

I met History once, but he ain't recognize me
—Derek Walcott, "The Schooner *Flight*"

On pilgrimage down damp steps, deep inside
the British Museum, among boxes stocked
roof-high, I rummage. And sniff like a dog
and pause, snout snuffling for nearest quarry,
for the tacks to my own, final shit.

Which box fell from father's cart
knocking about through the Karoo, farm to farm
as he tendered his art to anyone
who'd pay him a bauble or some jot of tripe
for shearing a sheep, planting a split pole?

In regulation tatters, did we children
skulk behind mother as father would
talk over terms of trade with the farmer
or foreman: yes, you may pitch there
draw water here; firewood you find yourself?

Did we all pitch in, unpack and pile
box and sack and pole, and father swore
and hammered, tied all into a bigger box,
our pitching home for a few days
until we had to cart it off again?

Did I search for the giant spiders
tempered overnight into tangles of dead wood,
their many legs that make good kindling
shadowed like webs under gutless bodies?
Did I drag back bundles, scrawling long lines

that led to our fire at night?
And how then we did dream. Learning to play
the bow, did I pluck at hamstrung song, coddling
my instrument? And the others rocked?

Swinging his dregs out in a dark arc

did father cough and rise, and from his box
fetch shears, a jar of black, used oil
and a heavy lump wrapped in greased cloth;
then, hands trembling as if it were our saving
charm, bare the ever-dwindling whetstone?

While my string thrummed, stopped, quivered again,
like the incomplete tongues troubling in me,
was the slap and slick of stone on iron
father's reluctant percussion?
Did he sing? And mother too? The young ones

staring at the flame and coal; and I fixed
on the stars to try hold the course of my string?
Was this how sleep stalked us, as song rang
in our cambering heads, the children
soon propping each other, then carried

to bed down in the smells of smoke and sand,
of gods and people burled like *kooigras*?
And we did sleep until dawn brought the clang
of cup and shears strung to father's waist
as, stooping, out he went to work?

Did I later take him shards of potbread
spread with fat? Kneeling on the spine
of a sheep, did he withhold his shears, look up
and say the sheep are nearly done, tonight
we roast tripe, but tell mother to pack

we go north tomorrow; yes we go north. . . ?

Did we then lose the box, when we left? ·
Fallen from the cart over some unbidden bump?
Or with wind in our heads did we forget
the box, a lone tombstone among footprints
the tools a rattle of charms, like bones,

like runes without which we were turned

from farm to enclosed farm? But north,
always north we trekked,
until we hung from the cracked lip
of a vast, somnolent desert?

And did we stray there many days?
Did we turn south again and, hungry
at the first fence, did father unroll
his bow and quiver,
long forgot?

                        *

But all that came later. And somewhere
in these many cunning passages must lie
a box that holds our shears and whetstone.
For now, I reach for the nearest box.
It shifts and pitches in my hands

as unknown weights rollick inside.

I steady it and place it down, kneel
and blow at the dust. Then wait for history
to settle around me. Is this box my own
making? To hoard a craft predating carts
and shears? Or did I roll into it

among others tossed too like bones
predicting life running, wandering, skulking?
And death? And after death
enclosure in boxes? And kept from
boxed-in earth and sky?

Did we see it coming? And now can do
nothing but roll and bump our heads?
And stare visionless, with sockets
hollowed by science and filled with baubles,
at our own lives our interrogators?

My lips drawn but caught in mid-cry
as I screamed not for help but yearned

the province of the mantis? Stalled
in prayer, cut off from grace?
Because in supplication we refused

the first fences that already ran
from sun-up to where night pummelled the sky?
And kept our arrows trained on cattle?
Belly-slow after a feast,
could we not run fast enough? And sought

to meld with moon, rock, inadequate shrub?
Close to the ground, did we hear the hooves
drum, the horsemen, the dedicants of prophecy?
Did we crouch and wait
for seven muskets hanging from the clouds

like unequivocal fingers of some foreign god?
And then lead balls did prod us
to silence for the real work
of bayonets punching stars in our bodies?
Stagnant stars that in days would turn blue?

Blue stars by whose unsounded frequencies
vultures would tack on course, dip into
cartwheels and circle unseen above us,
to triangulate the closest hopping distance
so that in feast they may unburden the earth?

By then our disremembered bodies
asserting their span of land only
by the reach of that temporary smell
of bloat? All this unseen by us boxed-in
heads, heading for port?

How we did feel the thrum of blades
on our necks. Like gods run amok
under the skin, the madness that sings
before the first nick; as the nick promises
the first inch opening, and so on,

unzipping further as bayonets sawed

through our necks. Was I alive still?
Even as in their cold ecstasy stars
untimely had spangled my body like some pox?
And I did feel and smell the hand

that tilted my jaw and had not charity?
Did I scream then and it was cut
out of me, stopped short of godhead? And how
did they negotiate vertebrae, cartilage?
And did a bookbinder, fingers adept

at pampering vellum, tuck flaps of neck-skin
under our jaws, sealing thus the servants
of the praying mantis in their foreheads?
Our souls now caught as recompense
for some flank of beef just-begotten?

*

Is this then the infirm box I stall before
and play at wiping gloves of dust
from me, as an intercom intones
closing time: five minutes to go
before I'm enclosed in the museum?

Will I leave this box unopened too,
heads unrolled onto my lap, and break
in a brisk walk into damp London?
And will a drizzle soon clot the dust
on my clothes as I run for shelter,
fugitively wiping at my knees and elbows?

The Naked Song

MANDLA LANGA ▼▼▼▼▼▼▼▼▼▼▼▼▼▼▼▼▼▼▼▼▼▼▼▼▼▼▼▼▼▼▼▼▼▼▼

On the day the Stock Exchange dropped a couple of points following the announcement of Nelson Mandela's confinement to hospital for a prostate operation, a somewhat depressed Leonard Gama sat in his office, watching traffic rolling by on a restless street. Elevated above street level stretched a freshly mown playing-field so green it could have come out of the pages of a children's picture book. A gaggle of black and white boys in grey trousers and white shirts and loosened ties passed a football around, dribbling and executing jubilant jigs.

Gama cast around in his head whether to read the morning papers or intimidate the secretary into making him a cup of tea. Magriet, a throwback to the good old days when blacks didn't give orders, was forever busy faxing her curriculum vitae to companies and organisations which still pandered to nostalgia. One evening, finding the gents' toilet inaccessible, Gama took a chance and emptied his bladder in the ladies' where he gazed with wry amusement at the legend scribbled with a koki pen on the whitewashed wall: *Affirmative action is sommer'n klomp kak!* Gama considered himself lucky in not having struggled to find a job. It could have been due to the shortage of black psychologists; most companies snapped up the few there were and exhibited them like hunting trophies in board meetings. He was employed by the Sandor Centre, a group of consulting psychologists who specialised in psychotherapy, assessment and mediation. This was where Gama had to make hard-nosed decisions regarding a rumour that there was a sympathetic black man who dispensed free advice, leading to all sorts of people beating a path to his door. Before starting a consultation, Gama informed the client that time was money. It wasn't always easy.

Returning to his homeland after two decades of exile had sensitised him to the difficult path his fellow citizens trudged every day. The government ministries and departments were usually housed in the same buildings or offices of the repudiated past. The personnel at the gates leading to the corridors of power remained as formidable as ever. Men as tall as cedars—and as wide—with moustaches resembling municipality brooms, towered above one and extended a hand the size of a graveyard shovel to accept one's written memo to see the Minister; the memo, as if frightened to death, shrinking in size to a postage stamp. Some of the ministers looked small and lost in chambers roomy enough to fly a small airplane.

Gama stopped and pondered, knowing that he was falling into the trap of cynicism; it was easy to cast stones at the fragile glass of the new democracy.

But it still rankled that he was increasingly having to deal with instances of inefficiency which could hardly be attributed to the legacy of apartheid. He handled many cases which needed co-operation and support from government departments; he wasn't making any money. His other partners who acted as stewards to an endless stream of white neuroses made a killing. Most of Gama's clients were—for the mere reason that they had been cast so low as to need someone to advise them—not in an admirable income bracket. Furthermore, paying for advice was not at the top of most black people's agendas; hell, it would be like paying for an uncle's beneficence. The majority of defaulters were former exiles who had missed the vehicle which had catapulted their more fortunate brethren to lofty heights.

Sounds of a scuffle in the reception area interrupted his train of thought. Magriet, blonde tresses swishing threateningly, stormed into Gama's office. Her blazing eyes were an indication of her combative mood; at the same time she seemed to be struggling with her own personal demons.

"What's the matter, Magriet?" he asked distractedly, knowing that he was beyond surprise. The surprise would have been a whole day spent without a surprise; that came with the territory.

"These people," Magriet said, half her visible figure shoving off somewhere unseen behind her, blocking their entry. "They just barge in here without any appointment. What kind of business do they think we're running here—a blerry shebeen in a *skomplaas?*" As if on cue, the skirt of a serge greatcoat flapped into view, followed by a trousered leg, until a small, wizened man stood in the doorway. He grunted a greeting and rubbed his nose with the back of his fist. Magriet, her worst fears confirmed, rolled her eyes and, her frame rigid with indignation, stormed out of the office, leaving behind a lingering fragrance of wild flowers. The visitor was of indeterminate age with a dome-shaped head of uncombed hair peppered with grey. The eyes were quick, alert, at the same time maintaining that distant, downcast attitude of servility which most black people have honed to a fine art as a defence against white authority. Gama knew that most black people had been so beaten that they would tend to be tentative to other blacks who represented power. This knowledge that he could fill his countrymen with fear and trembling, did nothing to lift his spirits. Under the greatcoat, the old man wore a threadbare navy-blue suit, a grey shirt held at the collar by a red tie which brought to mind the tongue of a strangled bull. Magriet's fragrance was overpowered by a feral odour people would associate with the grave.

"*Siyabonana, Ndodana,*" the man greeted again.

"*Yebo, Baba,*" Gama said and pointed at a chair. "Please take a seat." He thought of offering to take the man's coat—the weatherman had forecast a sizzling day—but decided against it: he didn't want to leave this early caller bereft of what could well be his security blanket. "What brings you here?"

"My name is Nkosi, Mr Gama," Nkosi said after installing himself in one of the uncomfortable chairs. "And this matter is not about me, really, although it concerns us all."

Gama, elbows on the desk with his fingertips meeting to form a pyramid, nodded understandingly. Outside, the sound of traffic commingled with the gritty staccato bursts of a pneumatic drill. Loosely, he remembered an old friend who, after taking a couple of long drags from his *zoll* of Durban poison, made this observation: "You know, *Chumza?* Work *is* noise!" Gama smiled remembering the sickly sweet fumes of the prize weed. "Who is it all about, then?"

"My son, Richard," Nkosi replied and, in the same breath, bellowed, *"Richard!"* Gama was so surprised he started out of his chair, ears ringing. He had a distinct impression that the hum of the air-conditioning had stopped, as if its heartbeat had been disturbed. Gama wondered what Magriet was making of all this.

Richard, in his early forties, emerged. He was taller, stockier and infinitely sadder than his father. Dressed in a windbreaker over a yellow T-shirt, denim jeans and trainers, he might have been of a different breed, but he was definitely of the same seed. It was in Richard's eyes that Gama saw something which connected them both to a remote past. What was it?

Then it hit him. *Richard!* Of course, this was Richard, once a wiry devil who caused women to scream when he blew his tenor sax with the Amandla Cultural Ensemble in Angola. And that was, oh, how many years ago?

Gama went round his desk and strode to Richard. "Hey, *camarada,"* he said, "what are you doing here?" Praying for mutual recognition, he made to embrace Richard. But Richard took a step back and something harsh and disjointed came out of his lips. Gama looked past Richard's shoulder to see Magriet wearing a look with which parents favour a loved but headstrong child. She shook her head sadly.

"He can't talk, Len," she said.

"What do you mean he can't talk?" Gama asked, feeling stupid.

"Just that." The revelation of Richard's disability had softened something in her hard interior. This was one of Magriet's character traits which never failed to intrigue Gama; she could switch from being a witch possessing the sensitivity of a Parktown prawn to a candidate in the Mother Teresa school of piety. "Must be mute hysteria," Magriet put in. "You know how that is."

Gama, mentally riffling through the pages of psychology textbooks for case studies, turned to the old man. "How long has this been going on,

Baba?" The subject of the inquiry, Richard, perched himself on the corner of the chair, his whole pose indicating a readiness to flee.

"He was fine when he came back," Nkosi began. He turned to his son and gingerly placed a hand on his shoulder, the touch gentle, as if he feared the possibility of a further wounding. "You were all right, were you not, Richard? When you returned . . . from exile?"

Richard nodded and rubbed the bristle along his jawline. He seemed to shrink further within the windbreaker, much like a snail retracting into its shell after contact with salt. It occurred to Gama that, even if this young man with a ruined mind might be an issue of his father's loins, it would take volumes for the old man to start comprehending what Richard had gone through. Because, Gama knew, there was no such thing as returning from exile. Exile was not so much a geographic dislocation as a state of mind, something that consumed and branded and left one marked for life. Many, like animals whose limbs were left in a snare, walked through life crippled, their minds locked on that fateful moment of rupture.

Nkosi looked up at Gama. "I don't know what happened." He turned in his chair to gaze at Magriet, then back to Gama. "It has something to do with a woman he met some time back."

"My!" Magriet said. Shaking her head, she disappeared to tend to her secretarial duties at the front desk. Despite his irritation with her, Gama felt that he needed her support because this was promising to be a long day indeed.

"You can still write, Richard?" he asked.

Richard nodded. Gama pushed aside the papers on his desk. He retrieved a lined executive desk pad and placed it on the mahogany surface. Pushing forward a cracked earthenware jug containing an assortment of pens, he steered Richard to seat himself at the desk. "Since we can't conduct this orally," he said, remembering the time he wrote his own biography at the behest of the Recording Section of ANC Security in Angola, "we'll just have to make do with the written word."

He wished to sit down and tell Richard of his own bewilderment when he wrote his biography in Angola. The effort of trying to remember each detail of his past life. The fact that the Security comrades had the power to dismiss certain passages on paper as arrant nonsense. In a word, the powerlessness he experienced in recounting his life to strangers. Richard shot him a quick look. What was behind it? Recognition of a past kinship? Bewilderment? Gama couldn't tell. Richard then flipped the pad open, chose a pen and started writing. Gama went to the reception area, picked up the phone and ordered rolls and sandwiches, tea and coffee from the deli downstairs. Magriet put in for biscuits and cans of her favourite fizz. Obliquely, Gama recalled a television show where the black American nationalist, Stokely Carmichael, was being quizzed about his sartorial elegance. "Mr Carmichael," the unctuous interviewer, going for the jugular, asked, "how do you reconcile your Brooks Bros suit, your silk rep tie and Florsheims that must have cost a pretty penny with your verbal fusillades against, ah, American consumerism?" "Well," Stokely replied, not missing a beat, "you've got to eat while you suffer."

Richard and his father ate while they suffered; in the meantime Gama mulled over Richard's problem. In his line of work, he had dealt with numerous post-traumatic stress disorder cases. While these differed in degree and range of severity—some being referred to other institutions—the task had been made somewhat clearer and more manageable by the possibility of dialogue between therapist and patient. With Richard, Gama could not have the benefit of the sufferer's nuance, inflection or cadence of speech, nor could he seize on nonverbal clues suggested by a telltale quirk or mirrored through eyes, facial expression or body language.

But if he didn't meet this challenge, he asked himself, who would? For multitudes, the return to the mother country after years outside was as bewildering as the first experience of exile. Although quite a few had been in contact with their countrymen and women—and knew of the changes that were taking place every day—something about the actual experience of walking on the sidewalks still stained with the blood of innocent children, seeing the grim stone edifices which had financed the might that led to their flight— the unchangeable nature of a myriad of institutions—left a bitter taste in their mouths. Many, then, had evolved stratagems to redefine themselves and recreate a piece of their country in foreign lands. They played music and reminisced over moments whose glorious nature was limned by longing. To fight boredom and despair, some of the exiles sought succour in the bottle and the weed. Quite a few found salve in the arms of strangers and thus staved off the hungry beast of loneliness. Legions found that the beast existed somewhere inside themselves and could not be appeased.

It was in the eyes of their children that Gama saw how the flight from oppression to the journey back had taken its toll. Because the young would always be looking for the promised land, and that land resided in the well-being of the parents. The children were quick to learn that what they had been promised as they were readied for the homeward journey was long in coming, and the edginess of the elders would deepen their bewilderment. Those weaned on the culture of video arcades and pool halls and easy access to shopping malls would balk at having their movements restrained.

Gama's eyes were drawn to the playing-field; a ball arced high above the heads of the boys, its momentary after-image seeming like a parabola against the deep green of the trees, and bounced soundlessly on the turf. Even from the distance of his window, he could see the intentness written on the players' faces, these children, a metaphor for the glory that was yet to see the light of day. For a long while, the phrase *levelling the playing-field* had been so kneaded into the everyday language of the country that sharp township suitors were wont to employ it in their chatting-up repertoire: "Hey, sister, I wouldn't mind levelling *your* playing-field." The schoolboys, however, were concerned with neither politics nor sexual advances. Now they were playing exhibition soccer, passing the ball to one another with dazzling accuracy. Beyond them the trees seemed to groan under the midday haze which was as much a character of the city as was white to rice. On the pavilion sat a scattering of kibitzing schoolgirls, in shorts and tunics, their white T-shirts catching the sun, defining a range of the howlers' colours that spoke so eloquently of voyages, occupations and resistance. The Rainbow Nation, Archbishop Tutu had christened the children of the new South Africa. Gama wondered absently if these happy players and their reluctant supporters would ever find the pot of gold.

Of the many people who had come to the Centre on the second floor of the building, a few had left their memories clinging to the walls like wisps of smoke. There was Abner, who had been pursued by memories of storms. He told Gama that he was a rational man, but he was convinced—he saw it all—that the path to his house was lined with tombstones. He later took his life. There was Trevor, who had an obsession with doing everything right. He had stopped smoking and was by then a moderate drinker. Each time he went into his room he was convinced that someone had altered the arrangement of the furniture. This sense of displacement led to his spending long nights outside his house, staking out his domicile the way detectives keep watch over a dwelling in a contested divorce case. He would sleep in his bed and dream that someone who had taken over his body was also sleeping in a room which was a replica of his own, and was merely biding his time, waiting for the moment Trevor went into a deep sleep so that he could make the switch. At the end of the sessions, Gama had to refer him to the local School of Psychiatry. By then Trevor was absolutely sure that his room, the house and even the streets had been tampered with by someone, in his words, who wanted to fuck with his mind. There was, ah, there were so many. But this . . . Richard. . . .

Old man Nkosi finished his sandwich and gulped down his tea. Pulling Gama aside, he confided that he had taken Richard to the *inyanga* in one of the hostels of Soweto. For a week Richard had been manacled to an iron-frame bed. The *inyanga* routinely pricked him with a porcupine quill. This was supposed to expel the evil spirit that had taken over his body. He had been to the spiritualists, who had prayed for the young man, laying hands on him, engaging in rites and rituals to exorcise the demons. Because, in the understanding of the traditional healers, the young man was possessed. All these attempts at healing failed. And vast sums of money were spent in the process. "Richard trusts you," Nkosi said. "You must help him."

When he left the office for the bank and some personal errands in the city, Richard was still writing. Gama had fought the impulse to peer over the hunched shoulders for a glimpse of what must have been the most important—and painful—confession. He knew that this was Richard's private moment, even though his testimony would later be out there for Gama to read. Because, he knew, to strip oneself naked in front of others was the greatest expression of trust—and trust could not exist separately from love. When he came back, it was after two o'clock. Magriet had left for the gym. He wondered what she wanted there, really, seeing that she had the tight, trim figure scores of women immolated themselves to attain. Thinking about her, Gama experienced a hot flash of lust; but he was in the middle of a messy divorce and couldn't afford to complicate his life further. Moreover, he belonged to the school which believed that, in the words of a street poet, an African woman must cast a wide shadow.

Richard and his father had also left after rinsing the cups and consigning the remnants of their meal into a waste-basket. On the desk lay a brown manila envelope with the legend, *To Mr Gama, from Comrade Richard*, in a neat, sloping handwriting. The titles bespoke the existence of a gulf which needed breaching. Gama opened the envelope and scanned the pages, wondering whether the loss of speech also meant that Richard couldn't play music any longer. Was there any connection? Should there be a connection? Activating the answering machine, Gama chose a comfortable position and began to read.

Richard's story was at first typical. He was one of the thousands of young people who left South Africa after the slaughter of schoolchildren in Soweto and elsewhere in June 1976. He wrote like the musician he was, bringing out sight and sound in detail. His account was here and there inflected with humour, such as when he and three others crossed the Pitsane-Molapo river into Botswana. The exultation when their feet touched a piece of independent Africa. Then they saw a huge python coiled in a bundle across the path. One of the kids, who had never seen a live snake in his life, screamed, "Voetsek! Voetsek!" shooing the snake away as he would a township mongrel. Richard remembered that, before slithering into the bush, the snake shook its head as if saying, "Now I've seen everything."

If Johannesburg had been exciting and dangerous, Gaborone proved one long session of waiting. The sun beat down with a ferocious intensity, the monotonous chirping of the cicadas and the schoolchildren singing in different sharps and flats caused everything to seem as desolate as a desert. The Batswana treated the refugees with a mixture of kindness and benign contempt. In all this, Richard practised his scores and sat in with a couple of bands.

Those refugees who had not cast in their lot with the Movement milled about the President Hotel from morning to nightfall. One student from Maru a Pula, when asked what she would like to be when she finished school, said that she would like to be a refugee, who would sit and drink at the President, speak English the whole day and at the end of the month get thirty pula. This was the monthly stipend refugees received from the United Nations via the Botswana Christian Council.

A new wave of exiles came in, artists, musicians, writers. In 1977 the University of Botswana became so pivotal in cultural activity that the country sat up and took notice. Richard joined forces with trombonist Jonas Gwangwa, freshly arrived from the United States, who was putting together a contingent for FESTAC, the Festival of African and Black Arts and Culture which was to be showcased in Nigeria. It was also a period of heightened South African Security Police activity. Richard remembered standing in an immigration queue at the airport as the group of musicians and poets were on their way to Lusaka. Craig Williamson, corpulent, smug as a bedbug which battened on blood, was behind him, making small talk, a UN passport in his hand. He was to be central in the June 1985 raid on Gaborone when thirteen ANC cadres were massacred. Among them were Thami Mnyele, an artist of consummate skill, and Joe and Lindi Phahle who had been towers of strength, giving sustenance to the artistic community in many ways. "White South Africans," Richard wrote, "must not forget what has been done in their name." Gama had himself seen how, in the name of reconciliation, there was a tendency in many convocations of the good and the great to inculcate a state of national amnesia. The past, which had dripped with blood and venom as mango dripped with juice, remained unacknowledged. The silence, then, was filled with the howling of those thousands who had been wronged, who had stood at gravesides watching the earth swallow their loved ones. For these, and many more, what was not forgotten could not be forgiven. What became a piquant flavouring of this strange fruit was that many people sincerely believed that they had murdered and raped for the sake of their children. These children, then, whose collective brow was stamped with the blood of guilt, roamed, looking for comfort in arms which could bear to embrace them; this, in a world that forgot nothing.

Lagos proved an eye-opener for Richard. Here thousands of artists, united by how thoroughly the white world held them in contempt, performed and exhibited their craft. There were fire-eaters from Surinam, dancers from Harlem; the colloquia were dominated by the expulsion of Abdias do Nascimento, who had incurred the wrath of Nigerian hosts by suggesting that racism was alive and well in Brazil. Stevie Wonder performed on the same bill with Miriam Makeba at the Tafawa Balewa Square. It was on the obelisk fronting the National Theatre, all countries represented by their flags, that Richard realised that he actually had no country.

The high point of the festival was when the then ANC President Oliver Tambo and Thabo Mbeki, then ANC Chief Representative in Nigeria, visited the contingent at the FESTAC village. Tambo, who seemed preoccupied with grave matters, gave the contingent encouragement, stressing that culture played an important part in the struggle. Some of the men and women asked questions, but Richard sat, awed by the leaders' presence. That night, the South African musicians blew up a storm.

When his mother died and he could not go home to bury her, Richard grieved alone. He knew that she had loved him and now he wanted to tell her how much he loved her, too. He wanted to prove to her that he would make something of himself yet, and that he was not as full of the devil as she had thought. Her death brought to him the knowledge that he had been playing for her, that, even if the whole world would be struck deaf and dumb, she would be there to hear him. Now that she was gone, everything seemed meaningless. When playing music started losing its earlier appeal, he hit the bottle. In many instances he found himself in brawls or waking up beside a nameless stranger, his nostrils assailed by the stink of stale alcohol, bodily funk and joyless sex. A long moment of self-disgust would follow; cobwebs would clear somewhat after the first draught of Castle Lager, then the cycle would start all over again.

It was on such a morning when his mouth felt as if it housed the nest of a weaver bird when there was a knock on his door. Who could this be? he wondered. Collecting himself, he padded barefoot across the cement floor and opened the door. Two men, Keith and Scara, stood on the threshold. They looked so fresh and smelt so strongly of Lifebuoy soap that Richard felt his gorge rise. After a greeting, he reluctantly let them in. They didn't waste time telling him the reason for their visit. "Pack your things," Keith said. "There's a car waiting for you, you're going."

"Where? What?" Richard asked.

"You said you wanted to be a soldier, didn't you?" Scara asked. "People are waiting for you. Snap it up." He wrinkled his nostrils, making no attempt to conceal his irritation and impatience. Minutes later, when they were in the car, a cream Range Rover, Scara observed dryly, "Anyway, you should be happy about leaving that hole you call a room."

"That's where I live, Scara," Richard said, his face flaming. "That's where I compose my music."

"Ah, we've pricked the artist's sensitivity. Sorry."

"Cut it out, Scara," Keith said, "the man is a comrade."

Gaborone was still waking up. The streets were empty of traffic save for the occasional taxi ferrying a tourist to the Holiday Inn. The asphalt was wet, evidence of earlier rain, the early morning sun cooking up steam. It was at this moment that Richard surrendered himself to the unknown, understanding that, as of then, his life didn't belong to him. He thought fleetingly of the women he was in the process of leaving, the few friends he had made among the Batswana. In his dealing with people, something had told him to discourage intimacy. He knew that he lived in a world where alliances were tenuous and friendships flickered on and off like a candle in a storm. The shebeen queens, though, would miss him, he had been a good if combustible customer.

Gama remembered his own journey from Lesotho to Angola, via Mozambique. How Mozambique was so different from anything in southern Africa: the loud *capulana* wraps women favoured over western-style dress, the ubiquitous soldier in fatigues cradling an AK-47, the billboards and posters sporting Samora Machel smiling benignly, the soft Portuguese syllables delivered in rapid staccato. The flight to Lusaka where the trainees were processed and then taken straight to TAAG airlines. The long haul to Luanda, a city which should always be seen from the air at night. The giant picture of Agostinho Neto at February the Fourth airport—and soldiers of Fapla, Fapla everywhere, a glimpse of the élite Red Berets, their boots treading on the soil for which so much blood had been spilt.

The camps themselves spoke of the battles that had been fought, the walls of barracks and the administration block pockmarked by bullets, much like walls of firing squads. The smell of cassava, the awesome sight of a baobab tree. Here men and women submitted to the authority of the administration and the instructors. Commands delivered in English, Spanish or Russian—and the singing that went on and on as people marched to their work detail. Gama pondered over today's preoccupation with the language question; how would the new South African National Defence Force deal with commands such as "Attention!" or "Fall in!" in eleven different languages? He laughed at himself, knowing that this was a preposterous idea. As he read on, he remembered a favourite song of the camp named after one of Angola's illustrious sons, Hoji ya Henda.

> *Tambo uyawabona lamabhun' esibulala*
> *singenacal' athumelen' uMkhonto*
> *Athumelen 'uMkhonto*
> *uMkhonto we Sizwe[1]*

the trainees would sing, an exhortation for Tambo first to look at the Boers killing innocent people and then set uMkhonto we Sizwe loose upon them; singing, oblivious of the swarm of mosquitoes or bandit activity farther to the east of Malanje. Here, the children of South Africa enacted rituals which connected them to the heroes of the wars of resistance. Even if the training was hard and the instructors unyielding, something said to the trainees that, yes, they were part of a glorious legacy whose resolve would help liberate their bleeding land.

Richard took to training like a duck to water. Having finished the infantry course in Caculama, he was sent for further training to Moscow where he specialised in military combat work. Here, the instructors were hard, insisting on discipline. Even with all that, South Africans proved the truth of the maxim that you can take a *tsotsi* out of the township but you can't take the township out of a *tsotsi*. Some of the trainees managed to sneak out and carouse with buxom Russian women.

One trainee from Soweto railed against guard duty. "*Hoe kan die Russkies ons moet* guard?" he asked. "*Daar's baie Zulus hier, hulle moet* guard. *Hulle is* a nation *van mantshingelanas, mos.*" He maintained that the Zulus should be on guard duty since they were a nation of night-watchmen.

Their training done, the South Africans graduated; some were sent straight to the GDR, Richard's group flew to Luanda via Lagos. He was amazed that, after all these intervening years, the airport was still named after Murtala Mohamed. The Nigerian leader had been assassinated in a go-slow.

Angola had also not changed much. Luanda showed that, even if the Portuguese had left in anger, the city was still stamped with their presence.

---

[1] In Zulu:

> Tambo, you see those Boers killing
> Innocent people
> Assign Umkhonto (the Spear)
> The Spear of the Nation.

Apart from Kimbundu and the *trocar*-friendly slang of the Zairos, Portuguese dominated in the tavernas, at the marketplace in Kinaxixi or during the celebration of May First, the *Dia do Trabalhador*. The colourful processions by OMA, the women's movement, and UNTA, the workers' organisation, constellated into a *festa* on the Primeiro de Maio plaza. Sometimes, Richard would come across Cuban troops in their aquamarine fatigues, their AKMs strapped across their backs. The Cubans never showed any strain of being far from home. It was in Luanda, at the ANC print-shop that was run by a Finn, Markku, that Richard came across Jonas Gwangwa again. Gwangwa was heavier and quieter—and walked with a limp. He had been injured in a car accident on the streets of Luanda after an Amandla performance. When the trombonist saw Richard, his face broke into this incandescent smile. After the two men had embraced, Gwangwa said, "*My laaitie, jy's so klein en jy's klaar 'n terroris*—you're so young and already you're a terrorist."

Gama's remembrance of Angola and the role South Africans played was of a vast expanse of greenery, gigantic trees and untamed woods. The MK comrades were unlike any people he had ever come across; they were mostly uncomplaining about their lot. The long, long years in the camps. Malaria, which sometimes required that a camp functioned at half-strength. Then there were the rains that carried on interminably, making physical training a veritable torture. But in all this people maintained their humour. They sang their songs repeatedly, marching, laughing—sometimes crying—thinking of the day when they would finally lay down their heavy load. When Amandla visited some of the camps, it was carnival time. Gama remembered Richard when the group accompanied Tambo, who also acted as a conductor on special occasions. One such time was in October during the celebration of the Day of the Heroic Guerrilla. This was a ceremony of reaffirmation, a rallying of the troops. Richard looked gaunt, the saxophone seeming a heavy load in his hands. It was when he straddled the instrument and blew notes that had neither beginning nor end that it was clear that the man possessed and was possessed by his instrument. He blew with his head canted to the side as if waiting for a corroboration from the rhythm section. When it came, it was as if he had been pulled from a long and endless darkness onto steady ground.

Amandla toured several European capitals; they went to Brazil and returned with stories about women who were incredible. In the ensemble, Richard had finally found a home. But this elation was short-lived. In 1984 a mutiny broke out and he was in the detachment assigned to defend Pango. It was the first time he had been involved in action; it dismayed him that this action was against his own people, no matter how misguided they might have been. For many nights, he thrashed and writhed under the assaults of nightmares, the images of bone shards, gristle and gore and brain tissue staying with him in all his waking hours. *Brother, brother*, he would sing in his head, *there's just too many of you dying.* . . .

When the group went to Sweden, he had to remain because he was laid low with malaria. On recovering, he was told to pack his things. Then he was on a flight to Zambia, Lusaka. He worked with the Security Department, ensconced in Libala. It was in Lusaka that he met Nozi.

By Richard's own admission, Nozi was a woman brought by gods to save him from himself. Small and sinewy, Nozi challenged him when he was slack, encouraged him when he began to falter. She would laugh at him when he hummed for her snatches of tunes he had composed, her face transformed by her joy. Since she worked for the underground structures, they hardly had time together. The few moments they had, they enjoyed to the full. They decided to get married. The ceremony was at the Lusaka Civic Centre, where a slow-speaking Marriage Officer pronounced them man and wife. Nozi continued with her work, crossing the border from Botswana into South Africa. She set up dead-letter boxes for messages and arms caches. Then some of the comrades were captured, but Nozi managed to escape back to base.

It was in her eyes that he saw there was trouble. She remained in Lusaka for six months, and she was sure that she had been grounded. He was with her in 1989 when Walter Sisulu and seven other leaders were released from Robben Island. In January 1990, Nozi told him that she was again assigned to go inside. That night their lovemaking was full of sweetness tinged with unutterable pain. She held him as they rocked and rocked, both cursing the possibility of the hour of departure. As she cried out, Nozi gazed into his eyes as if engraving his face on the substrate of her memory.

A month passed without word from her. Then the ANC was unbanned and Nelson Mandela was released. Confusion reigned in Lusaka, where some of the comrades felt they had been left without direction. For those whose lives had depended on the continuation of the struggle, it was a moment of decision. Many applied to go to school, knowing that the future dispensation would have no role for them. Others girded their loins and readied for a long war of destabilisation which they knew the dying regime would wage. Richard was sent home in the same contingent with Oliver Tambo. He recalled the tumult at Jan Smuts Airport when the Old Man walked out of the Zambian craft, the women ululating, the workers pausing in the middle of serving, and running all the way to the tarmac. Then there was the

Consultative Conference at Nasrec, the first sighting of Mandela. He could not express his joy.

He stayed in the country long after the conference, scouring township after township, knocking on doors, looking for Nozi. A year passed, then another. Even when the thought came that she might be dead, he banished it. For some reason, Richard was convinced that she would never die without giving him a sign.

By day he worked in the ANC Security Department at Shell House in Plein Street; by night he jammed with musicians in the city. This routine was interrupted by preparations for the elections. Day in and day out he worked with other cadres, visiting the flashpoints of violence, trying to bring sanity to communities that were certainly going off the rails. The elections came and went; at the victory celebrations at the Carlton Hotel, Richard, who wished Nozi were with him to share the moment of glory, got motherlessly drunk.

On the morning after election victory, Richard was still nursing an evil hangover when he heard a knock on the door. On opening, he saw two comrades; this filled him with a strange sense of déjà vu. "Come in," he said. His room was a mess.

One of the men, Steve, Richard knew, had worked in Ordnance. He was a tall Indian fellow with an infectious grin. Today he was quite grim. His partner, Tebego, worked with the Military Headquarters.

"Comrade Richard," Steve said after sitting down, "I guess we have some bad news for you." He glanced at Tebego, who was still standing, cradling a satchel. "We've brought you some of Nozi's things."

Richard experienced the kind of fear which left him numb. "Where is she?"

"She's dead, Com," Tebego put in softly. "We were with her in Special Ops. This was the time when we were in Natal. She was caught up in an ambush."

"An ambush," Richard echoed, failing to comprehend. "Why wasn't I told?"

"It was difficult." Steve's uneasiness increased. "You see, at the time of her death she was under suspicion. One of the comrades had branded her, said she was working for the Boers. I guess, her going out and trying to pull an operation single-handedly was her way of absolving herself."

"But," Richard said, "Nozi was a careful person. Surely, she couldn't just go out on a mission unprepared. . . ?" He let the sentence trail off. When he next looked into their eyes, he saw a flicker, a subterranean message communicated by the two men. He was then hit by a realisation which left his mouth dry. "Why don't you tell me the truth?" he asked. "She was set up, wasn't she?"

"That's what we suspect," Tebego said. "Comrades are still investigating. She must have been killed trying to find the real enemy agent in our unit. There are lots of people whose deaths still need checking. Unfortunately, at the moment people are still caught up in all these commissions."

All these years. All these deaths. He thought of the sacrifices men and women had made; the betrayals which had led some of the best warriors in the land to a bloody end. Quite a few were interred in graves without headstones, unknown and unmourned in inaccessible sites.

"Sorry, Com," Tebego said with real tenderness. Then he handed a stunned Richard the satchel. "This is where she kept her notes. I'm sorry that we had to read everything."

"When did this happen?"

"In February 1990, just before they announced the unbanning of the Movement." Steve seemed as if he were close to tears.

"Four years," Richard said atonally. "Four fucking years and you chose to tell me now. . . ." He couldn't remember when or how the two men left. He was in a daze for the whole day. In the afternoon, he ventured out of his Berea flat into scenes of jubilation. Thousands of people on the streets, even foreigners, all exulting in one of the greatest victories of the century. He went back inside, sat down and emptied the contents of the bag on the tangled sheets. Journals, notebooks. A letter in an envelope, dated simply 1990.

Dear Richard

I don't know where you are and in what frame of mind you might be when this letter reaches you, if it reaches you. I am all right in body and I guess that doesn't say much for my spirit. Certain things have happened here. I have been happy in my work and the comrades have been great. There is a small matter which all of us have to face as revolutionaries. It happens, now and then—and people sometimes pay a heavy price for this—that one falls under suspicion. In my case, I know that what is being whispered is not true. I love my country. I love the cause I have dedicated my life to serving.

There will possibly be a time when these nightmares will have become mere memory of a terrible chapter in the book of our life. Then I will tell you the whole story, or parts of the story because, who knows? No one alive will ever know the whole truth. In the meantime, know that I love you and cherish you. I only wish that you will understand, sometimes, when things don't turn out the way we wanted them.

Love,

N.

Richard flung the letter on the bed and howled and howled until his Mozambican neighbour broke down the door. They bundled him into a car and sped straight to Hillbrow Hospital. Since the doctors couldn't find anything physically wrong with him, they released him. By then he had lost the power of speech.

The phone rang. Gama heard the click as the machine answered. Then a voice: "Hi, Leonard, it's Thembi. I hope you haven't forgotten. . . ." Gama sprang to his feet and snatched the receiver from the cradle.

"Thembi, hi," he said, speaking above Magriet's clipped syllables. "Sorry about this. How are you?"

"I'm okay," the disembodied voice said. "What's with the answering machine? Skiving off today?"

"No such luck. No rest for the wicked." He glanced at his wristwatch. "Jesus. Is it four already? Tell you what. Why don't you wait for me at The Yard of Ale. Get a drink and I'll meet you there. Then we can see the exhibition."

"Don't stand me up, Leonard Gama," Thembi said, "'cause if you think you know wrath, you haven't experienced mine."

"No, nothing like that. I need to talk to you."

"Can't talk now, I suppose? Client confidentiality?"

"Something like that."

"Okay. See you in a while." The line went dead.

Gama pondered over the exchange, cursing himself for the arrangement with Thembi. He had told himself that it was nothing, a case of like-minded people coming together and enjoying each other's company. Women still made him uneasy, he could never be sure where he stood with them. There were many cases where he had thought that everything was on the level and things had turned out otherwise. There were many women he had wounded. He certainly wanted to treat Thembi with respect, allow their friendship to bloom without complications. But then, he said to himself, Johannesburg had turned many a lonely person into a predator.

Stuffing Richard's papers into his attaché case, he switched off the lights and locked the office. On the way to the bank of lifts, he heard the booming of music from the adjoining studio. As he proceeded to the lift, he heard a sound not dissimilar to the whine of a distant mosquito; then four young men came out of the studio, singing in harmony. They were dressed in hip-hop gear and sported the high-top hair-do. These were to be the South African version of Boyz II Men. Gama admired their youthful enthusiasm. Nodding, he wished them luck. It was a tough world.

Richard temporarily forgotten, Gama concentrated on the road, giving the mini-bus taxis a wide berth. It was strange that these vehicles with bumper stickers proclaiming peace were driven by men not famous for peaceful activities. Just that afternoon, a mini taxi war had broken out in the city with a shoot-out in Bree Street, three dead. What amazed him was the resilience of the passengers who were squashed like sardines: what terrifying images went on in their minds? he wondered. But what really bothered him and raised his hackles was the lack of courtesy on the road, the big bozos in their German cars travelling at a hundred deaths an hour, cutting in front, only to be stopped by a red light. These should be exiled to Lagos, thought Gama, see how they deal with them go-slow apples. The idea of red-faced yuppies flailing their arms in the midst of an indifferent, treacle-slow traffic cheered him somewhat. That the traffic issue was a mess and public transport the pits could not be overstated. There was already a long queue on President Street, Friday people waiting patiently to get out of town. Poor Mac, Gama thought of what the Transport Minister had inherited. What does he make of all this?

As he pulled up into the parking area of the Market Theatre, he saw posters and banners announcing the opening of an art exhibition. Gama knew that art was supposed to play a part in therapy; how would he start introducing Richard to that regime? Immobilising the car before locking it, he scanned the late afternoon throng around the Market precinct. Wits-type men and women slumming it among the natives brushed shoulders with tourists who fought hard to disguise what they were. They were given away by their feet encased in grey socks under thong Jesus-style sandals, no different from cops in *mufti* being betrayed by their brown, size-eleven shoes. By their feet, Gama mused, ye shall know them.

The majority of the clientele patronising The Yard of Ale consisted of artists, playwrights, actors, singers and dancers. For members of the public, this was a favourite watering hole to visit while waiting for the shows to start. The atmosphere was usually pleasant, the drinks outdoors bringing to mind the pubs of London. Farther on along the paved area stood Kippies, which catered for the music lovers. It was closed today, for repairs. The gallery was next door to the pub; a knot of men and women in evening dress moved desultorily towards the entrance, invitation cards in hand. Gama espied Thembi at one of the tables near the door. She caught his eye and waved him over. She kept her eyes on him until he sat down across from her.

Although Thembi exhibited the confidence which came with her calm beauty, Gama knew that she could be very tentative in dealing with people. She was tall, angular—My Masai princess, Gama thought apropos of nothing—her height accentuated by her long neck. She wore her head in braids at whose ends was an assortment of coloured beads. Thembi was beautiful in that cold, distant manner discouraging to most men, with an ebony, chiselled face, large eyes and full lips which glistened with lip gloss. As she moved her hands, rows of gold bangles clattered; these set off her kaftan patterned in earth colours on a mother-of-pearl field. She regarded him with a mixture of kindness and humour.

"Hard day, huh?" she asked, taking a sip from a tall glass.

"You're telling me." Gama looked round. At a table across, a lively discussion over the merits of a new lager was on. The occupants, in a slightly advanced state of inebriety, were united in their endorsement of the old lagers. This new stuff, someone put in, tasted like a horse's piss. A pregnant horse at that, another wit added. The hapless salesman, sobered by this harsh judgement, collected his cans to try his luck among drinkers some two tables away.

"Bet you're happy you're not that guy," Thembi said. "That's a *kak* way to earn a living, trying to introduce those jackasses to a new product. . . ."

"Maybe the guy's sales pitch stinks," Gama said. "South Africans might be creatures of habit, but they know a good thing when they see one."

"Except in the Cape, of course," Thembi said, trying to catch a waiter's attention. "Those wouldn't know a good thing if it was served on a platter with their breakfast cereal. Shit, they made sure that Hernus Kriel became the only white *bwana* on the African continent."

At first, Gama was puzzled by the bitterness in her tone until he remembered that Thembi was originally from Cape Town. "Well," Gama said, "one day they'll remember District Six, and the vote that was taken away from them by the Nats. Maybe some will also remember with fondness all the callipers used to measure the breadth of the nose, and those pencils the Boers shoved into their hair to determine whether or not they were white."

"It's all that mountain air," Thembi said, flicking her wrist dismissively. "Maybe it's got chemicals which can turn activists into non-whites . . . ah, here comes the Messiah to deliver us from the drought."

They placed their orders. While they waited for their whiskeys, Thembi quizzed Gama on the progress of the divorce. It was a painful subject, one he would have preferred to avoid. But there was no side-stepping Thembi. She had a knack for extracting confessions that would have stood her in good stead with the Security Branch of yore. Briefly he told her that his wife was up in arms, wanting to take him to the cleaners, saying that he earned more than he had disclosed.

"Says I'm on the gravy train," Gama said, shaking his head. "If people really knew how much I get . . . it's sidewalk soup."

"Thin sidewalk soup," Thembi supplied, rearing her head and letting out a ripple of laughter.

"It's not funny."

Their drinks came. Gama and Thembi toasted each other and listened to the silences inside themselves. The time came to go to the gallery. Inside, they found men and women resplendent in their finery, celebrating the undying tradition of art. The artist, a young man from Sebokeng, wore a white shirt under a blue blazer, a pair of grey slacks and a pair of trainers. He seemed ill at ease, not at all the flavour of the month. His paintings depicted scenes from everyday life in the troubled East Rand: barricades, the graffiti of hope and rage against a backdrop of burnt houses and blazing bodies. The critics and the art lovers were united in fulsome praise, all marvelling at the artist's unerring eye for detail, strong lines and exquisite executions. The lights danced above the coiffured, moussed or permed heads of the gallery patrons, investing them with the fire which burnt in the young man's imagination. When Gama and Thembi came across him at the drinks table, he was tearing at chicken wings and washing them down with red wine. He confessed that he hadn't had a square meal in two days. He also had no transport. The two passed him a fifty-rand note. Thereafter, Thembi and Gama decided to tear themselves away from the appreciative crowd.

Later, they sat and ordered more drinks. The experience in the gallery had left them with a great disquietude. It was as if they had gazed upon a mirror which reflected all the unflattering aspects of their selves. Because, Gama asked himself, what have we done for the artists? For the Richards of the world who come and expose the more unpalatable features of our society and are then left alone to groan under the weight of discovery? We patronise them with exhibitions and gigs where they are paid paltry sums by a bloodless clientele which reaches an orgasm over a glimpse of how the other world lives. That other world does not live, it dies. It dies from the accumulated rage which renders it mute, where it sees the eyes of children without a future and women without hope begging on the streets, some with cardboard placards bearing the legend of the wretched. It lives in hospital wards where abused infants with broken limbs stare and stare in mute horror at the havoc adults are capable of wreaking.

"You're angry," Thembi said. She covered his hand. "Is it about the exhibition or is there something you wish to tell me?"

Gama felt on the verge of a breakdown. When he told her about Richard, he was actually telling her the story of his own life. He knew as he talked that he was also undergoing a therapy session that all South Africans, the guilty and the innocent, should undergo. Richard, he convinced himself, would be given the kind of occupational therapy befitting a musician. Gama saw the whole process unfolding before him, how music would be used to evoke memory and stimulate imagination. He would hold him, Richard, a brother, and tell him that there were people out there who loved him and who would make sure that, if he stumbled, they would hold him. Gama would remind Richard of his mother who had died while Richard was confronting himself in exile, and that, wherever she might be, she also loved him. There were many people, men and women, who would be there to walk the long road with him. The people would rejoice with him when a moment of joy presented itself, and they would weep with him, too, because Richard was of their flesh and their blood.

Some of the women, their walk and the way they carried themselves—the lilting laugh and the cadence of their speech—would remind him of Nozi. Gama would tell him that, yes, all the women involved in struggle are Nozi. They are there, these women, in the shacks of our country, trying to maintain their dignity in the face of abuses; they are there in hospitals, looking upon the eyes of men, women and children who have been ruined by disease and poverty. They are there, these women, singing their sad songs as they bury their loved ones cut down at a tender age by our collective cowardice. They will be there at the victory hour, when poverty and strife, pestilence and death are finally eradicated from our soil—and it is not a blasphemy to love them, but the highest tribute to Nozi's memory. Some of the sessions would be painful, as when he would let Richard re-experience the trauma, but he, Gama, would make him feel safe. We will play music together, he said to himself, and improvise. At the end, we'll let ourselves go.

Hot tears sprang into his eyes and streamed freely down his cheeks. Thembi leant forward and dabbed at his face with a tissue. "Let's get to my place," she murmured. Before he could respond, she shook her head. "We don't have to do anything."

The hubbub of drinkers and diners and the clink of glasses, the soft strains of piped music from somewhere inside the pub, the roar of traffic along Market Street punctuated by an angry blast of a hooter, the whispering wind which deepened the gathering of shadows and segued into the soft footfalls on the paved ground, the wail of a distant saxophone solo, the siren signalling the dawn of a new life or the dripping urgency of an expiring one, all cohered into a savage symphony of joy, a feature without which the Market region would die.

"Yes," Gama said. "Let's go."

Telegraph to the Sky

SANDILE DIKENI ▼▼▼▼▼▼▼▼▼▼▼▼▼▼▼▼▼▼▼▼▼▼▼▼▼▼▼▼▼▼▼▼▼▼▼

Stay with me
when the sun rises
from a western sky
with silver spears lashing
at earth and our youth
when the eastern horizon
hangs smoke
as celebration to a fading dream.
Will you take my blistered hand
to a kiss?
That journey
between reflex action
and conviction
where moments flash
from substance to emotion
and where we count seconds as instinct
we live in times where we are against time
and impulse rules over us
as undirected, unelected factor
we live cliché as fact
and fact is cliché
to the one beat of change.

Will you stay with me
when I have no more hallelujahs
to your name
and instead offer dallilahs
to your anonymity
when my knees refuse to bend at your beauty
but my eye of growth
raises an altar to your soul
that power that dreams awake
the Brazilian forest
or in its strength of wish
reawakens our dead
at Kassinga, Biafra
or wherever your heart lives
among the innocent dead.

Will you really
stay with me
when I stand up
and sing to the world
its magnitude
its greatness
for an ability to turn itself
upside down
while the inhabitants still believe
in its constancy

unaware
that their heads are facing downwards.

Nowadays
they don't hang you by the neck
till you die.
They dangle you by the feet
till the blood comes to the brain.
It's a high feeling that makes you reach for sky
but touch earth as limit
as ecstasy
of reaching some end
because some journeys are so long
and much longer
when you live in a dream forest
called poetry.

They say
it is not by bread alone that we live.
I know.
It is by poetry alone that we survived.
With poetry dancing on our tongues
we wiped the blood from our mouths
we charmed our torturers
we dangled freedom bells on our shackles
we made music out of sirens
we made homes out of prisons
we redesigned parliaments out of corrugated iron
we petrol bombed our angry past
we blasted our martyrs out of our brains

and we made shrines out of their graves
we wove forgiveness onto our T-shirts
and with last remaining droplets of blood
we tried to paint peace on angry dark skies
we silenced our solitude
we mated our humility with our anger
with hammers and chisels
we punched hope deep into our hearts
we swam, we danced and we played water games in our tears
and now,
now we wave flags so bright
sometimes brighter than our future
but stay with me.

Stay with me
when the jungle has no tree
when the wind has no breath
when the rain has no sea
the desert has no sand
the stars have no eyes to see
God has no mercy
and the devil is making barbecue out of the land.
Now, will you stay with me?

Stay, so that we sing
songs from experience
we sing, ideas from consciousness
and let's cultivate destiny
from the bareness of this,
this history.
Stay with me.

Will you?
Please?

Rituals for Martha

Zachariah Rapola ▼▼▼▼▼▼▼▼▼▼▼▼▼▼▼▼▼▼▼▼▼▼▼▼▼▼▼▼▼▼

Mmarita gave birth to her first child when she was seventeen. That did not cause a scandal in a township where sex was an addiction and child-bearing nothing unusual among fourteen- to eighteen-year-olds. The fact that most of the new-borns were girls soothed most families because of the prospects of lobola. At least, that's what I thought until, after my marriage, I started attending weddings (only occasionally, for weddings were indeed a rarity in our township), funerals, and burial society meetings. I was a neighbour of Mmarita's parents.

It was always the younger participants who exhibited irritation at Burial Society meetings. Understandably so, when agenda items would be sacrificed so that the old people could indulge in their laments. Who could blame the young for becoming irritated with this, for it was they and their peers who were the chief subjects of these dirges. Fathers moaned about sons who were lazy and seemed to enjoy no occupation except fathering kids. Mothers bemoaned their daughters, whose heads were only filled with boys, whose cleverness was only realised in dark alleys where they let boys strain the tissues of their firm breasts until they were left sagging. Who could blame those old people for lamenting when girls forgot to kindle fires at five o'clock, forgot to attend to their pots around six or seven and wasted precious time and youth staring into the eyes of boys. . . ?

> What! Not only boys. Wena! Those girls
> are wanton. They are not ashamed of stripping
> a man old enough to be their father.
>
> Not during our times, Mmawena.
>
> Ohoo! Do you think there are any men left
> around? These boys are not scared of leaving
> a child with a suckling baby.

It was a perpetual circle. Fathers blaming mothers, and mothers blaming fathers. Each accusing the other of either spoiling or not teaching the children manners. Sometimes those accusations and counter-accusations resulted in beatings. Some of these developed into fist-fights as more and more women started asserting their independence. Those fights at times made their way into our local newspaper. And we would relish the stories, at times even making press cuttings which we would photocopy and circulate.

But at the same time, peace was quickly forged:

> How am I expected to cope. I am supporting not only my own children, but broods of those little bastards, whose mothers and fathers don't know the meaning of "Support."

> Let alone "work." How many of them have ever experienced the tyranny of waking up at four o'clock every weekday for a full nineteen-year stretch. . . .

> Don't you wonder why they settle for "Vat en Sit." Useless bastards—can't afford lobola.

> Hear this one: my son asked for money to buy bread the other day. You know what I said to him: "Buti! You are a man. If you can so quickly master child-making, boy! You are man enough to learn the art of money-making."

> Yours is better, Rra Tommy. Mine is always borrowing money for taxi fares—to where?
> I don't know. So yesterday he came again: "Eer . . . Ou Lady, ke vraiza tiger daa. . . ."
> "What?" I said.
> "Can you lend me ten rands," he repeated.
> "Hau! You surprise me. Wasn't it you last week who was boasting about having bought a leather suit worth three thousand rands?"
> Hee! After that he tucked his tail between his legs and disappeared.

Sometimes those conversations, or rather laments, would be punctuated with roars of laughter. And at a distance one would think the old people were enjoying the rewards of life.

As I have already said, Mmarita's child-bearing did not cause a scandal. Though what it led to some years later would be a scandal of unparalleled proportions in the whole township. A dozen daring priests introduced it into their sermons. Burial Society meetings would always digress from their agendas to ponder that scandal.

But why begin at the end ? Mmarita's real name was Martha, but everybody called her Mmarita, an Africanized version of Martha. Her aunt, Aunty Pheladi, who was known to have been schooled only up to standard three, was said to be the source of this name change. She was also known to be possessed by ancestral spirits. It was said that this would have led to her becoming a diviner or medium, but then she failed her initiation rituals. She was then advised by her muti mentor to select somebody in the family, preferably a female, to replace her. And she chose Mmarita.

When Mmarita was a pretty little baby, her mother composed a lullaby for her:

> *Mmarita—yoo, Mmarita—*
> *Kgarebe tsa geso di sa yo tansa*
> *dikgekolo le dikgarebe di—*
> *boa ka madila. . . .*
> *Kgarebe tsa geso di sa you tansa masogana le baditi*
> *ba boa ka dikosa-thunsa-lerule*
> *Mmarita—yoo, Mmarita—*
> *Kgadi-ya-Mma tsea lebese.*[1]

That song is now forgotten. The voices that used to render it are tuneless. The ears that used to rapture to its soothing melodies are now deaf, sealed by the oily wax that has been accumulating since childhood. The song was forgotten even as Mmarita grew up, her ears readjusting to other frequencies, the rasping voices of males.

The bearers of those voices came with different presentations—some sly and evasive, some soft and suggestive, others confident and persuasive, others confused and hesitant. But their tune was the same. In time her curiosity was fuelled when she would hear older women laughing:

> Hahaa! Ora Jacky. He couldn't even finish one sentence without biting his tongue. . . .

> Not my Ruben—that one! On our first night together he kept on rushing to the toilet with a running stomach. I took pity on the poor thing and pretended to fall asleep. And you know what, the poor thing came creeping to bed . . . and had a peaceful sleep. The running stomach miraculously cured.

Mmarita took up with one boy of sixteen. She wondered how the "poor thing" would make his proposition. She wondered how he would behave on

---

[1] In a combination of Sotho, Tswana, and Pedi:

Mmarita—oh—Mmarita
Our young girls have gone for a dance
Old women and some of the girls are drowning themselves in liquor
Our girls have gone dancing
Young men and mountain school graduates are stomping the ground in song and dust
Mmarita—oh—Mmarita
Mummy, baby come feed on milk.

their first night together. By then she was twelve. It was at this stage that Aunty Pheladi resolved to start preparing her niece for her future role. It was appropriate that she inform the girl what it entailed undergoing initiation as a medium and getting approval of the ancestors. The first rule was chastity—chastity until the trainee graduates. One had to observe a strict code of abstinence at certain times.

Of course those were extremely complex issues for a girl who savoured soap operas, her favourites being "Loving" and "The Bold and the Beautiful." No sexual contact the night before attending to a patient. . . . Ridge and Brook drowning in passion . . . no lustful thoughts when attending to male patients. . . . Ava and Jack smouldering with desire . . . and she was to be a vessel for ancestral spirits!

It seemed Aunty Pheladi never properly communicated her choice of Mmarita to the ancestors, for no ancestral communiqués were transmitted to Mmarita. She carried on with her life like any other fourteen-year-old. She marvelled at seeing her breasts swell. She panicked at seeing blood flow out of her body, until her cousin introduced her to sanitary pads. Thus she graduated from a township "sqwaka," who use folds of toilet paper, to an "ousie." She then naturally stopped talking about boys with girls who still used folded toilet paper. She also started curling her hair, and wearing jeans.

All these things started troubling Aunty Pheladi.

> "Aowa, don't worry. She's simply sampling life," said one of Mmarita's neighbours.

> Mma-wena! All mothers always say that—She's sampling life—next time you see them, eyes rolling in their sockets, belly swelled and their tongue stiff in their palates.

How sad and true it was. More and more of them would swell and bulge, the sad reality fermenting inside them. It was at such times that parents acknowledged that lobola was as elusive as a son-in-law. It was also at such times that they awakened to the fact that little Dorah or Phuti or Lerato was a failure. The girls, in turn, confirmed their failure as parents. And their parents would wait for the next burial society meeting, silently rehearsing their sad tales. There they would bow their heads as they listened to each other pouring out sorrows and disappointment in their daughters—on whom they had placed all their hopes. Some would lament the price society was paying for its drive to progress. And all would wish they had only sons. At that, parents whose sons were culprits would pretend their ears were itching and would start scratching them with match sticks or grass stalks until that part of the conversation was over.

Mmarita started evening excursions, supposedly to attend neighbourhood Group Studies. The shine that permeated her face on her return would always tell another story, though.

> Mmarita ngwanaka, please my child, take care.
> You are the only one I and your father have.
> Not all the sweet melodies in the valleys
> originate from the lips of larks. Always
> remember that malnourished snakes also
> learn to sing so to entice their prey. And some
> of them appear in the form of men.

Of course, Mmarita repeated her mother's counselling to her friends. They burst into laughter. One or two of them repeated the words to their boyfriends. Their boyfriends did not laugh, though. They merely stroked their darlings affectionately, and repeated with emphasis the need for them to be open and confide in each other—as true lovers are supposed to.

Throughout the neighbourhood, the girls' "Hihihiii!" would be heard. Then the boys' "Kwa-kwaaakwaaaa!," a near sadistic laugh that emanated from fragile vocal chords already starting to rust from cigarette and alcohol abuse.

The young people in our township did not regard making love while standing as a disgrace. But the older people viewed it with contempt.

> "What kind of an offspring will come out
> of such copulation?" they used to sneer.

And because of that they always insisted that young people should wait until after marriage. But time, to young people, was anathema. It was as if they suspected that death would rob them of the pleasures that love had in store. There was also the fact that fornication was a non-existent word in their vocabulary.

Mmarita got tired of her sixteen-year-old boyfriend. She gave the reason that she was tired of "hitchhiking," for that is how young people in our township called vertical lovemaking. She also confided in her friends that she was bored with her young lover's lovemaking:

> A ke sa di kena, he is always nervous, hurried and
> repeatedly looking and ready to run whenever he
> hears or sees someone approaching.

How could he not? He was not sure of when Mmarita's mother or father would apprehend them. Or when one of the older "toughies" would bump on them, pump a bullet through his head before "jackrolling" his Mmarita.

In his place she got herself a taxi driver. Luckily he owned a backyard shack, which proved cosy for their intimate sessions. Like all girls of her generation, and those before, and probably even those to come, she knew it was hard to come by a millionaire in the townships, but divine intervention could still deliver her own personal chauffeur. Besides, Mmarita had to get herself a taxi driver boyfriend because all her friends had one. For them it confirmed graduation into a higher social order. Of course this group looked down upon those who still dated schoolboys, even if they used sanitary pads and curled their hair as well. What was the bait? A mini skirt? Tight-fitting pants? A pretty face? Wrong! Every girl growing up knew the mentality of taxi drivers. Play-act coyness and delicacy. And frequent their haunts. Mmarita followed that to the letter. And so she got her "lunch boy."

As punctual as his nickname, her taxi driver would appear every school day around lunch time, bearing a package of Chicken Licken or Kentucky. Later on she informed him that the now-thing was Nando's. That added an extra four kilometers of detour from his main route. But, like any solicitous lover, he endured. His Sundays were given over to transporting her and her friends to Moretela Park. He knew it was one detour the taxi owner wouldn't have taken to kindly, but the yearning lover in him instilled a sense of adventure and boldness.

And the old people continued with their laments.

> This Moretela Park of theirs! Kare, it is their new-found church.

> I say they can't even afford merge lobola, but are wasteful on these Moretela Park outings of theirs.

Who could blame the old people? Theirs was an era long effaced from the brow of reality, an illusion they occasionally brought back to life in their memory, a rainbow diluted by the tears of lamenting gods.

What a shame! Indeed, the girl who was at the forefront of a generation of fornicators was tired of vertical lovemaking. She need not have spurned it though, for that was exactly the position she would be in three years later when she conceived. The physical features of her baby confirmed speculation that children conceived vertically suffered defects. Just to be sure, dozens of people thronged over to her place to see the baby.

Afterwards some of them started spreading the rumour that at birth the infant had been as upright as a reed. Some even said his little penis maintained an erection, which collapsed soon after someone mentioned the little bastard's father by name.

Agaa! Who can believe those township gossip-mongers.

The first reaction of Aunty Pheladi on hearing that Mmarita was pregnant was to consider rushing her for an abortion. But then she recalled that nothing can be hidden from the ancestors. And she knew that her pretty niece was lost.

Like Jezebel! Like Lot's wife! She will suffer the vengeance of the gods.

And there was nothing mortal man could do to save her. All diviners shied away from her. For they declared tampering with her would be akin to challenging the ancestors.

Like Prometheus, her heart would feed the wild birds of prey. Like Joan of Arc, her flesh and bones would rekindle the greatest bonfire.

I was one of the many sceptics about these prophecies of doom. We were justified in that. Hadn't we grown up on the precipice of apocalypse, orated by Watch Tower evangelists throughout the years? Warnings that have not only proved wrong, but also turned the messengers into buskers, and their testimony into a mockery. I held firmly to my doubts until 1982. That is when I saw a man being roasted with three tyres around him. Later I saw mongrels fighting over parts of his charred remains. Then I realised that certain things are realised with the maturity not of time, but of perception.

Like all reluctant grandparents, Mmarita's parents had a grudging fondness for their grandchild. Fate decided that they would become his legal guardians, for a couple weeks after the birth Mmarita was knocked over by a car on her way from "Kwa Muhle," where she had gone to file a paternity suit. Her taxi driver disappeared, and resurfaced months later, driving around with one of her friends.

Initially we thought she had been committed to an institution. But no— it was only that she was never seen venturing out except at night. It was Aunt Pheladi though, who ended up at Witkoppen. It started with her exclaiming the tragic fate of her niece. When two hours had elapsed with her still mumbling the same words, a sangoma was called. After a couple of minutes with the patient, she told the family that there was nothing she could do.

A long consultation followed. Some of the relatives recommended taking her to Giyane, others said Mozambican muti men were better equipped to handle such a case. It was at the mention of taking her to Phafula, great muti men in the Northern Transvaal, that Aunt Pheladi stood up and bolted. Two days later the traffic police apprehended her marching up and down Ben Schoeman Highway. She was naked and still lamenting the fate of her niece.

The first sighting of Mmarita, or rather her silhouette, occurred at twenty to nine on the night of the twelfth of April 1987. It was on the eighth anniversary of her self exile into darkness.

Her son, Kgetsi, was then, of course, eight years old. It was as though she had never existed for him. Whenever asked about her, he would always respond by mentioning his grandmother.

"No—I mean your mother, your real mother."

He would pause, thinking the question again: "Mmmm-my mother, she is at work. She does washing and ironing piece jobs. . . ."

Kgetsi didn't suffer a complex though, as most people feared. He was an adventurous, daring boy. Maybe that is what proved to be the cause of his downfall. Together with other boys his age, he would taunt and jeer at young girls their age. That was understandable. They were past the age of playing husbands and wives, fathers and mothers with those girls. And they asserted their "bigness" by the girls. Their play-time was now preoccupied with TV heroes like Zorro and McGuyver. However, they always got confused when those heroes of theirs exhibited attraction to pretty women. This dilemma was solved by the bright Kgetsi. He called a council and reviewed the play rules. He employed his eloquence to win over the other boys' doubts. Soon his proposal was taken by all.

> Yaa! There is Mantwa. There is Zodwa. There is Thembi. From today they will be our women.

And he chose for himself the fairest Zodwa. She was nine then.

On the sly he got the girls to accompany them to a run-down abandoned house. There they had the time of their childhood. Playing familiar and recently invented games . . . until the beckoning of the serious one, of copulation, which men and women play in their bedrooms.

It was probably curiosity that led Zodwa to take off her panties. It was probably the same curiosity that led Kgetsi to take off his underpants. "Let us do it like they always do on TV."

They were still marvelling at the strange and funny sensation of each other's bodies when Mmarita pounced on them. She went for Kgetsi's throat and started squeezing. It was the first time in eight years that she had ventured out in broad daylight while her parents were at work. Trailing behind her were some of the neighbours.

When they managed to free the little boy from her grip he was already unconscious and frothing. Later, the neighbours saw his limp body being hoisted onto a stretcher by frantic ambulance attendants. Still later, they told the police they had first been alerted by Mmarita's screaming:

"Get off me . . . get off meee!"

Habari Gani Africa Ranting

LESEGO RAMPOLOKENG ▼▼▼▼▼▼▼▼▼▼▼▼▼▼▼▼▼▼▼▼▼▼▼▼▼▼▼

(eureka europe gathers the dust of a fallen berlin wall
africa rolls in the mud of its tropical brain-fall)
habari gani africa
so free & unconscious where you sit
drowning in complacence's shit
a national situation it's universal station top of the pops
pulled off the shelf when the rand drops
it takes a self-exultation\struggle ticket to ride the train
fortune-wheels in cranial rotation
slaves of example now masters of spectacle
hoarding seed crushed in loins labour broken
his/her/its imperial majestic(k) token
vacuum cleaning out a skull turning the brain cocaine
spliffing powdered bone/membrane rolled up in a dollar bill
terms of revolution's dictation not for the negotiation seal

habari gani africa
government's hammering & anvilling consent
quoted out of pavlovian con-text
self aggrandisement's god complex in ascent
self-eulogises til images of own creation believe the guise
soulthiefblindbelief demonsermonmindrelief gnu consciousness
in bloodstreams loo crass reflections of pork righteousness
nation's birth's midwife's face upon currency
wrath's head stamping the image-making of democracy
historical revamping drumbeating politicking
upon a slime bomb's ticking
bent-backing for international mother fucking
epiloguing your orifices puckering to nuclear waste puking

habari gani africa
operation eradication death movement's in stealth
declaration of good intention by tin-godly decree
poverty's amelioration a military spending spree of corpse-wealth
morality's education for the living in health
a spiritual fulfilment read the gospel of saint general
in the satan staple book-write of denial

smiles of mirror practise/tv screen cosmetise flies on disease
spotlights out on melting americanised scream/ice-cream expression
& fatsweat's a sweet taste to thirst of emaciation
dark incontinent orwellian sequence content in emancipation
liesmacks soundtrack the powermonging in conference
crack-polished-bone-mirages affluence & wretchedness confluence

habari gani africa
for everything the media sells
foul winds of small change fanning both flag waving & burning
on both sides clogged-up brain-cells
commerce's judas coins always spinning
tails or heads of state turning
& vanity before humanity only beasts beauty contesting & winning
sankara-sermon-legacy's silent witness
wash our marks of millennial cains in blood of self-sacrifice
adam-father's sin-seed nakedness in the skin of his genes
fallen smashed upon earthheaven's kilns to fashion artifices/
edifices tegumental monuments luciferean at human genesis
graveyard upheavals of self-revelations

habari gani africa
dross rehearsal in cock-suction for intravenereal progression
a grain of wheat away from descent to maggot-fattening ingestion
land of sunshining on the constellation-bound in lead-starroles
& cold deep in butt-plugged holes where sit in shit scarred souls
scorncobwebbed for intestincineration by nuclear excretion
amputated arms held out for world rank alms of bob or two doles
fake deliverance in providence's corruption
bred on breadmoulded destitution
not diarrhoea or constipation your innards revolution
birth of the incubus bursting the umbilicus in eruption
commerce acidsluiced out your intestines
barrenstoned from lusty look of land-barons' medusa concubines

habari gani africa
criminal-against-humanity-element become subliminal celebrant
hour of the serpent's servant in power's fervent dance
to the slashed drum's heartbeat in despoticardiac arrest
king-poet-pus sings president sore's praises
faeces on tongue's feet pound to the sound of a wound's abscess

stagnation's ambition putrefaction's ad/ministration
arrived as implosion of oppression's child
have you survived explosion of liberation gone wild
nightfly hover above deceit heated under muckiness' cover
new worldly empty embraces of darkness' lover
black despair/regency shame borne coldfear's catarrh as trophy
ignorance's arrogance destruction's slave-agent of catastrophy

habari gani africa
bloodstains on morguesheet sweat of impotence
born to die lie dead in the street the lie of omnipotence
scarstripes on the soul sign of demention/delusion
look of drugged minds hidden behind illusion
& outside the grenade-reality-cracked window the botched moment
licemen of the west bearing gifts rearing rifts of torment
come to perform reconciliation a land's abortion operation
nuclear wasted to the world's acceptance/assimilation
a disembowelment your creation cursed to a braindeathblow
manchildwomanimal NOWHERE left/right/middle/O . . .
sixfeetdownbelow
glow longknifenightsessionsplashed blooddroplets in the sewers
fleshpieces from crossed Xs / axes of man-made-wood hewers

habari gani africa
purification rite-sight/site unset for handheldfirstworld viewers
no hard meat & bone news chewers
parental guidance adviced to toothless pensioners of civilisation
radioactivation messages of rage beyond broadcast of the age
riding gossamer telewaves the royal educated savage
thunder before morning conceived of night's ravage
squash for wine the fleas on which you dine serpentine
brine-soaked oaken to the druid broken barkbacked dried out
spinal-fluid hangs a lifeline/capitalisticked sucked bloodmine
mortality/age on morgate steal-deal tables fangstacked
(eureka europe gathers the dust of a fallen berlin wall
africa rolls in the mud of its tropical brainfall)

Tiresias in the City of Heroes

KAREN PRESS ▼▼▼▼▼▼▼▼▼▼▼▼▼▼▼▼▼▼▼▼▼▼▼▼▼▼▼▼▼▼▼▼▼▼▼▼▼▼

1. In the city of heroes

Not only the unexploded bombs in their hearts
but these sweet pools of honey in each pair of hands
cupped to sip, being
a past that lit the night all the way to this
ending: dry air in a still, old city.

Memories are the daylight, in a place with no present.
The map with the closed rooms along the way unfolded
and you arrived with all the closed rooms in your years
throbbing, you arrived beyond the boundary of your map
saying, here I am, and from the closed rooms
such voices answered you: here I am.

If they had known the script
these heroes in the city of heroes
would have become statues and stopped waiting.

As it is they sat so still all day
but not—composed,
something in the angles of the amputated limbs
always implying movement of the ghost of movement,
even though absent, not finished yet

      x

waiting.

      x

Over the square the pale dust of the dry season sifts;
from jacarandas and flamboyants desiccated petals
in the victory colours fall.
Air murmurs.

The jungle licks the walls on the home side;
reticent waves attend at the outer edge.

The ground transmits biographies
of movement and hesitation,
vibrations of uneven footsteps circling
this city, this transit camp, this photograph of the time
before the end of struggle,
souvenir of the old days,
still breathing.

The jungle rustles with satisfied laughter.

It opens no path, yields no messenger,
darker and darker green, ancient.

     x

After the war there are always heroes
to be forgotten until they are dead.
There can be no heroes in times of peace.
Inside every song the words are buried:
Stay away, heroes of our struggles.
Let us paint pictures of you, let us tell stories.
Stay away where we can imagine you.
If you return now you will crumble like ancient kings
untombed in our corrosive air.

     x

These are not refugees, good god—
it isn't help they need, coins and crutches.
These men and women left in a column of fire
and will return garlanded with their deeds.
These men and women went in order to return,
not fleeing they were singing the jungles open,
setting up mirrors all the way to look back,
to send light and their faces back to the homeland
waiting for their deeds to arrive.
Not seeing the jungle grow up in their mirrors
new and permanent.

     x

These heroes are heroes,
triumphant on the long, long way home,

their silent days in this city
are a journey and it will end.

> And they will become kings and queens in their own land,
> and multitudes will welcome them
> with candles and flowers and firstborn children
> to bless with their golden pain.

    x

2. Tiresias remembers

A man came, unfortunate bridge. Tiresias:
with his dangerous memory come to the city of heroes.
Foolish man, looking for a woman
to watch her say again, go away.
Melting memories into dreams with a blind longing,
the hot longing that opens darkness,
melting the dreams of heroes into memories,
aching, aching.

    x

A man arriving is an emissary or an enemy.
Tiresias holds his poor broken heart under the shedding jacaranda
as the heroes undo him with questions.

"Tell us the story of the war we won."
Like children looking for a history to wear.

What do I remember? Standing in the sun for hours listening to speeches
while my feet burned on the ground. Walking along streets where women
stood at every door crying. Hacked bodies. A little man who followed
me for three kilometres and when I finally tried to grab him he begged
me to teach him to sing, but I thought he was lying and killed him. A
baby with its stomach carved out and a policeman standing next to it,
vomiting. Being given a computer and told to write. The smell of beer
on dead men's lips. Sitting in a shebeen drinking brandy after brandy
and getting so happy I felt like flying. A woman laughing as another
woman's house burned down. Yellow cars and vans: that thick flat yellow
like sweet icing on a cake. The noise of helicopters. My mother saying

don't go, or don't come back. My child screaming when I tried to pick him up. Meat roasting at my child's funeral. A book with my photo in it. Crowds becoming silent. A man who shot his wife in a meeting. The noise of helicopters. My burning feet. Bodies in the street covered in blankets. My home is a place I'm frightened of. It's a big sore inside me that burns when I touch it.

"Are you not bigger than your own backyard?
In that war each of us became the nation:
the whole nation entered into each of us.
Tell us that story."

That story. That story:
In Sharpeville your arms died.
In Uitenhage your tongues died.
In Boipatong your eyes died.
In Katlehong and Bekkersdal and Empangeni you died and you died and you died.
That's what I remember.

In Pretoria your fingernails became joint chief of staff:
In Pretoria your teeth ran the central bank.
In Pretoria your hair was the president.
That's what I remember.

In Jo'burg your heart was tortured and died.
In Cape Town your skin joined the enemy police.
In the veld and the mountains your memory buried its children.
That's what I remember.

That's what I remember.
All this dead and defeated, is your story.
Only the hair and the shadow still growing,
responding to sunlight, and I ask myself
which body were they grafted onto, in that moment of darkness
before total victory was declared?
My home is a place I'm frightened of.

The heroes leave him in the marketplace
like an old newspaper, blurred with the truth,
Sifting the dry breeze for her scent.

x

In a cool room she lies on a mourning mat.
Themba, he says, Themba, Themba.
You are still here.

You are still here, she says with the voice of dead bullets.
He is gone and you are still here.
Why couldn't they kill you?

x

There's nothing to remember.
what remains is here.
Its origins will repeat themselves.
How this man got his power
and that man starves
will not glue joy to your heart.
Sing or dream
or keep silent inside your bandages.
Don't dig, it only cuts the roots
and whatever is growing now will wither
like what came before.
Silence is big enough to hold the present
wide open for you to breathe in.

x

3. *To save what must be saved*

Heroes are those who will kill to save what must be saved.

Mnyaniso comes to the doorstep where Tiresias sits
carrying the knife, the long curved blade, a hook for a man's heart.
Once before he has excised a heart from his body
unmarked and fresh, a bulb stored in the dark room
of his return.

"Ah, Mnyaniso, do you remember
how as a child you could carve open the stem of a lily
without snapping it? How the lily continued to grow,
receiving its sap in two rivers now instead of one?"

"We could do such things, such things, Tiresias,
such expansions of the spirit in us.
Now my hand is a vulture on my dead days."

"But remember, Mnyaniso, remember your hand, remember."

All night Mnyaniso cut the bougainvillaea petals,
and in the morning Tiresias was a tree
with a million blood-red birds singing in its branches.

Eternity Is
a Hell of a Thing to Waste

NATASHA DISTILLER ▼▼▼▼▼▼▼▼▼▼▼▼▼▼▼▼▼▼▼▼▼▼▼▼▼▼▼▼▼▼

The arsonist stood at the side of the road. His sins did not weigh heavily on him. He was not that kind of man.

The woman in the bakkie drove along the road. The dry Karoo heat made the inside of her vehicle throb, as though the air were being beaten and begged for mercy. She drove in silence, enjoying the long road that spread itself before her invitingly, the insects that hurled themselves at her windscreen with kamikaze fury. She loved the feeling of travelling. She may have been running from something, as the arsonist was, but if so it was nothing serious, unlike the arsonist. She certainly did not seem like someone who has something to hide. The arsonist stood, the woman sat, one tapped his foot, one pressed her foot down, one stayed still, one travelled inexorably forward. As though they were bound together by fate, the different strings of their lives woven together in a vast tapestry, the weft and woof of destiny that had to meet to complete a picture, they hurtled towards each other like the mutilated insects had seemed to dash towards the brutal expanse of glass and as the planet moves always through space, spinning on an axis, rotating a fixed path with something charging towards consequence on its surface. If the arsonist was the windscreen, the woman was in trouble.

The sun smote, the road stretched, the insects died, the arsonist waited. The bakkie appeared in the distance. The arsonist smiled. He raised his thumb. The car slowed. Why did she stop for him? Perhaps because in the New South Africa people are safe now. Perhaps, unwittingly, she was merely a thread in a Muse's delicate hand. Perhaps foolishly, she had no sense of guilt, no awareness of sin for which punishment was needed. Wheels crunched the gravel on the edge of the highway, digested silently as the arsonist climbed into the passenger seat, then spat the stones out again as the car pulled off and rejoined the road that ran like tears towards the future.

As they drove, as she tried to chat politely, as he brooded and schemed, the small humpbacked hills that lay beneath the far o'erreaching firmament gradually grew height and teeth as the bakkie approached the Drakensberg. The sky was perfectly clear above them, and there was no wind. The pickup travelled smoothly along.

Safe from the lethal road, dassies froze in picturesque terror as a sudden, low rumble filled the world.

"Sounds like guns," said the arsonist.

"Thunder," agreed the woman. Glancing up she thought that it was strange to hear thunder when there were no clouds. She mentioned this, but the arsonist remained silent. Shortly afterward another peal resonated, shaking the air. It could have been thunder or guns, except that the landscape seemed to respond to the sound in a most unusual manner. The scrub wanted to twist away in fear, and the hills almost shuddered in distress.

As they continued on the path that would lead to danger, his brutality and her pain, the rumble became louder and more frequent until it was a roar, until it rolled through the air in a continuous, reverberating moan. She wondered if she was guilty of the all-too-human error of anthropomorphizing nature. After all, they say dolphins don't smile and dogs don't laugh and laboratory rats don't matter at all. She thought of poisoned seas and mutilated forests and slimy lakes and blasted, barren land and piles of small corpses and trembling bodies strapped to tables with their eyes clamped open and frantically pacing leopards in cages and cuttlefish in small tanks rapidly changing from ivory cream to stormy mottled grey with misery, fluttering in agitation, and she almost wished they were right.

The road swept gracefully to the left and the car swung along like the spiral arm of the galaxy, into mystery. Reality shook as the basso continuo grew into a lament and then exploded into a bellow of pain and despair. The woman slammed her foot onto the brake pedal, the little pick-up squealed in protest, skidding to a shocked halt, and a lesser man than the arsonist would have been glad that the road behind them was empty. But once more the arsonist was silent. The quality of his silence had, however, changed.

They stared out of the speckled windscreen, faces perfectly still except for a small twitch in the corner of the arsonist's eye. Before them, chained to a huge mountain that reared up out of the landscape inside the curve of the road, was an enormous man, a Titan, although the arsonist certainly did not know that, since he had directed his intellectual energies elsewhere. The colossus was bound with shackles that pinned his gigantic feet, each one twice as big again as the fragile pick-up truck, and his hands, palms outwards, to the rock. He was spread-eagled, and the flesh of his hands was blistered and peeling from long exposure to the sun. He seemed to have been there for a while. The woman could see the skin of his cuticles and around his nails (which were long and cracked from twisting and tearing at the cruel rock behind them) was burned black, cracked and pared. Perhaps it was dried blood. He had long, thick fingers and she could see the intimate patterns the skin made in his palms. She could trace the deep groove of his love-line.

The gargantuan man's head was against the mountain, his chin lifted to the sky, his eyes closed and his mouth open as he howled agony. An extremely large eagle, beak bloodied and eyes glistening, circled around his torso, and the woman noticed for the first time a gaping jagged wound in the creature's side, strips of muscle hanging like streamers amid caked blood and raw edges of flesh. Even the arsonist winced. The giant flung his head from left to right, smashing his ears against the crags, tearing sinew and leaving long, dark, wet streaks on the boulders as he cried and cried and cried, the roaring breaking down into great sobs that started deep in his soul and forced themselves up past his pride, through aeons of agony and hopelessness, to wrack the great body and tear down his strength, wear away at his endurance, undermine his sense of self until all he knew was pain, more pain, and sorrow. He knew that when the sun began to set, long shadows would reach out towards him and chill his tortured skin until the stealing cold of night would coat him deep inside with ice. He knew that when the dry hacking convulsions ceased, and the great burning hole in his side began to close with teeth-gritting pulls at the bruised muscle, then the eagle would scream in triumph, and wait for the new day.

The woman said, very, very softly, "That's Prometheus." The name may have sounded vaguely familiar to the arsonist, but more surprising than his continued silence was their unquestioning acceptance of what they were seeing. They both knew it was too real to be a dream. The kind of pain and desperation that emanated from the writhing, gasping figure dominating the horizon in front of them drove deep into the world around them, and echoed with a kind of truth that accumulated through remorse, centuries, hundreds of thousands of millennia of suffering. The arsonist swallowed. Then, wanting to look away, he looked up.

Above the head of the scapegoat, a yawning hole in the sky echoed the wound in the Titan's side. Ozone crackled and bled as the atmosphere struggled to hold itself together. The sky does not heal overnight. The broiling turmoil seemed to emulate the sensations writ in sweat on the giant's tortured brow, on his abused form, in his throat-tearing screams.

The woman wondered, briefly, if he ever got hoarse.

The violated ozone cried. The giant Prometheus cried. Time, uncaring, did not stop for either of them.

"We have to help him."

For the first time the arsonist spoke. "What?"

"I said, we have to help him. Do you know how long he's been there? We can't leave him like that!"

Grimly determined, she yanked the gear lever into first and started driving towards the mountain and the monster. They had a fairly long way to go before they pulled up at the enormous toenail. It was ingrown, and weeping pus. They had to step carefully through the yellow liquid to get closer. The arsonist did not protest—he was not a man of words—but he had begun to sweat heavily. If he weren't so overwhelmed, he might have been a lot less co-operative. As it was, he was experiencing a growing sense of dread, an unpleasant gnawing sensation he could not name, this arsonist, this abuser of fire.

Staring up at the hairy toe the woman cleared her throat. She glanced sidelong at the pale arsonist. Prometheus heaved. A single tear splashed to the ground, drenching them in salty misery. "Come on," she said. "Nobody deserves this." Hauling a hiking pack out from the back of her pick-up, she hoisted it onto her shoulders with a grunt, tightened the laces of her new Hi-Techs, grabbed the arsonist, and began to climb.

Two hours later they were sitting atop the iron band strapped across the left foot. It was easily broad enough to accommodate both of them, the backpack, a small gas canister which the woman had pulled out of her pack, the scattered provisions, ample leg room, and six sticks of dynamite. The canister was lit and a stainless steel camping pot perched on its detachable cross-bar bubbled away, emitting the aroma of Royco Pasta 'n Sauce (Cheesy Tomato and Herbs). The arsonist looked yellow, which was not an improvement. He was decidedly the worse for having been cut off from his empowering explosive rods.

"This is the plan," said the woman, as she handed him a tin plate and indicated that he should help himself from the pot. "We climb to each shackle, stick a piece of dynamite where the iron is bonded to the mountain, climb down again, and detonate. He'll probably get a bit burnt, but I doubt he'll notice." A tormented whimper surrounded them. They could feel the vibrations in the iron. Somewhere, an eagle called.

The arsonist shuddered.

"Well, what do you think?" she asked. "Will it work? I'm not familiar with the stuff. Can you rig it up to do that?"

"No," said the arsonist.

"No? What do you mean, No!" she shouted. "Why not?"

"I don't carry kilometres of fuse around. Not easily concealable, that."

"What are we going to do?" She looked at him wildly. "How can we end this anguish?" The arsonist shrugged sullenly. The woman frowned.

"Listen here," she said. "I can't do this without your help. You obviously know something about explosives, though why you carry half a dozen thingies of dynamite around is beyond me. You have to help. How can you just sit there and ignore the big guy? Don't you feel for him? Aren't you being just a little bit selfish by refusing him your aid? Don't you want to help out an ancient myth in need? Why don't you think of someone else besides your-self? Shouldn't you. . . ."

"All right, all right already." The arsonist reached inside his black leather jacket, which he had refused to leave in the car despite the heat and the coming exertion. From the murky depths of his terrible obsession he drew out what looked to her to be a large lump of rather dirty putty, and four small alarm clocks. "Plastique," he said.

After lunch, they decided on plan B. They would set the timer on the plastique placed at the join of rock and iron where they now sat, for twenty-four hours. They would climb up to the left arm, which should take approximately six hours if they worked fast. Setting the timer there for eighteen hours, they would then climb across the vast chest and along the arm to the right hand, E.T.A. four hours, set the timer there for twelve hours, and then rest for two. Next they would climb down to the right foot, set the timer for six hours, and this would give them a four hour leeway for delays and to get out of the range of falling debris before detonation.

And so it was. Climbing past the rapidly closing wound was particularly unpleasant. By the time they traversed the huge expanse of chest, clinging onto coarse black hairs to get across, night had fallen, and the body had mercifully quieted to great snoring rhythms, with only the occasional sniffle. The exhalative force of the heavy breathing was astounding, particularly when they were directly below the nasal cavity, and there were a few close calls where they had to cling desperately to the wiry filaments to avoid getting blown away. Throughout this arduous task the arsonist seemed kept in hand, less by the bravely maintained haranguing of the woman than by the presence of the giant, whose every movement sent the arsonist scurrying to cower ever deeper in himself. They worked hard, and by the time they were halfway through they were exhausted, despite occasional rests snatched from the precious minutes that ticked steadily away on the faces of the four identical clocks placed snugly in the inside corners of the four identical iron clamps.

One thing they had not counted on was the eagle. Three quarters of the way down towards the right foot, their final destination, the eagle which had perched atop the mountain like a headless statue during the night and had been ominously circling since sunrise, began to screech in anticipation. It was about seven 'o clock in the morning. The woman looked at the arsonist's sunken, bleary eyes and at the prickly shadow that had spread like a rash along his grim jaw. She ran a hand over her own face. Her muscles ached, her hands were raw from climbing, and she had blisters from her new Hi-Techs. She felt like hell. A vast shadow fell over her. She didn't know if the arsonist was aware of what was about to happen, and she was almost too tired to care.

"We have to hurry," she whispered. They scrambled and slid down the remaining rock to the last iron band. As they got there, Prometheus awoke with a scream as the eagle dive-bombed into his side, ripping at scar tissue and tender scabbing with adamantine claws. A terrible sucking, squelching sound was heard. The woman grabbed the arsonist and pulled him down. They lay, covering their heads, and heard the sharp clacking of a beak, bellows of pain that threatened to burst their eardrums and break their hearts, a terrible rending, and they were showered with hot sticky liquid, bits of skin and muscle, and mucus and tears from the giant's streaming facial orifices. For the longest time they lay in Prometheus's gall, desperately trying to shut out his tortured cries. Realizing that their time was running out, that they could not wait for the eagle to complete its terrible task, the woman glanced anxiously at her wristwatch. 9:49. They had about three hours to set this timer and get off the giant.

She shook the arsonist, who seemed to have fallen asleep. "Move, damn you," she hissed. "We've got to move." Reluctantly, carefully, he and she crawled along the flat iron surface made treacherous by slick blood and pieces of sinew and bits of other, softer things that she did not stop to examine. They made their way over to the join. Pushing the plastique into place and setting the nifty travel-size timer did not take the adept arsonist very long. Then they began the last leg of the journey, past the massive calf, down the side of the foot whose toes were curling and uncurling in helpless wretchedness (dislodging quite a few small boulders which proved an additional obstacle for the climbers on the way down). They reached the ground with about forty-five minutes to spare. The woman sprinted, the arsonist stumbled, the car shuddered into life and they sped away from the Titan.

"He may fall," reasoned the woman, so she set off back along the road, realising that if the creature stumbled it would be at a right angle to the road, across the curve. She stopped when she heard the explosion. They both climbed out of the car. Holding onto the sides of the bakkie for support, they viewed their handiwork.

One of the eagle's wings had been partially blasted away, and the bird, scorched and dying, lay at the feet of the Titan. The vast iron clamps had not, as she had hoped, completely melted, but they were loosened, and as she watched the mighty creature, in slow motion, pulled a hand outward, straining his arm so that the wasted muscles bulged and tore. The iron band, with a teeth-wrenching wail bent away from the mountain. One hand was released. Slowly, slowly, as if he had forgotten how to move, the colossus freed himself. As the last bond gave way and he tried to push himself off the mountain, he did indeed stumble, and fell onto his knees with a thud that echoed through the earth. Minor quakes were reported around the country. However, instead of rising up off his now grazed and bleeding knees, the giant gave a cry more terrible than any he had uttered before, and crashed to the ground completely, crushing the smaller hills beneath him. He was Prometheus, which meant he was chained to a rock in everlasting agony. Now, he began to die.

His death was as long, as slow and as dark as the deepest recesses of murky mythological beginnings. Slowly, slowly, Prometheus died.

Stupefied, empty, shaking, she watched. She knew they had killed him. Finally, all that was left was an incredible, supernal silence, and a vast pile of big bones, cracked and splintered, in a translucent ooze that gently trembled like the final sighs of a jelly.

For hours they stood, then they sat, then finally they got into the car and drove away slowly. Neither of them looked back, neither of them saw that, although the giant was gone, the raw wound in the sky was still there. As he realized that the Titan was no longer, as he looked at the weeping woman clutching the steering-wheel on his right, the arsonist began to feel better.

Glossary

A ke sa di kena—I'm out of it (Sotho)

Ag, moenie worry nie, boet—Oh, don't worry about it brother (Afrikaans)

APLA—Azanian People's Liberation Army, the military wing of the Pan Africanist Congress during apartheid

Asyn—vinegar (Afrikaans)

Babbie-shop—Indian trader store

Bakkie—pick-up truck

Biltong—dried meat

Bleddy—bloody

Blerry—bloody

Boerewors—type of sausage

Boet, sien jou môre—Brother, see you tomorrow (Afrikaans)

Bokbaard—goat's beard, similar to a goatee (Afrikaans)

Borrie—turmeric (Afrikaans)

Bredie—stew (Afrikaans)

Broederbond—right-wing organization promoting the economic and political interests of Afrikaaner nationalists (Afrikaans)

Buti—brother (Xhosa and Zulu)

Bwana—comrade, irrespective of gender; master, sir (Swahili)

Camarada—comrade (Portuguese)

Caspirs—police armoured vehicle

Chumza—chum

Cortina—a type of car made by Ford, popular in South Africa in the late 1960s and early 1970s

Daar's baie Zulus hier, hulle moet—There are many Zulus here, they must (Afrikaans)

Dagga-roekers—marijuana smokers (Afrikaans)

Dassies—small animal resembling a rabbit known elsewhere as a hyrax

Deepavali—Hindu Festival of Lights (Tamil)

Diepvlei—place name meaning "deep lake" (Afrikaans)

District Six—mixed race neighborhood of Cape Town whose inhabitants were forcibly removed under apartheid; most of the area was razed

Doek—cotton scarf worn on the head (Afrikaans)

Doppies—empty cartridge case (Afrikaans)

Durban poison—variety of marijuana

Fapla—acronym for the Angolan armed forces (Portuguese)

Festa—festival or party (Portuguese)

Habari gani—what's the news?; how are you? (Swahili)

Hadidah—onomatopoeic name for a large ibis

Hau—expression of surprise, wonder, joy, or a range of other emotions (Zulu)

Hoe kan die Russkies ons moet—How can the Russians (do something with or to) us? (Afrikaans)

Hulle—they (Afrikaans)

Inyanga—African traditional herbalist (Zulu)

Ja—yes (Afrikaans)

Jackrolling—taking a young woman by force for the purpose of gangraping her

Kafferboom—type of deciduous tree (coral tree); name is associated with the denigratory word *Kaffir*

Kaffirs—offensive term for a black person, associated with the height of apartheid; derived from the Arabic word for "nonbeliever"

Kak—excrement (Afrikaans)

Kannetjie—can (Afrikaans)

Kare—I say

Karoo—dry plateau

Khakibos—type of weed, bush (Afrikaans)

Knobkerrie—short stick with a knob at the end used as a weapon

Koeksisters—traditional cake soaked in syrup (Afrikaans)

Kooigras—a kind of shrub; literally "bed grass," probably used for bedding (Afrikaans)

Kwa Muhle—justice office for laying charges against and seeking redress from men who abandon the mothers of their children

Kwaai—fierce, bad-tempered (Afrikaans)

Lanieskap—aspirations to yuppiedom; main love interest (Afrikaans)

Lobola—bride price (Xhosa and Zulu)

Maagpyn—stomach-ache (Afrikaans)

Mal—crazy (Afrikaans)

Mbira—hand-held instrument (Shona)

Mealie—corn

Mebos—dried apricot sweet

Meths—methamphetamines

Milo—brand-name chocolate drink

MK—uMkhonto we Sizwe, Spear of the Nation, armed wing of the ANC

Morogo—edible, leafy plant (Sotho and Tswana)

Moskonfyt—thick syrup prepared from grapes (Afrikaans)

Mufti—plain-clothes, used by someone who traditionally wears a uniform; has implications of a disguise (Arabic)

Muti—medicinal or magic charm (Zulu and Xhosa)

My laaitie, jy's so klein en jy's klaar 'n terroris—My boy, you're so young and you're already a terrorist (Afrikaans)

Naai—screw, an extremely rude term (Afrikaans)

Naartjies—tangerines (Afrikaans)

Nats—member of the conservative National Party; National Party Government

Ndicel' ukuy' etoilet?—May I please go to the toilet? (Xhosa)

Ngwanaka—my child (Sotho)

Otchy chornyeh—black eyes (Russian)

Ou Slams—old Muslim (Afrikaans)

Ousie—old sister (Sotho and Afrikaans)

P.T.—Physical Training (what gym class was called in Bantu education schools)

Pere—horse shit (Afrikaans)

Praznie butilki—party bottle (Russian)

Res.—student residence hall

Rra—Father (Tswana)

Roti—Indian flat bread (Hindi and Urdu)

Sambal—relish or side dish salad of Malay or Indonesian origin, usually accompanying hot food

Samoosas—deep-fried Indian food which are triangular pastry snacks stuffed with various fillings (meat, vegetables, etc.)

Sangoma—traditional healer who divines and has the ability to see into the spiritual world (Zulu)

Sankara—Thomas Sankara, Burkina Faso's prime minister, killed in 1987

Shebeen—unlicensed house selling alcoholic drinks

Shebeen queens—women who run shebeens

Sies—exclamation of disgust

Singises—heavily accented pronunciation of *things*

Siyabona, Ndodana—Greetings, young man (Zulu)

Skat—term of endearment, like "darling" (Afrikaans)

Skelling—scolding (Afrikaans)

Skollie—hoodlum (Afrikaans)

Skomplaas—scum place (Afrikaans)

Sommer 'n klomp kak—Just a load of shit, nonsense (Afrikaans)

Slooshahytyeh pahzahloostah—listen please (Russian)

Sout—salt; warning to run for cover (Afrikaans)

Sqwaka—fool; someone still wet behind the ears

SRC—Student Representative Council

Stoep—veranda at the front of the house

Storff eennoussmin—heavily accented pronunciation of "staff announcement"

Thlokomelo Nja—beware of dog (Sotho)

Thunnee—Indian card game similar to poker

Tickeyline—cheap

Toyi-toyi—defiant chant and dance

Trocar—exchange, trade, or barter (Portuguese)

Tsotsi—hoodlum

uMkhonto we Sizwe—Spear of the Nation, armed wing of the ANC during apartheid

Unisa—University of South Africa

Vaalpens—derogatory term for an Afrikaaner (Afrikaans)

Van mantshingelanas, mos—from security guards (township slang)

Vat en Sit—shack-up outside marriage

Vetkoek—doughnuts without sugar (Afrikaans)

Veld—open grassland

Viva amandla—Long Live! Power to the People! a rallying cry of the ANC

Vlakplaas—clandestine paramilitary death squad

Voetsek—scram, fuck off; contraction of "Voort, se ek" (Afrikaans)

Voorlaaier—firearm, rifle (Afrikaans)

Wena—you (most southern African languages)

Witdoeke—vigilante group that collaborated with and was organized by the apartheid police; active in the squatter camps around Cape Town in the 1980s, its members wore white headbands to distinguish themselves as they went on the rampage; literally "white headband" (Afrikaans)

Witkoppen—institution for the mentally disturbed; also used as a reference to dismiss or degrade people

Yebo, baba—Yes, father (Zulu)

Zoll—marijuana joint (Afrikaans)

About the Contributors and the Editor

JEREMY CRONIN was born in South Africa in 1949. He studied at the University of Cape Town and at the Sorbonne in Paris. He became active in the political underground in the late 1960s. He was arrested by the security police in 1976 and sentenced to seven years for "terrorism" (the printing, publication, and distribution of "illegal" newsletters). Cronin's first poetry collection, *Inside* (1984), based on his experience in Pretoria Maximum Security prison, won awards and went into four editions, and poems from the collection have been translated into many languages. Cronin's second collection, *Even the Dead,* was released in 1997. The title poem won the Sid Clouts poetry award. Cronin is presently the Deputy General Secretary of the South African Communist Party and on the national executive committee of the African National Congress.

ACHMAT DANGOR was born in Johannesburg and has lived a somewhat nomadic life. Sojourns in many rural South African settings as well as metropoles such as London and New York (where he taught literature at City College) have exposed him to a wide variety of influences. Politically active since youth, Dangor was "banned" from 1973 to 1978. This five years of enforced solitude bred in him an almost stubborn individuality that is constantly revealed in his writing. He has published two novels, a volume of short stories, and a number of poetry collections. His latest work is *Kafka's Curse*, a novella and four stories.

INGRID DE KOK'S work has been published widely in South Africa and has appeared in journals and anthologies in the United States, Canada,

England, Denmark, and France. Individual poems have been translated into French, Japanese, Spanish, and Dutch. Her first collection of poems was entitled *Familiar Ground* (1988), her second *Transfer* (1997). She also writes on cultural topics; she edited, with Karen Press, *Spring is Rebellious* (1990); and was advisory editor for *World Literature Today: South African Literature in Transition* (1996). She works at the Department of Adult Education and Extra-Mural Studies at the University of Cape Town.

SANDILE DIKENI, born in Victoria West in 1966, was educated in the Ciskei and at the University of the Western Cape. He began writing while in detention in 1986. He writes and performs in Xhosa, English, and Afrikaans. He is an ex-editor of the political journal *Die Suid Afrikaan*. His first collection of poetry was published under the title *Guava Juice* in 1992. He has completed a second book of poetry, *Telegraph to the Sky*, and is currently Arts & Lifestyle editor at the *Cape Times*.

NATASHA DISTILLER was educated in Johannesburg, Cape Town, and Oxford. She works in teaching, training, and the voluntary and statutory sector. She plans to combine these with further study and research in South Africa.

FINUALA DOWLING, a freelance writer, was born in Cape Town in 1962. She taught English at the University of South Africa for eight years. Her short stories "Shakespeare & Co." and "We Shall See What We Shall See" won prizes from *Cosmopolitan* magazine and the Commonwealth Broadcasting Association.

GRAEME FRIEDMAN has won three literary awards, including first prize in the *herStoria* Short Story Competition for the story included in this volume. His first novel, which won second prize in the Macmillan Boleswa/Pace Writers' Competition, is to be published under the title *Fruit of the Poisoned Tree*. He is the co-editor of *A Writer in Stone: South African Writers Celebrate the 70th Birthday of Lionel Abrahams*. He is currently completing a second novel, *The Fossil Artist*, and a non-fiction book on South African soccer and society. He lives with his wife and two sons in Johannesburg, where he works as a psychotherapist.

PUMLA DINEO GQOLA was born in the Eastern Cape and grew up mainly iDikeni (in Alice). She teaches African, Indian, and Caribbean literatures at the English Department of the University of the Free State. Her short stories tend to be based in the Eastern and Western Cape.

LOUISE GREEN, born in Johannesburg in 1968, grew up in Melkbosstrand and Cape Town. She won the Sydney Clouts Memorial Prize for Poetry for a piece entitled "Sharer." Her poetry has been published in various journals. The poem in this volume was first published in *New Coin*. She is a research fellow at the Institute for the Study of English in Africa, Rhodes University.

JONATHAN GROSSMAN is a lecturer in the Department of Sociology at the University of Cape Town. He writes, "My main interest is in the collective processes, organisations and actions through which ordinary workers survive, make, and change history. I have been active for a long time in popular organisation and education." His e-mail address is grossman@socsci.uct.ac.za.

HEIDI GRUNEBAUM-RALPH grew up in Johannesburg. She spent some years intermittently travelling, studying, and doing odd jobs before recently completing a master's degree in French literature. Her work has been published in *Current Writing* and other journals. She is a Ph.D. candidate at the University of the Western Cape.

MAUREEN ISAACSON'S stories have been published widely in anthologies and magazines both in South Africa and overseas and have been broadcast on radio. Her collection, *Holding Back Midnight*, was published in 1992. She has co-edited two books, *The Fifties People of South Africa* and *The Finest Photographs from the Old Drum*. A journalist, she lives in Johannesburg and is the books editor for the *Sunday Independent*.

RUSTUM KOZAIN was born in Paarl, Western Cape, in 1966. Most of his university education has taken place through the University of Cape Town; he also spent ten months in the United States, as a Fulbright scholar, in an M.F.A. program. He has published poems, reviews, and essays in various journals and anthologies in South Africa, France, and the United Kingdom. In 1989 he won UCT's Mandela Prize for poetry and in 1997 the Philip Stein Award for a poem entitled "Talking Jazz." He is a Ph.D. candidate and assistant lecturer at the University of Cape Town.

ANTJIE KROG writes mostly in Afrikaans. She has published eight volumes of poetry, several of which have been translated into European languages and have won local and foreign prizes. Her most recent book is *Country of My Skull* (1998), about the Truth and Reconciliation Commission.

MANDLA LANGA grew up in the KwaMashu township of Durban. After being arrested in 1976, he spent 101 days in prison on a charge of trying to leave the country without a permit. He was sentenced but skipped bail and went into exile in Botswana. He underwent military training for the MK in Angola and lived in Botswana, Lesotho, Mozambique, Zambia, Hungary, and the United Kingdom, holding a variety of ANC posts while abroad. He has published three volumes, *Tenderness of Blood, A Rainbow on a Paper Sky,* and *The Naked Song and Other Stories.* A weekly columnist for the *New Nation,* he lives in Johannesburg.

EDWARD LURIE, a civil engineer living in Cape Town, has won several South African literary awards. His novels have been published locally and internationally.

PAUL MASON was born in Johannesburg in 1963. He took degrees in literary studies from the universities of the Witwatersrand and Natal. He has published arts reviews, poetry, and fiction in literary journals, magazines, and an anthology of South African poetry. He is currently based in Cape Town, where he writes and coordinates creative writing workshops.

DAVID MEDALIE was born in Bethal, South Africa, in 1963. His first volume of short stories, *The Shooting of the Christmas Cows,* was published in 1990. "Recognition," the short story included here, won the Sanlam Award in the unpublished category in 1996. He holds degrees from the University of Witwatersrand and Oxford University. He is the editor of *Encounters,* an anthology of South African short stories published in 1998. He lives in Johannesburg and works as a lecturer in English at the University of Witwatersrand.

JOAN METELERKAMP was born in 1956 and grew up in the Natal midlands. Her first collection of poetry, *Towing the Line,* was published in 1992 and was a joint winner of the Sanlam Literary Award. "Portrait," the central poem in her second volume, *Stone No More* (1995), won the Sydney Clouts Memorial Prize for that year. She has taught English at the universities of Natal and the Western Cape.

LUVUYO MKANGELWA has published poems in *New Coin, New Contrast, Carapace,* and *Tribute.* He received his primary education in the Transkei before moving to Cape Town, where he studied at the Cape Technikon.

SEITLHAMO MOTSAPI was born in 1966 in Bela-Bela, Warmbaths. He published *earthstopper/the ocean is very shallow,* a collection of poetry, in 1995. He has worked as a school teacher and is currently a lecturer of English at the University of the North.

BERNADETTE MUTHIEN writes, "I was born in Cape Town over thirty years ago, the seventh of eight children to a Coloured mother and an Indian father. Poverty and politics was my daily feed, and poetry my reward. Not much has changed since, as I still agitate for more social, political, economic change, and work for a nongovernmental organization for minimum wage, and write."

ROSHILA NAIR was born and raised in KwaZulu Natal. She studied English and literary studies at the University of Natal. She has published in various South African journals and anthologies. She currently lives and works in Cape Town.

KAREN PRESS has published four volumes of poetry and her work has appeared in journals and anthologies in South Africa, the United Kingdom, and Canada. She lives in Cape Town and works as a freelance writer and editor.

LESEGO RAMPOLOKENG, who was born in Soweto, performs as well as publishes his poetry. He has put out a CD/tape entitled *End Beginnings*. His other collections are *Horns for Hondo* and *Talking Rain*.

ZACHARIAH RAPOLA was born and grew up in Alexandra Township. He studied filmmaking locally, then proceeded to France and Denmark. He has written and directed two short features. He attended creative writing workshops under Nadine Gordimer in the 1980s; has published poetry, short stories, and book reviews; and is currently working on a short story collection entitled *Beginnings of a Dream*.

MONGANE WALLY SEROTE has published several major works of poetry and prose, including *Yakhal'inkomo*; *Tsetlo*; *No Baby Must Weep*; *Behold Mama, Flower*; and *To Every Birth Its Blood*. Born in Sophiatown in 1944, he spent nine months in solitary confinement in 1969 and was then released without being charged. He is currently a member of parliament.

IMMANUEL SUTTNER has written extensively for radio and television. He has published poetry and short stories in *Cosmopolitan, Tribute, New Coin, Jewish Affairs, Slugnews, Botsotso,* and *Imprint*, and his work has been included in the *Hippogriff Anthology of New South African Fiction*. He is the author of a collection of interviews with South African Jewish activists entitled *Cutting through the Mountain*.

CHRIS VAN WYK, born in Soweto in 1957, has published poetry, short stories, children's books, and booklets for newly literate adults. His poetry collection *It Is Time to Go Home* won the Olive Schreiner Award in 1980. His books for children include the well-loved *A Message in the Wind* and *Petroleum and the Orphaned Ostrich*. *The Year of the Tape Worm*, his first novel for adults, was published in 1996. He lives in Johannesburg, where he works as a freelance literary editor and full-time writer.

IVAN VLADISLAVIĆ was born in Pretoria in 1957. He studied at the University of the Witwatersrand, worked as a translator, and later as a fiction and social studies editor at Ravan Press. He has been publishing short fiction since the early 1980s, and his work has appeared in journals and anthologies in South Africa and abroad. His fiction has been translated into French and German, and has won several awards, including the Olive Schreiner Prize and the CNA Award. He has published a novel, *The Folly* (1993), and two collections of stories, *Missing Persons* (1989) and *Propaganda by Monuments* (1996). In 1998, he coedited the volume *blank_____ Architecture, apartheid and after* with Hilton Judin. He now works as a freelance editor.

FELICITY WOOD was born in 1961 in Cape Town. She is a lecturer in the English Department at the University of Fort Hare. Her short stories have been published in a number of anthologies.

ISABEL BALSEIRO is Associate Professor of Comparative Literature at Harvey Mudd College, The Claremont Colleges, in California. Her work has been published in journals in the United Kingdom, the United States, and South Africa. She is currently editing an anthology on South African cinema and a book on Caribbean literature and culture.

ISBN 0-325-00231-2

EAN

9 780325 002316

HARDCOVER BAR CODE